SEAWINGS

. . . *Whenever I find myself growing grim about
the mouth; whenever it is a damp, drizzly
November in my soul. . . . then, I account it high time
to get to sea as soon as possible.*

HERMAN MELVILLE

*The fated sky
Gives us free scope.*

WILLIAM SHAKESPEARE

Behold the sea . . .

WALT WHITMAN

SEAWINGS

An Illustrated History of Flying Boats

EDWARD JABLONSKI

ROBERT HALE & COMPANY
London

For CARLA,

who loves romances

Contents

SEAWINGS

An Illustrated History of Flying Boats

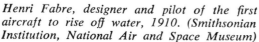

Henri Fabre, designer and pilot of the first aircraft to rise off water, 1910. (Smithsonian Institution, National Air and Space Museum)

Man's first successful seaplane. Power was furnished by a seven-cylinder Gnome rotary engine mounted at rear of fuselage. Note how main spars of wing and tail are not enclosed within them, but serve as a support from which they were simply suspended. The three small floats were remarkably efficient, just as the controls were primitive. A heavy rod actuated the small horizontal elevator; foot pedals, via wires, warped the wings. The rudder placed directly before the engine was fixed. Fabre's flights were never so extended that he ever had to consider turning his craft around for a return to the spot from which he had taken off. (Musée de l'Air)

Prologue

En l'air! *Fabre's flight over the Gulf of Fos on March 28, 1910. Man's first successful take-off from, and landing on, water. After a few such flights—and a bad dip—Fabre gave up aviation while still intact. His contribution was not so much to the design as to the proof that a seaplane could be built and flown. (Musée de l'Air)*

The first man in history to devise an aircraft capable of lifting off and landing on water is little known in the annals of aviation. His name was Henri Fabre, and like so many early French pioneers of flight, he was no aviator at all. He was, in fact, a marine engineer, which may account, to some extent, for his success in designing the three floats that sustained his little craft on the water.

If Fabre was no aviator, his contraption could hardly qualify as an aircraft. It looked more like an unfinished length of fence to which a wing and various other appendages had been attached. The engine, a fifty-horse-power Gnome rotary, was mounted at the rear, directly behind the wing and the rectangular fixed vertical rudder. Below all this, on either side of the rudder, were two winglike hollow wooden floats. Fabre sat about midway on the top crosspiece of his flying fence. Two horizontal elevators provided some degree of lateral control; beneath the elevators was a third float. Additional control was maintained via foot pedals, which caused the tips of the craft's wings to bend and twist, a form of primitive aileron.

The aircraft was remarkably stable, considering Fabre's limited knowledge of aerodynamics. The Gnome engine, which spun around at about a thousand revolutions a minute, was not equipped with a throttle, and in the cliché of the time, ran at two speeds: Off or On. Fabre's success with this embryo seaplane is all the more remarkable, considering that other, more experienced "airmen" had failed in the earlier attempts at off-the-water flight.

Five years before Fabre's flight, Gabriel Voisin of the brother team of pioneer aircraft designers (the other member being Charles), had produced a glider on floats. This had been built for Ernest Archdeacon, a Paris attorney and aviation enthusiast. Voisin, who was a graduate architect, assembled two sets of giant boxkites (an idea borrowed from Australian pioneer Lawrence Hargrave) and mounted them on floats.

Towed behind a motorboat, the Voisin-Archdeacon float glider actually lifted off the surface of the Seine River in the summer of 1905. Later in the year, this same craft—with added modifications—was tested at Lake Geneva, but with no success at all.

Another float glider was produced by Voisin, also in 1905, for another aviation enthusiast, Louis Blériot. Of somewhat different design from the Archdeacon glider, the Blériot, with its stubbier wings, proved less stable than the former. On July 18, 1905, following a successful trial with the Archdeacon, Gabriel Voisin climbed into the Voisin-Blériot (which Blériot called the *Blériot II*) and signaled for the motorboat to begin its run.

The pullrope tightened with a sprinkling of water, the glider moved, lifted off the Seine, made a sudden banking turn, and sideslipped into the river. Extricating himself from the dripping wreckage, nearly

A pre-Fabre attempt at a water glider, the Voisin-Archdeacon design of 1905. Attempts to lift the plane off the water by pulling it behind a motorboat were moderately successful, but hardly proved much. (Musée de l'Air)

A pre-Fabre failure, the Voisin-Blériot, built shortly after the Archdeacon float-glider. The craft is shown on the surface of the Seine being prepared for a tow by boat, Gabriel Voisin seated in the "cockpit," such as it was. Moments later he was floundering in the river, nearly trapped in the wreckage of the plane. (Musée de l'Air)

drowned, Voisin decided to give up on the Blériot design.

Blériot, on the other hand, not having suffered submersion, was undaunted. By May of the next year, 1906, he ordered Voisin, who now owned an aircraft factory at Billancourt on the Seine, to build another float plane of Blériot's own design. It was, indeed, a strange device: both wing and tail were ellipsoidal and of the same size. A major difference was the addition of an Antoinette engine (the design of Léon Levavasseur), which drove twin propellers mounted just in front of the wing. Blériot dubbed it, with characteristic modesty, the *Blériot III.*

This craft was placed upon the waters of Lac d'Enghien in May of 1906—and it

stayed there. So did the *Blériot IV* that followed, despite the change to a Wright brothers type of wing. Even with the floats removed and wheels added, it, so to speak, never got off the ground.

Blériot, daunted finally after these experiments, eventually abandoned the biplane type for the monoplane. Water never lost its fascination for Blériot, however, and in 1909 he became the first man to fly the English Channel in a heavier-than-air craft in his *Blériot XI,* a single-winged landplane.

It remained for Fabre, therefore, to solve the riddle of getting a powered plane into the air off the water. This was accomplished in his "flying fence" on March 28, 1910, in the Gulf of Fos at Martigues, near

Blériot's own conception of what a float plane should be, the Blériot III of 1906. Besides the unusual, and quite beautiful though impractical, design, Blériot added an engine, the famed Antoinette designed by Levavasseur. But neither the engine nor the configuration could get the plane off the surface of Lake d'Enghien. (Musée de l'Air)

Marseilles. The strange contraption lifted off the surface of the bay, remained in the air for a few seconds, and landed, without mishap, on its three scientifically designed floats. Encouraged by this success, Fabre continued flying his plane for the next few weeks until May 18, when in attempting to climb he caused the plane to stall and splash into the Mediterranean. Although Fabre was unhurt, the plane was badly broken up—and Fabre daunted. He chose to exit from the pages of aviation history while still intact. The plane itself was salvaged, rebuilt, and flown a year later, but the design itself, excepting the floats, had not proved capable of further development.

Meanwhile, the American aviator-designer, Glenn Curtiss, had also become engrossed with the possibilities of flight from water. This idea had no doubt been spurred by his flight in 1910 from Albany to New York; this was the highlight of the "Hud-son-Fulton Celebration," as the flight of Curtiss would traverse the routes of Hudson's ship *Half Moon* and Fulton's *Clermont.* A prize of ten thousand dollars was offered by newspaper owner Joseph Pulitzer to the first man who could accomplish this. Curtiss was the man, and he did it in his *Albany Flyer,* a landplane that presented him with many ticklish moments as he flew over the surface of the Hudson River.

A practical mechanic, Curtiss first tried to mount one of his planes in a canoe and attempted to get it off Lake Keuka, New York. This miscegenation of conveyances proved to be neither sea- nor airworthy. Another vain attempt, but a step in the right direction, was the installation of pontoons onto his prize-winning plane, the *June Bug.* But the float design was inefficient and served only to keep the *Loon,* as Curtiss renamed the plane, in the water. The

An early Curtiss try at a seaplane—mounting one of his racers on a canoe. This appears to have provided instant inherent instability. The problem never really came up, for the plane never got up. The setting is Lake Keuka, New York, 1909. (National Archives)

engine was incapable of lifting the added weight, nor could it overcome the pull of the water on the pontoons.

Determined and resourceful as well as pragmatically inventive, Curtiss shifted the scene of his search for a seagoing aircraft to the gentler climes of California. He set up shop at North Island, near San Diego, and continued experimenting with various types of pontoons. He finally struck upon a curious design that looked like the thick middle section of the wing of aircraft to come. Fashioned of a very light spruce, the pontoon was attached directly under the

Curtiss moves to North Island, near San Diego, California to continue with his "hydroaeroplane" experiments. As a group clusters around the plane, a couple of workmen on the left have begun constructing a hangar. This photo was taken on January 20, 1911—six days before Curtiss made his first successful flight. (Historical Collection, Title Insurance and Trust Company, San Diego, California)

One of the early Curtiss hydroplane designs that did not prove to be very successful. Various float positions were tried before Curtiss found the right one. The stubby float was where, on the original plane, the main wheels were placed; the front wheel was replaced by the little, narrow, float. This had a tendency to dig into the water. During tests this plane skidded and damaged the main pontoon. (Historical Collection, Title Insurance and Trust Company, San Diego, California)

Curtiss's successful hydroplane with a newly designed single pontoon, although without step. It was in this craft that Curtiss made the first flight from water in the United States on January 26, 1911. (Historical Collection, Title Insurance and Trust Company, San Diego, California)

Curtiss out to lunch. After taking off from North Island, Curtiss flew to Coronado for lunch at the Hotel Del Coronado, after which he flew back to North Island, again demonstrating the advantages of the world's first amphibian. (Historical Collection, Title Insurance and Trust Company, San Diego, California.)

The Curtiss Triad, a refinement of the hydroplane. Curtiss sits at the controls of the plane after a flight and brings the craft ashore in demonstration of its triple functions: on sea, in the air, and on land. (Historical Collection, Title Insurance and Trust Company, San Diego, California)

The Navy takes an interest in the airplanes, the inception of the Naval Air Service in 1911. This earned "G.H.," as Curtiss was called by his associates, the title of "Father of Naval Aviation." (Historical Collection, Title Insurance and Trust Company, San Diego, California)

center of the plane, thus to sustain the weight of engine and pilot. This Curtiss "hydroaeroplane" succeeded in taking off on January 26, 1911. It was the first such flight made from American waters—and a full year after Fabre's in France.

Having succeeded, unlike Fabre, Curtiss was determined to go farther. Within three weeks he devised an improved pontoon— longer, more streamlined—and perked up the interest of the U. S. Navy by flying out to the cruiser U.S.S. *Pennsylvania* in San Diego Bay. The hydroaeroplane was hoisted aboard ship and, after a pleasant visit, Curtiss had the seaplane dropped back into the water and he took off to return to his base at North Island.

This was the beginning of the Navy's interest in aircraft; shortly after, the Navy Department placed an order for its first hydroplane. This was delivered by Curtiss, at Hammondsport, New York in July of 1911. The Navy's official designation was "A-1"; Curtiss called it the *Triad,* because with the addition of wheels the plane had become an amphibian capable of performing on land, sea, and in the air. Along with the order for the aircraft came the necessity for training the Navy pilots to man them. This was the foundation of the U. S. Navy's air arm.

It remained only for two more Curtiss ideas to complete the evolution from the capable-of-rising-off-water gadget to a genuine flying boat. One of Curtiss's most important innovations was the introduction of the "step" into the design of his pontoons. This break in the line of the bottom of the pontoon made it easier to overcome the suction of the water, which had kept so many of his earlier experiments glued to the water.

The second idea dispensed with the pontoon or float and, in a sense, equipped the hull of a boat with wings. Of course, the hull design was related to the Curtiss experiments with pontoon development rather than to ship architecture. The first Curtiss

flying boat capable of carrying two passengers, flew off the surface of San Diego Bay on January 10, 1912. Before the year ended Curtiss had produced a refined version of this boat, the Curtiss *F-Boat,* which were purchased by the U. S. Navy and Army as well as wealthy sportsman pilots.

For his contribution to flying from water, Curtiss was awarded that same year the Robert J. Collier Trophy for "the greatest achievement in aviation in America, the value of which has been demonstrated by use during the preceding year." In 1913 Curtiss received the Collier Trophy again for his work with the flying boat.

The success of Curtiss inspired and encouraged others, among them the enterprising Burgess Company of Marblehead, Massachusetts. Founded by a Harvard graduate in engineering and naval architecture, one W. Starling Burgess, the Burgess Company, originally functioning as a shipyard from around 1904, appears to have switched to aircraft around 1909–10. This may be attributed to the association of Burgess with a nongraduate of the Stevens Institute of Technology, Augustus M. Herring (who became a voluntary dropout when his paper on flying had been rejected by the Institute).

Herring's airmindedness extended a fair time into the past: As early as 1895 he had worked with Samuel Pierpont Langley— himself a pioneer of over (or rather "into") -water flight. Langley's unsuccessful *Aerodrome* of 1903 was launched from a houseboat on the Potomac River, ending up twice in the cold waters of the river. By this time, however, Herring had left Langley and became associated with another pioneer, Octave Chanute, and eventually, thanks to Chanute, witnessed some of the flights of the Wright brothers, some of whose secrets, it was suspected, he took with him when Herring decided to join the Wrights' rival, Curtiss, in 1909. That partnership—the Herring-Curtiss Company—was not long-lived, and when it dissolved Herring teamed up (for about a year) with Burgess.

It was Herring's temporary drifting into Marblehead that turned Burgess to aircraft, most of them Curtiss-type biplanes equipped with skid landing gears. With all the excitement over Curtiss's seaplanes, Burgess also turned to this type of plane, as did other aircraft manufacturers.

The first of the Burgess planes to fly off water was actually a Wright biplane with floats (Burgess was licensed to produce Wright planes), and named the Burgess-Wright *Hydro*.

Soon after, the company was joined by an exhibition flier Howard Gill, who besides testing Burgess planes brought publicity to the firm because of his daring aerial exploits. His presence in the Burgess Company resulted in an interesting design built to compete for the Edwin Gould Prize of fifteen thousand dollars. This was offered in 1912 to the man or company that would produce a twin-engined hydroplane that was capable of flying also on a single engine. The result was the Burgess-Gill hydroplane, the final design of which was powered by two engines turning four propellers. Tested by Gill in May of 1912, it proved a worthy craft—and capable of the single-engine flight. But when he arrived to compete for the Gould Prize Gill was surprised to learn, although there had been other entrants, that he was the only one to appear. Gould reasoned that since there were no other contestants, there was no contest, and he withdrew the prize, which ended Gill's enthusiasm for seaplane design.

Burgess persisted, however, and by 1911 he had produced an original design designated the Model H, a biplane intended to serve as a military biplane. In time, this plane too was equipped with floats and was developed as a seaplane and refined into the later Model I or the Coast Defense Hydro. The Model H, more officially known as the Burgess Military Tractor, was used both

Howard Gill testing the Burgess-Gill float-plane in May 1912. The contest for which the craft had been designed and built never took place because only Gill appeared on the day it was to have occurred. The plane was capable of remaining airborne with only one engine operating. (U. S. Air Force)

The Burgess-Wright H, twin float plane that was used by the U. S. Army prior to the First World War. Although evolved out of a Wright design, it owed more to the Burgess design staff than to Wright. It was powered by a French Renault engine. (U. S. Air Force)

Jean Conneau (professionally known as "André Beaumont") flies over the Seine River, near Paris, in the Donnet-Lévêque *flying boat. (U. S. Air Force)*

Glenn Curtiss gracing the hull of the America, *his conception of a transatlantic flying boat. (Smithsonian Institution, National Air and Space Museum)*

as a land-based plane with skids and wheels and also as a water-based aircraft by the U. S. Army prior to the First World War.

The influence of Curtiss was not confined to the United States as far as seagoing aircraft were concerned. His design having evolved from float plane to flying boat, Curtiss found that others developed their ideas along similar paths. In France the designer Denhaut produced a successful variant on the Curtiss idea in his *Donnet-Lévêque* pusher biplane. It was both a handsome and efficient design and was flown by the famed Jean Conneau (who, because he was a naval ensign, flew as a civilian under the pseudonym "André Beaumont"). Conneau was one of the first of France's celebrity pilots and participated in many of the early air meets and races in Europe. He used the *Donnet-Lévêque* in two aquatic air meets in 1912, neither of which he won, although in September of that year, after participating in a competition sponsored by

the Aéro Club de Belgique, he was awarded a trophy donated by King Leopold, for his performance in the flying boat. Interestingly, the meet had been held to determine the possibility of using seaplanes in the Belgian Congo.

In 1914 Curtiss was commissioned by Rodman Wanamaker, heir to the Wanamaker Department Stores fortune, to build

The America, *one of the earliest of flying boats. (Smithsonian Institution, National Air and Space Museum)*

The first "airliners," Benoist seaplanes of the St. Petersburg–Tampa Airboat Line—the world's first scheduled airline—flying over Central Yacht Basin, St. Petersburg, during the spring of 1914. The plane on the right, a Benoist Model XIV, is No. 43, the plane with which the line began operations on January 1, 1914. (City News Bureau, St. Petersburg, Florida)

a large flying boat. Wanamaker had decided to back a venture nurtured by Lord Northcliffe, owner of the London *Daily Mail,* which offered a prize of fifty thousand dollars for the first transatlantic flight. The flying boat, named the *America,* was the largest aircraft produced in the United States up to that time. It had a wingspan of seventy-four feet and was powered by two engines. The *America* made its first test flight at Lake Keuka in June 1914. Hiring British pilot Lieutenant John C. Porte, Wanamaker hoped that a successful crossing of the Atlantic by air—a joint British-American endeavor—would demonstrate "the importance" of "aeronautics" to "every nation," celebrate a hundred years of peace between Britain and the United States, and prove once and for all that it

was time for the entire world to disarm. The oceangoing flying boat, Wanamaker hoped to prove, would render war futile.

Ironically the project was ended with the outbreak of the First World War. Also, despite its two ninety-horsepower Curtiss OX-5 engines, it was highly unlikely that the *America* could have lifted a load of fuel sufficient to make the crossing. The type itself was used by the Royal Navy as patrol boats and evolved into the larger flying boats of the U. S. Navy. The Curtiss concept of the large flying boat had come to stay.

Short-lived, however, was an attempt—also in 1914—to establish what might have been the world's first scheduled airline. The St. Petersburg–Tampa Airboat Line began operations on New Year's Day using a Benoist flying boat, designed by Thomas

Benoist of St. Louis and bearing a striking resemblance to the Curtiss flying boats. The twenty-mile flight saved a passenger a drive of thirty-six miles and a good deal of time (twenty minutes by air, two hours by auto—maybe). Capable only of carrying pilot Tony Jannus and one passenger (who paid five dollars for the flight), the Benoist actually made two round trips a day for four months before the company went out of business. The idea was good: to combine the large flying boat with a regular passenger-carrying service, but it had come prematurely.

Conspicuously missing from this summary of the evolution of the flying boat is the name of Wright. Wilbur and Orville Wright, the two self-taught mechanical geniuses from Dayton, Ohio, had proved in 1903 that man could truly fly in a powered, controllable aircraft. They were hardly rewarded with instant fame and fortune, but quietly went on with their developments. In 1907 they began experimenting with cylindrical pontoons equipped with hydrofoils in preparation for making their *Flyer* capable of operating from water. This line of study was interrupted when a sudden spurt of interest in their invention sent Wilbur to France in 1908 to promote their flying machine.

Although the Wrights were finally widely hailed and their plane accepted, their contributions to the further development of aviation began to peter out some years prior to the First World War. They became embroiled in a bitter lawsuit with Curtiss and expended more energy on protecting their patents than on further research. Meanwhile, other designers and manufacturers, among them their arch-enemy Curtiss, added refinements to the original Wright idea of the practical vehicle of the air (such as wheels, for example, in place of the Wrights' runners).

Early in 1912, Frank T. Coffyn, a Wright protégé, equipped a Wright Model

"B" with large skilike aluminum pontoons to produce the first Wright hydroplane. He entertained New Yorkers by taking off from the ice-laden Hudson River near the Battery, at the southern tip of Manhattan, flying up to Grant's Tomb, returned, circled the Statue of Liberty, and landed again in the water. The next week he again performed, this time by flying under the Manhattan and Brooklyn Bridges. While the very efficient pontoons proved seaworthy, it might be remembered that Curtiss had already produced his more sophisticated flying boat by this time. The Wright hydroplane, except for the pontoons (and less obvious refinements), looked little different from the Wright *Flyer* of nearly a decade before.

If fairly constant litigation curtailed the Wright imagination, the death of Wilbur of typhoid fever on May 30, 1912, dispirited it completely. Within a couple of years Orville Wright retired, selling out the business and copyrights. The name, however, continued, and in 1913, in fact, the Wright Company manufactured its Model "G" Aeroboat. Although Orville Wright was still associated with the firm, the Aeroboat was the brainchild of a young aeronautical engineer, Grover C. Loening, who had joined the company in June.

The wing and tail configuration was typically Wright, but the addition of a graceful hull and floats near the center of the

The Wright Model G Aeroboat, *designed by young engineer Grover C. Loening in 1913. (U. S. Air Force)*

Lawrence Lewis, in the spring of 1916, takes off from the water near Tampa, Florida, in his small, hulled flying boat, a Lawrence-Lewis A-1. Structure of this craft appears to be rather flimsy, although the hull looks tough. Skilike projection of hull in front of the plane is interesting—as if the craft were mounted on a surfboard. (U. S. Air Force)

lower wing were the touch of Loening. Eventually Loening struck out on his own and formed a successful aircraft company, specializing in the manufacture of seaplanes.

Others besides the "big names" in aviation were experimenting with water-based aircraft in the period before the United States went into the war. An interesting though little-known design was flown by Lawrence Lewis off the waters of Tampa, Florida in the spring of 1916. In this craft, which appeared to have been constructed of balsa and covered with tissue, the pilot sat far back, aft of the step, in an unprotected cabin. An oddly shaped rudder was placed beneath the elevators and a tiny float kept the tail above water. Although little seems to survive so far as information of the plane's performance goes, it was reported to have lifted off the water in less than five seconds. It appeared to have the makings of a fine little private seaplane that might have carried a couple of passengers.

The coming of war accelerated the development of all aspects of aviation, from aircraft design to engines and specialized aircraft types. Curtiss' *America* design served as the prototype of the wartime flying boats that were employed by the British in their life-and-death struggle with the German submarine. Two Curtiss H-4s ("H" for Hydroplane), were delivered in Britain as early as November 1914. Subsequent models, generally fitted with more powerful engines than the Curtiss OX-5s, led to improvements in the design as well as to greater size. The first American-built aircraft ever used in aerial combat was the Curtiss H-12, delivered in July 1916. As were its predecessors, the H-12 was underpowered. But fitted with two Rolls-Royce "Eagle" engines, it proved to be one of the best of Britain's patrol boats. In May of 1917 a crew of an H-12 caught a German Zeppelin—this was the L-22—over the North Sea, pulled up alongside, and shot it burning into the sea. A few days later another H-12 crew succeeded in sinking a German submarine.

The British produced their own variant of the Curtiss boat, adapting the Curtiss wing and tail surfaces to a stronger hull design (the work of quondam *America* pilot, John C. Porte), and identified by "F" numbers. The "F" stood for Felixstowe, the Royal Navy Air Station where experimental work in flying boats was carried on. The F-5, the last of the series, was a large aircraft for its day—the wingspan was slightly over 103 feet, its hull was forty-nine feet from stem to stern.

Curtiss developed an improved, and enlarged, H-12 in the H-16, which had a ninety-five-foot wingspread, besides a double step hull, balanced rudder, and improved armament. These great flying boats saw service with both the Royal Navy and the U. S. Navy in the latter months of the war.

It remained, fittingly, only for Curtiss to provide the link between the wartime flying boat o' war and the peacetime ocean transport. In the summer of 1917 the U. S. Navy asked for a flying boat capable of flying the Atlantic "to avoid the difficulties of delivery." Such a craft was to be as seaworthy as it was airworthy. To Curtiss, around this time dreaming of a large flying boat, the Navy's specification amounted to an invitation. The result was a joint Navy-Curtiss venture, with contributions made to the over-all design by both parties. Thus began the project that resulted in the NC flying boats, four of which were built. The NC-1 flew for the first time on October 4, 1918, too late to participate in the submarine patrols for which it was intended.

The NCs were the largest aircraft built in the United States at the time. The top wingspread was 126 feet and the hull, unlike that on most Curtiss designs, was short—forty-four feet; the total length of the plane was sixty-eight feet. Power was supplied by

The Curtiss H-12, which had evolved from the early flying boat design by Curtiss. The first American-built aircraft ever used in aerial combat. It was bought by Britain in 1916 and improved by the installation of Rolls-Royce engines. (Navy Department, National Archives)

A Porte/Felixstowe flying boat of 1917. These F-boats were inspired by the Curtiss but generally modified by John C. Porte, who was to have served as the transatlantic pilot of the America. Actually there was a series of F-boats, the last of which of the Curtiss variants was the F-5. Plane in the photo is an F-3 of 1917, which had been built by Short Brothers. It was the last of the F-boats to be used in the war. (Short Brothers & Harland, Ltd.)

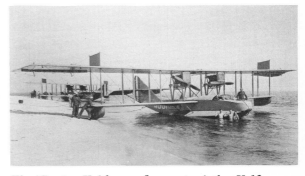

The Curtiss H-16, a refinement of the H-12. The Navy version was powered by the wartime Liberty engine (the British version used Rolls-Royce Eagles). (Navy Department, National Archives)

The Navy-Curtiss flying boat, in this instance the NC-4, jointly developed by the U. S. Navy and Curtiss in 1917–18. Intended originally as a bomber, the plane was completed too late to be used in the war. (U. S. Air Force)

The NC-4, first aircraft to cross the Atlantic, in May 1919. Crew consisted of A. C. Read, commander of the flight; E. F. Stone, pilot; W. Hinton, copilot; J. L. Breese, pilot/engineer; H. C. Rodd, radio operator, and E. Rhodes, machinist. (U. S. Navy)

four wartime Liberty engines, three pulling and one pushing. Top speed was about 90 mph, and the range nearly fifteen hundred miles. The plane carried a crew of five: commander/navigator, pilot, copilot, and two engineers.

The Navy, thwarted in its hopes for the NCs, did not despair merely because the war ended before the giant flying boats could be put to use. The Atlantic, free of the hated U-boat, continued to beckon. Also the London *Daily Mail* revived its offer of a prize of ten thousand pounds for the first men to cross the Atlantic by air. While the Navy Department had scant concern for the money, the prestige and honor that might accrue from such a feat was most attractive.

This inspired the decision to attempt the first crossing of the Atlantic by air with the coming of spring. An intensive period of training and preparation followed, during which the NC-2 was dismantled for spare parts. On May 8, 1919, the NC-1, NC-3, and NC-4 left Rockaway Beach, New York, en route to Trepassey, Newfoundland, for the flight across the Atlantic. On May 31 the NC-4 landed at Plymouth, England, the

only plane to complete the flight. The NC-1 and NC-3 had been forced down at sea; the former sank while being towed into port and the latter ended its flight in the Azores with a damaged engine after a fifty-two-hour, two-hundred-mile journey as a surface vessel. No crew members were injured in these mishaps.

Despite the two-thirds failure, the flight of the NC-4 was a triumph, and a milestone in aviation history. Its flight had not been nonstop, but it had succeeded in bridging the Atlantic by air. The flight was the overture, if a little prematurely, to the dawn of a new era in aviation: the simultaneous conquest of the sea and the air.

Not all efforts at creating aviation history, particularly as associated with operations from water, were crowned with even the qualified success of the NC-4. The intent of one of the classic failures of 1919, however, pointed to the future as had the flight of Commander Albert Read and his crew in the NC-4. The Navy men had shown that the Atlantic could be crossed by air. In that same year Italian designer Gianni Caproni, who had produced giant bombers and flying boats during the war, came up with a grand idea: no less than a hundred-passenger flying boat, the Caproni 60. With a sixty-six-foot hull, nine wings, and eight 400-hp Liberty engines, this flying houseboat weighed more than thirty thousand pounds. The passengers were to be housed in the "houseboat" upon which the wings and engines were affixed; the crew was stationed directly behind, and slightly above the center engine. The crew consisted of a pilot, two copilots, and three engineer-mechanics, who obviously could roam about working even while the plane was aloft.

An outstanding feature of the Caproni 60 was the spacious passenger accommodations—all of which was planned for transatlantic service. However, what with underpowered engines, the massiveness of the plane, the miles of wire, struts, the resistance of all this made it impossible to get the plane off the surface of Lake Maggiore, let alone over the Atlantic. After two trial flights and a subsequent splintering sinking into the lake, Caproni abandoned the idea implicit in the Model 60. But it was an idea.

Caproni Model 60 on the surface of Lake Maggiore, Italy, in 1919. The designer's hope was to produce a hundred-passenger transatlantic flying boat that could be operated economically with a crew of five. The idea of using no less than nine wings resulted in a unique, but highly unsuccessful, aircraft. The **Model 60 barely flew. The hull measured sixty-six feet from stem to stern.** *(U. S. Air Force)*

1: "Gentlemen Adventurers"

The big boom in aviation that aerial dreamers had predicted would follow the Great War did not materialize. The war, if little else, contributed to the development of aircraft design, the progress of engine evolution, and a general expansion in scientific thinking about aeronautics.

While this might have provided the means for a burgeoning of the once infant industry, it simply did not follow. This was especially true in the United States. Instead of boom, there was a decided apathy. American aircraft manufacturers, caught short by the war, had just about found themselves professionally when the end of the war brought further embarrassment. The American aircraft market became glutted with surplus planes; sturdy old de Havilland DH-4s and the multitudinous Curtiss JN-4s, the "Jenny." Hundreds of enthusiastic Army-trained pilots, bitten by the aviation bug, who wished to pursue their new love could buy one of these planes for as low as three hundred dollars and become a professional aviator.

The problem confronting such an enthusiast was that, once outfitted with "crate" and a dashing flying costume, there was little demand for his services. Having proved itself a rather deadly, not to say romantic, weapon, the airplane was relegated by the American public back to its prewar category of oversized toy. What might have been developed into an instrument of transportation was diverted into a prop for entertainment. This ushered in the era of the "gypsy flier," who traveled from hamlet to village to cow pasture diverting the yokels with his stunting and, if persuasive, talked the brave and the carefree into taking a ride in a flying machine.

On a more businesslike level, American aviation was utilized in carrying the mail, though with no great conviction nor with much success. This service, initiated by the Post Office Department in the summer of 1918, did not boom either after the war. Even so, more and more of the larger population centers were joined by air following the Armistice and into the twenties.

Civil aviation in Europe, however, placed an emphasis upon the transportation of passengers. Surplus aircraft formed the fleets of the first airlines, the very first of which was formed within two months of the Armistice. This was Germany's Deutsche Luft Reederei, which began operations using old, converted A. E. G. (*Allgemeine Elektricitats Gesellschaft*) reconnaissance aircraft to carry passengers between Berlin and Weimar, home of the new German Republic. Although the Versailles Treaty would, in time, place a handicap upon the German aircraft industry, thus also on its civil aviation, the Germans found means whereby its strictures could be circumvented. These wily methods made it possible during the period between wars to revive the German aircraft industry in Italy, Switzerland, Denmark, Sweden, and Soviet Russia, among other peace-loving nations; in Russia also the German Air Force was brought back to life.

Germany's civil airlines were thus supplied aircraft that might have been denied them, according to the Versailles Treaty, and flourished with the direct aid of the German government. By the early twenties German-owned airlines were in operation as far

away from Berlin as Colombia and Argentina in South America.

France and Britain trailed Germany only slightly in inaugurating regular passenger service between England and the Continent: France with its Lignes Aériennes Farman (Paris to Brussels, later London) in March 1919 and Britain's Aircraft Transport and Travel in August of the same year. Europeans were among the first to recognize the flying boat as a commercial aircraft. As early as 1920 the Levy Lepen was used by the Belgian airline Ligne Aérienne du Roi Albert (LARA) in the Belgian Congo.

A LARA Levy Lepen in the Belgian Congo, 1920. The plane carried only two passengers plus pilot and was used to connect Leopoldville and Stanleyville by air. LARA was eventually absorbed by Sabena Airlines. (Musée de l'Air)

CAMS-53 flying boat, Air Union's major aircraft, on its North African run during the middle twenties. Seaplanes were highly useful in the colonies of European nations because of their capability of operation from undeveloped areas without airports and runway facilities. (Musée de l'Air)

A three-place seaplane, the Levy Lepen could carry only two passengers per trip, and when the line closed up two years later it had carried a mere ninety-five passengers during its entire history. The French were fortunate in North Africa, where Air Union operated CAMS (Chantiers Aéro-Maritimes de la Seine) flying boats. By the mid-twenties Air Union was operating the CAMS-53 on this route, connecting with the Paris-Marseilles flights from Europe. Air Union, in time, was merged with other French lines to form Air France.

About midway in this period the U. S. Navy's NC-4 became the first aircraft to cross the Atlantic. The significance of this accomplishment had not escaped a young Yale student who wrote in the Yale *Graphic,* even before the event, that the Navy tour "would demonstrate that a flight across the Atlantic Ocean is a perfectly safe and sane commercial proposition and not a gigantic gamble."

No callow prophet, the youthful student based his view on some experience, at least. During the war he temporarily dropped out of Yale to enlist in the Naval Reserve Flying Corps, where he earned his wings as a qualified bomber pilot. In the spring of 1919 he returned to Yale where he organized the Flying Club the following year. Among its charter members were such "socially prominent" war-trained fliers and friends as John Hambleton (of a Baltimore banking family), Cornelius V. Whitney (better known as "Sonny" of the New York Whitneys), and William H. Vanderbilt, of the railroad Vanderbilts, and himself, Juan Terry Trippe.

Like his classmates, Trippe had come from a comfortable, monied background. His family history in the United States could be traced back to the earliest English settlements in Baltimore. His father, Charles White Trippe, had established himself in Wall Street, the New York Stock Exchange, and the *Social Register*. When expecting

the birth of her first child, Lucy Terry Trippe was so certain the baby would be a girl that she had alrealy selected a name—Juanita Terry, the name of her favorite aunt.

But on June 27, 1899, a boy was born to the Trippes, then living in Seabright, New Jersey; loath to let a name go to waste, Lucy Trippe merely adopted the masculine variant of her aunt's name, and thus Juan Terry Trippe. This small touch of whimsy of Trippe's mother would have its further, more practical, Latin connotations in his future.

Upon finishing at Yale Trippe, ostensibly following in his father's footsteps, set out on a career in Wall Street as a bond salesman. The untimely death of his father at the age of forty-eight led to a greater concentration on business and less on flying for Trippe. But he was able to contend with the paperwork of Wall Street for only a year, being as he was a man of vivid imagination, an almost aggressive ambition, and no heart for earthbound routine.

In the summer of 1923 Trippe, after having talked his friend John Hambleton into becoming his partner, acquired nine surplus Navy Seaplanes at a cost of five hundred dollars each. With these and his small amount of remaining cash, he formed Long Island Airways. In this venture Trippe served in every capacity from president to pilot to mechanic. Despite its rather impressive name, Long Island Airways was actually an air-taxi service and not an airline in any sense. Trippe or one of the gypsy fliers he hired would fly wealthy patrons around the New York-Long Island area to fashionable beaches and resorts. A charter flight, now and then, would extend the little airways' flights as far south as Florida, or north to the fishing waters of Canada.

Although he tried to run his line on a businesslike base, Trippe's major problem was with his pilots, who affected a quite casual attitude toward such vexing details as schedules. On a day off a gypsy might earn as much as a hundred dollars or so,

Aeromarine floatplane, similar to the type with which Juan Terry Trippe went into the airline business. (U. S. Air Force)

by taking passengers for short joy rides and then celebrate his good fortune with wine, women, and song—mostly wine or stronger spirits—and then not show up the following day at Long Island Airways.

Another problem was the aging seaplanes; keeping them in flying condition was as much of a drain on the company's exchequer as hungover or no-show pilots. Within two years little Long Island Airways collapsed under the weight of financial, materiel, and personnel problems.

Despite this misfortune, 1925 was not a bad year for Juan Terry Trippe, it being also the year of the passage of the Air Mail Act, more popularly known as the Kelly Act. This was in honor of its sponsor, Representative Clyde Kelly of Pennsylvania, the "Voice of the Railway Mail Clerks," who agreed that the government should get out of the mail delivery service by air, thus no longer competing with the railroads and "encourage commercial aviation . . ."

The Post Office Department would ease its way out of the air mail business by helping private operators establish air lines between major cities with payments for the transportation of mail. This amounted to a government subsidy, as was already being paid out to the railroads and steamship lines. Even so, it amounted to very little compared to the subsidies granted by European governments to their airlines, which also carried passengers as well as the mail. The United States, with its massive railroad system, at the time saw little profit in passenger airlines that could but rarely carry a passenger at a cheaper rate or even a faster speed than the railroads.

Thus the emphasis upon the mail.

When the Post Office Department let it be known that certain air mail contracts were to be let, thousands of inquiries began to pour in. At first, the plan was that only short feeder lines would be privately established. These would connect with the already well-regulated transcontinental route run by the Post Office. Significantly, the

Opening of the first Boston–New York air mail service on July 1, 1926 by Colonial Air Transport. Group includes Leroy Thomson, H. I. Wells, and Major T. O. Freeman, who delivers the bundle of mail to Colonial's managing director, Juan Terry Trippe. (Pan American)

first contract let, Civil Air Mail Route 1, which operated between New York and Boston, was awarded to Colonial Airways —significantly because the driving spirit behind Colonial was Juan Terry Trippe. Almost as soon as he had given up on his disintegrated taxi service he had heard of the Kelly Air Mail Act. He approached his Yale Flying Club friends, John Hambleton, Sonny Whitney, and William Vanderbilt, to help him back a line running between the two eastern seaboard metropolises. This line he planned to call Eastern Air Transport. But then he heard of a Boston-based group that had the same plan; this was Colonial Air Transport.

Moving quickly, Trippe approached the other group and suggested they combine capital rather than compete with each other.

Trippe and his friends were all comparative youngsters, so it was decided that to give Colonial a mature, businesslike façade one of Colonial's men, General John F. O'Ryan (who had achieved some distinction in the war) be made president. Trippe was named vice president and manager. When the new line began operations in the summer of 1926 it hopefully announced that "passengers may be carried if there is sufficient demand." Trippe obviously was not pleased with the prospect of aircraft merely carrying paper.

The following year, on April 4, 1927, Colonial Air Transport did, in fact, inaugurate scheduled passenger flights between New York and Boston. The next month Charles A. Lindbergh flew the Atlantic alone in a single-engined monoplane and dramatically changed the course of aviation history. In one captivating exploit Lindbergh demonstrated that the aircraft was not a toy, that it could travel over great distances nonstop, that engine design had reached a peak of reliability, and—quite simply—that man could truly fly. This last was no mean contribution, even at that late date.

Consequently, a spurt in aviation followed Lindbergh's flight and he himself, when he returned an international hero, began speaking out for passenger-carrying airlines.

This coincided with Trippe's thinking also, but he had run into trouble with his conservative board of directors at Colonial. Trippe had recognized the airline potential of the Fokker F-7 (the main workhorse, by then, of the pioneering Dutch airline, KLM, which had been operating since 1919). The trimotored Fokker, introduced into the United States by Anthony Fokker himself in 1925, in Trippe's view had an excellent payload capacity and, with its multiple engines, a built-in safety factor. So he ordered two for Colonial Air Transport. This expenditure ($37,500 each) for uninsurable equipment greatly upset the board.

Then during a survey flight to the south,

in company with Fokker and Hambleton, Trippe ran into further trouble. First one engine went out, then another, so that the Fokker came in to a landing on a single engine. The plane was slightly damaged, but the three men were only a little shaken up. The board of Colonial was greatly shaken, however. Trippe, who was out seeking new lines to set up to the south, believed that their landing had proved his confidence in multi-engined aircraft; the board was convinced that Trippe suffered from overgrown ambition.

The board meeting that followed Trippe's adventure in the Florida Keys lacked decorum, and before the smoke cleared away, Trippe and his two friends, Hambleton and Whitney, sold their stock in the company back to Colonial and left to begin their own airline. Colonial was later absorbed into what became American Airlines.

Trippe and company formed the Aviation Corporation of the Americas, a rather formidable name for a line connecting New York and Atlantic City. But that was only for the summer season of 1926; by the spring of 1927 Trippe had begun to move again. He had heard that the Post Office Department was interested in issuing a mail contract for a route connecting Key West, Florida, with Havana, Cuba—a distance of about ninety miles.

When he arrived on the scene in Florida he found two competitors already on hand; Florida Airways, which had been formed by two wartime fliers, Reed Chambers and "Eddie" Rickenbacker, and Pan American Airways, Inc., which was the brainchild of Major Henry Arnold. As a U. S. Army Air Corps information officer Arnold had seen reports sent by a military attaché in Colombia. These furnished "repeated data about a German airline, SCADTA, run by a Captain von Bauer, and operating between Barranquilla and Bogotá. All pilots, mechanics, and equipment of this line, running up the

Magdalena River, and far too close to the Panama Canal to be ignored, were German."

Military Intelligence being what it was in the latter twenties, some of Arnold's information was not quite accurate. SCADTA, a name derived from the initials of its full name Sociedad Colombo-Alemana de Transportes Aéreos, was an Austrian-German-financed pioneer airline (there was no government backing, however) that had been formed in 1920 by Dr. Peter Paul von Bauer. It was the first successful airline in South America and one of the most efficiently managed. Not the least of the reasons for its success was the fact that all employees, whether of Austrian or German birth, had become naturalized citizens of Colombia. This, technically at least, made SCADTA a home-owned airline, which pleased Colombian nationalists considerably; in turn SCADTA was favored with such concessions as the operation of its own post offices, the establishment of air mail rates, and the retention of all revenues received.

The result was that SCADTA became a profitable operation, and Bauer visualized himself as a builder of an aerial empire. He began in 1925–26 to petition for landing rights in Central America, Panama, and ultimately Florida. It was at this point that Arnold and his associates, among whom were two other Air Corps majors—Carl Spaatz and Jack Jouett—plus an ex-Navy air enthusiast, John Montgomery went into action. The latter served as the fund-raiser for Pan American Airways and had succeeded in interesting two money men, Richard Bevier and Grant Mason, in the idea.

Before Trippe appeared on the scene Pan American had already secured a contract from the Cuban government to carry the mail between Havana and Key West. Trippe, unaware of any future threat to the security of the Panama Canal by SCADTA (actually there wasn't), saw Pan American

Airways as a threat to his idea of building an airline into the Caribbean. With characteristic élan, he and Hambleton visited Cuban dictator Gerardo Machado and received an exclusive flying permit. This meant that no other airline could land or take off from Cuban territory—which, in turn, rendered Pan American Airways' mail contract worthless.

Meanwhile, Florida Airways (whose main lines connected Atlanta, Georgia, with Miami, Florida) was having its own troubles. Two of its three planes had suffered accidents (the third was seized by the sheriff) and the backers suffered qualms, forcing the firm into receivership. It was then Pan American's turn: Arnold, who had backed outspoken General William Mitchell in his fight for a separate Air Force, decided he could not quit the Air Corps under fire to head the new airline. Likewise, Spaatz; so not only was Pan American without a permit to land in Cuba, it was also lacking its president (Arnold) and operating director (Spaatz).

Trippe, of course, held all the cards, what with his winning of an exclusive permit from Machado. So it was that whatever remained of Florida and Pan American were absorbed into the Aviation Corporation of the Americas. All the real airmen—Chambers, Rickenbacker, Arnold, and Spaatz—simply dropped out of the picture, although some of the money men remained in various positions in the new company—at least for a time. Once again a more mature board chairman was selected—Richard Hoyt (of Florida) was placed at the head of the Aviation Corporation. Trippe was to head the new Pan American Airways, Incorporated, as the operating subsidiary of AVCO.

Having eliminated his immediate rivals, and having lined up the backing, most of it through his wealthy friends, Trippe was about ready to begin operations. Not quite,

The modest birth of Pan American Airways; Cy Caldwell's Fairchild FC-2 floatplane, in which Pan American inaugurated the first air mail service between Key West and Havana. The Fairchild belonged to West Indian Aerial Express, which was later swallowed up by an expanding Pan American. (Pan American)

Pan American Airways, Incorporated

FLIGHT REPORT

TYPE and registrationmarks of the Airplane...........

Pilot.......... Cy Caldwell

Assistant Pilot..........

DATE: October 19, 1927

Purpose of the journey.......... Mail

Duration of the journey.......... 1.08

Mileage of the journey.......... 90

MINALS: Departure from Key West at 6:28 A.M. | Arrival at Havana at 7:35 A.M.

Intermediate Stations:
Arrival at..........A.M. Departure from..........A.M.
Arrival at..........A.M. Departure from..........A.M.
Arrival at..........A.M. Departure from..........A.M.

		PASSENGERS								MAIL					EXPRESS AND EXCESS BAGGAGE					
NUMBER		NAME	FROM	TO	Ticket No.	Return Ticket No.	Fare Collected	Insured For	CLASS OF MAIL	No. of Bags	Weight	FROM	TO	CLASS	No. of Pk'gs	Weight	FROM	TO	Freightage Collected
Paying	Free																		
									F.M.4	7	251	R.M.S. KW	Havana						

STATIONS	Time of Observation	VISIBILITY	LOWER CLOUDS		Wind Direction	Velocity
			Height	Amount		
Key West	7:30 A.M.	Unlimited	1000	solid	North	39

REMARKS:

EXAMINED BY:
Administrative:
Traffic:
Manager:
Statistics:

A document of historical note: Cy Caldwell's flight report of October 19, 1927, marking the birth of Pan American Airways and the delivery of seven bags of mail at Havana, Cuba. (Pan American)

however; the Fokker trimotors Trippe had ordered had not been delivered.

According to the agreement with the Post Office, Trippe was to begin flying the mail between Key West and Havana not later than October 19, 1927. On this date there were still no Fokkers on hand in Key West for the historic inaugural flight. In fact, there was no one on hand at Key West but a very frantic manager, J. E. Whitbeck, scanning the morning sky for a trimotored aircraft. The mail sacks had already been delivered from the mainland. As for Pan American's executives, they were equally frantic, in Washington, hoping to gain an extension of the opening date from the Post Office.

Whitbeck stood around literally holding the bag. Then, also literally, out of the blue a speck appeared. It was no Fokker F-7, but a little sputtering single-engined Fairchild floatplane that splashed gracefully into the water and pulled up to the landing ramp. Whitbeck rushed out to greet the pilot, who turned out to be the colorful Cy Caldwell, on his way to Haiti, making a refueling stop.

Would he, for a consideration of $175, make a round trip flight to Havana carrying the mail?

He would of course, for such arrangements—informal, spur-of-the-moment—were not unique in the early days of flying. So, after refueling the Fairchild, Caldwell took off with seven bags of mail in the cabin. The flight, thanks to a tailwind, took him a little over an hour. In fact, he arrived in Havana an hour before the cablegram announcing his impending arrival was received. Then ensued a four-hour encounter with Cuban customs officials before Caldwell could complete the circle.

His departure was again cabled ahead and, again, Caldwell arrived an hour before the cable. This was the rather frenzied improvisation that marked the first official flight of Juan Terry Trippe's Pan American Airways: one man, a quantity of mail, and a single-engined floatplane—all of which added up to a mighty acorn, indeed.

There were two elements that nurtured this acorn into a forest of great oaks. The first was the remarkable business acuity, the imagination, and sheer drive of Juan Trippe. The other was the benevolence of the United States Post Office Department. Once Pan American had proved it could fulfill its obligation to get the mail to and from Cuba (within eight days of Caldwell's "Inaugural Flight" the two Fokkers had been delivered and daily flights were begun), its most generous silent partner was the Post Office.

With the passage of the Foreign Air Mail Act in March of 1928, under which Pan American was issued Foreign Air Mail Route No. 1, a second "first" for Trippe, Pan American was well on its way into an entrenched position in the Caribbean.

Trippe and the men who had joined him in this enterprise were issued what in the seventeenth century amounted to a Royal Charter. Like those earlier "sundry Knights, Gentlemen, Merchants, and other Adventurers" they were comfortably monied but venturesome and seeking to expand their horizons and willing to risk both their money and their futures. In turn, a benevolent monarch (in the case of the Virginia Company, King James I; in the case of Pan American, Postmaster General Walter Folger Brown) granted them a wide latitude of privilege and power.

2: Flying Down to Rio

In selecting the Caribbean for his province, Trippe had chosen wisely, for by the time he and his friends had been bought out of Colonial Air Transport the domestic airline picture was virtually complete. The Caribbean, and points south, were practically virgin territory.

Not totally untouched by foreign hands, however. As early as 1919 the enterprising Inglis M. Uppercu had inaugurated regular flights between Key West, Florida, and Havana. Uppercu's Aeromarine and Motor Company had gained much experience with seaplanes, building them for the U. S. Navy during the war. That finished, Uppercu founded Aeromarine Airways, and in No-vember 1919 began flying passengers, mail, and freight between Key West, Florida and Havana. The aircraft were Navy surplus F-5-Ls (actually the Curtiss flying boat con-verted to civil use) that had been manufac-tured by the Naval Aircraft Factory. Be-sides transporting the mail and freight from the United States to Cuba, the function of Aeromarine, as legend has it, was primarily to fly pleasure-seekers out of Prohibition-dry United States to wet Havana, where the spirits flowed freely.

Aeromarine's operations were seasonal, and although reasonably regular, it was not a truly full-time airline. When the winter season ended in Florida, the planes were

An Aeromarine F-5-L (a Curtiss design produced by the Naval Aircraft Factory, Philadelphia) moored off Havana, Cuba, late in 1919. This operation was one of the precursors of the Pan American operations that would begin just a few years after Aeromarine went out of business. (Smithsonian Institution, National Air and Space Museum)

flown to other ports to provide air service between New York and Atlantic City and another, across Lake Erie, between Detroit and Cleveland. These, too, were seasonal. Even so, considering that it lasted for four years, Aeromarine could be regarded as the first operational airline in the United States —if the embryo effort of the St. Petersburg–Tampa Airboat Line is placed in proper historical perspective. Aeromarine also was the first American-based airline to operate internationally and was the first to be awarded a foreign air mail contract.

But despite Uppercu's foresightedness Aeromarine did not flourish, even after a merger that joined the firm with West Indies Airways to form Aeromarine West Indies Airways. Uppercu even expanded the service, establishing flights between Miami and Nassau, in the Bahamas, stopping off en route at Bimini. But the operation did not pay off, besides which mail payments were withdrawn, and Aeromarine floundered in 1924.

Still another pre-Trippe enterprise was initiated almost simultaneously with Aeromarine, although its history went back farther in time. In fact, this one had its beginnings in the 1914 attempt at crossing the

Atlantic in the Curtiss *America*. Rodman Wanamaker, who had sponsored it, hoped to form a transoceanic airline—which he did in 1916 as America Trans-Oceanic Company. Nothing came of this, except cementing Wanamaker's association with Curtiss, because of the war.

The war ended, Wanamaker once again reactivated ATO with the intention of connecting certain Florida coastal towns by air and also to make flights regularly to the island of Bimini, mainly because of the location there of the posh Bay Rod and Gun Club and the availability of strong waters in British territory. The general manager of ATO was David McCulloch (who had served as the pilot of the NC-3) and it was he who was also pilot, with John Miller, when ATO's first flight to Bimini took place on February 24, 1920. Their craft, which could carry a crew of three (George A. Page, Jr. came along as engineer), provided space for about ten passengers. It was also one of the most striking flying boats ever seen. In deference to the president of the Bimini Bay Rod and Gun Club, Charles Thompson (who had once landed an exceptionally large fish), the converted Curtiss H-16 was decorated to look like a fish. It was named, appropriately, "Big Fish," and made the trip between Miami and Bimini quite regularly (generally a round trip every day, in season). This lasted for a couple of seasons, but this particular operation of ATO faded out. The "Big Fish" was used also, off-season, in New York to fly paying passengers to various lakeland pleasure spots. The life of the "Big Fish" came to an end in 1921 during a landing at Port Washington, New York, when the bottom of the hull buckled and the plane sank. That ended the international operations of the America Trans-Oceanic Company (at least until it was revived in 1927, when Wanamaker sponsored the transatlantic flight of Richard E. Byrd). In time, like Aeromarine, ATO also faded from the scene. It remained for Juan Terry Trippe to come upon that scene, study it, understand it, and make it work.

The terrain of Trippe's chosen domain was perfect for aircraft: water, jungle, and mountain. A journey that once had taken days, even weeks could be accomplished in a few hours by air. All things being equal, that is: provided the weather was right and provided that there were airports. Chopping such facilities out of the jungle, even with local political aid, was no simple job. Nor was it inexpensive. And it took time, some times as long as six months from the moment a locater sack of flour was dropped in a selected spot at the edge of a jungle until the Fokkers could land there. Work crews would trek to the spot, find the flour splotches, and prepare the site, hauling all their supplies by burro, by canoe and boat, or having it dropped from the air. Even fuel had to be brought in on the heads of local Indians (who greeted the intruders initially with arrows and stones). Thus was an air route cut through the jungles of the Honduras through to Panama.

The "Big Fish" during one of its northern jaunts in the Florida off-season. The setting is Lake Keuka, New York, near Hammondsport, where Curtiss had his factory. Various other Curtiss flying boats line the beach, although "Big Fish" attracts the most spectators. (Smithsonian Institution, National Air and Space Museum)

It was Trippe's plan to ring the Caribbean with Pan American air tracks. He worked his way from Panama southeastward, chopping and building, and buying out, if necessary, as his airline expanded. Soon flights were possible almost daily to Haiti and Santo Domingo, then more directly southward to points in the Leeward and Windward Islands and eastward again to touch the northeastern coast of South America at Georgetown, in British Guiana, and Paramaribo in Dutch Guiana. For the moment Venezuela and Colombia to the west remained a break in Trippe's circle —the former because dictator Juan Vincente Gomez, better known by his more popular name as the "Butcher of Venezuela," hated flying machines; Colombia remained off limits because of the entrenchment of SCADTA under Dr. Peter Paul von Bauer.

To close the circle between Panama and Florida the obstacle of Yucatan remained. The problem was natural, not manmade. To carve an airport out of some spot on the coast of Yucatan seemed impossible until someone suggested that a small Caribbean island, Cozumel, just off the Mexican coast, was accessible from both Havana and the Yucatan.

It was about at this point that a certain other feature of Trippe's domain impressed itself upon everyone. If there were mountains and jungles to cross, so was there plentiful water, always close to the major shipping and population centers. That water could present a threat at times. In the early months of Pan American's operations in the Caribbean the Fokker F-7s were used, and these could only operate from land bases. One pilot (now faded into legend) who had taken off from Key West on the Havana run flew into a tropical storm over the Gulf of Mexico. The Fokker averaged about eighty miles an hour, but the hurricane was making ninety. For an hour the hapless pilot pushed the Fokker

Pan American initiated its overwater flights in a landplane—at first the Fokker F-7 trimotor and, two years later in 1929, the F-10. This photograph was taken on the introduction of the F-10 to the Miami-San Juan route on January 9, 1929, at the Santo Domingo stopover at San Pedro. On the left, nearest to the camera, stands Basil L. Rowe, once of West Indian Aerial Express, who had just joined Pan American when his firm had been absorbed by Trippe's company. He would prove to be one of Pan American's most "intrepid" pilots during its early years. (Pan American)

through the murk until, his fuel dwindling, he decided he would have to give up and make the best of the quite hopeless situation.

Throttling back, he pushed the stick gently forward and descended into the clouds. Certain that he was lost somewhere over water, he was more than surprised to see the outline of land breaking through the weather. There was an even greater surprise: He found himself directly over the airfield he had left an hour before.

Another Pan American pilot (perhaps the same one, for he remains equally anonymous) returned from a survey flight along the western coast of Central America to make the classic comment upon the more than ample supply of water. "It rained all the time," he said, "it rained so hard that there were three inches of fresh water on the surface of the ocean."

With all of that water everywhere, Trippe reasoned, why not put it to use? Why not employ an aircraft capable of carrying a good payload, combine it with the safety factor of multiple engines and the ability to operate from both land and water?

To provide a solution to the problem of joining the Yucatan with Cuba and Florida by air, it was suggested that the lagoon at Cozumel off the Yucatan coast be utilized as a seaplane base. The problem then was to find the plane for the job that could, incidentally, also be flown over the watery stretches of the eastern Caribbean.

The American aviation scene had changed a good deal since the early days of Wright and Curtiss; by the late twenties neither of these pioneers were active (by the thirties the names of these two irreconcilable antagonists would be ironically joined in a single firm, the Curtiss-Wright Corporation). Neither Wright nor Curtiss (who had been the early leader in the field) had pursued the design of seagoing aircraft after the war.

Trippe then turned to a struggling firm located at nearby Roosevelt Field, Long Island, known as the Sikorsky Aero Engineering Corporation. The company had been formed around the aeronautical genius of a Russian refugee from the 1917 Revolution, Count Igor Sikorsky. Before his arrival in the United States in 1919 Sikorsky had already established himself as a leading figure in aviation as the designer of outstanding multi-engined aircraft. It was while flying in one of his early planes, forced down by a mosquito-clogged carburetor, that Sikorsky conceived the idea of an aircraft powered by more than one engine. Another Sikorskyan theme was giant aircraft—with four engines, a remarkably advanced idea in 1912—with wingspans spreading to more than ninety feet. During the war Sikorsky produced an even larger plane, the "Ilia Mourometz," with a wing measuring just over 101 feet—one of the first of the "heavy bombers."

The coming of the Revolution ended Sikorsky's Russian aviation career, and he fled to France. He found no permanent niche in French aviation either, and emigrated to the United States in 1919. The postwar slump and the general low level of American aviation at the time forced him into a teaching career until some four years later, in 1923, friends and students (most of them fellow Russians emigrés) who had

been aware of his contributions to aviation before the Revolution, banded together and helped form and finance the Sikorsky Aero Engineering Corporation.

The first venture of the embryonic and financially uncertain firm was a twin-engined, all-metal transport, the S-29-A (the first letter standing for Sikorsky and the last for America), which held promise but did not establish Sikorsky on any solid fiscal footing. But the company continued to develop, filling nonspectacular orders, including the ill-fated S-35, built for French war ace René Fonck. This was during the era of the "Atlantic crossing fever," when airmen were anxious to be the first to make the transatlantic flight that would win them the Raymond Orteig prize for the first flight between New York and Paris. Through no fault of the design, the S-35 crashed on its takeoff run, killing two men, although Fonck himself escaped. Stubbornly determined to make the crossing, Fonck ordered another Sikorsky plane—the S-37, which, although built, was not used by the French flier; the flight of Lindbergh in 1927 canceled its function.

Just before the advent of the S-35, Sikorsky had experimented with another aircraft, which like Fonck's plane, ended up unhappily, although without fatalities. Sometime in 1925 Sikorsky built a five-place floatplane that was to be used in South America by an oil company. This plane stirred up Sikorsky's imagination, and by the end of the following year a new type of plane had emerged from the little Sikorsky factory. This was the S-34, a twin-engined amphibian. The hull was shaped like an ordinary boat, with the two engines mounted at the top center of the single wing. Projecting from the trailing edges of the wing were two booms onto which the tail surfaces were attached—a curious-looking aircraft.

Unfortunately the plane suffered engine failure during a test flight while near the

Sikorsky's first attempt at an amphibian—the S-34. Designed to carry six people, it established the pattern for the Sikorskys that followed. This craft flipped over during a test, and so it was never learned whether or not it might have proved successful. (Sikorsky Aircraft)

water, and the pilot was forced to land downwind. A gust from behind flipped the S-34 over into the water, and pilot Charles Collyier, mechanic Hans Olsen, and Sikorsky, who was aboard as observer, managed to climb out of the sinking plane and held on until a rescue boat arrived. The plane sank, however, although the optimistic Sikorsky found in its design and failure "much that was later useful."

The loss of the aircraft and the loss of Fonck's S-35, which had preceded it, did not bode well for the struggling Sikorsky Aero Engineering Corporation. Then came Lindbergh's flight and the need for Fonck's new plane, the S-37, went with it (although the single example of the type, another large, twin-engined transport, was eventually sold).

However, the plane produced just before the S-37 was another amphibian, an improved modification of the S-34. This was the S-36, Sikorsky's first successful amphibian. Like the earlier design, it featured a high wing from which the boatlike hull was suspended; the twin engines were mounted into the underside of the wing, and two booms extended from the wing's trailing edge to carry the tail surfaces. One of the refinements over the S-34 was an enclosed cabin; taking off and landing in an S-34 would have been a most dampening experience. There was room for eight passengers in the S-36's cabin; the entire hull was thirty-four feet long, and the wings of the plane spanned some seventy-two feet.

Only five of this design were built, one being leased to Pan American for testing.

It was this single Sikorsky S-36 that opened up the pioneering flights by Pan American Airways into the Caribbean and South America. It proved to be a worthy if under-powered craft, indeed, with fine flight char-acteristics plus the duocapability of opera-tions over land and water. Pan American had its weapon for the South American conquest. Its implications were broader than initially imagined. As expressed by Pan American's chief engineer, André Priester: "A seaplane carries its own airport on its bottom."

Priester, Dutch-born, shrewd, outspoken, and colorful, knew aircraft. He had come to Pan American after a brief stay with the Atlantic Aircraft Corporation (actually the American-based Fokker), and before that he had worked in his homeland with the pioneer airline KLM. He thus under-stood both operations and machines. In the Sikorsky amphibian Preister recognized the plane that would serve the needs of Pan American's growing pains.

The success of the S-36 encouraged Sikorsky to develop the concept further, even as Pan American proceeded with its exploratory flights to the south. Despite its performance, the S-36 and its not very spec-tacular sale could not solve Sikorsky's prob-lem: money. Lindbergh's flight, however, had served to stimulate a general interest in aviation; Sikorsky believed that this boded well for the future, and he risked one further venture. Using the S-36 as a starting point, he deftly added refinements to the design.

Work was begun early in 1920 on a ten-place amphibian powered by two Pratt & Whitney "Wasp" engines of some 400 horsepower; practically the same wing as served for the S-36 was used, but the hull was extended about six feet—the new hull being forty feet long. The new ship, com-pleted in May, was the S-38, affectionately dubbed the "Ugly Duckling" and the "Fly-ing Tadpole," among other sobriquets.

The second Sikorsky amphibian, the S-36. Re-finements, as compared with the S-34, can be noted: Engines have been lowered to dangle under the wing, floats have been fitted under the sponsons, and—to the eternal gratitude of the pilot and passengers—the cabin is en-closed, which protected all from drenching. Hull design, however, had not yet been quite perfected, and getting the S-36 unstuck from the water was quite a job. (Sikorsky Aircraft)

An S-36 as a landplane, not yet quite a true waterbird. Pan American leased one (of five built) to test out the theory of operating in the Caribbean with amphibious, instead of land, aircraft. (Sikorsky Aircraft)

In appearance the plane resembled a shoetree onto which a wing, tail booms, and engines had been attached. It was, technically, a sesquiplane; its smaller lower wing had a span of thirty-six feet. This wing served to strengthen the lift structure, carried the floats, and shared some of the stress of the landing gear. The wheels did not fully retract, but were tucked in alongside the fuselage for water operations. For one-engine steering in the water, stability was achieved by lowering the wheel on the same side into the water. The S-38 was capable of taking off and climbing with a single engine and presented no problems in level flight.

The hull, divided into six watertight compartments, was flat as hulls went. This sometimes complicated takeoffs and landings—the former because the propellers sprayed water over the windshields, blinding the pilot until the plane lifted onto the step, or dampened the carburetors, which in turn led to engine trouble. In landings, the flatness of the hull caused some jolting discomfort if the pilot was forced, as in the event of rough waters, to stall in. The ideal landing was to come in on the step, settle down, and all was well. But this was not always possible.

The S-38, Sikorsky's first completely successful amphibian, at the Chicago Air Races in 1930. This is a later model with the sloping windshield, which was introduced with the twenty-second S-38B in 1929. (U. S. Air Force)

Despite these comparatively slight disadvantages the S-38 was an excellent ship and was quickly recognized as such; its advent saved the Sikorsky company, and it contributed to the expansion of Pan American Airways.

Trippe, although he possessed the aircraft he needed for what Sikorsky called "the peaceful conquest" of South America, was confronted with other tougher realities. The conquest, while not outright war, was not so peaceful. Trippe's business methods and his almost overwhelming success incited a general hue and cry of rape. However, the young adventurer took a grander view: "With the airplane of today America has the first chance to dominate the future highways of world trade since the days of the clipper ships of a hundred years ago."

Trippe's view was a kind of twentieth-century Manifest Destiny, honestly and sincerely held, in which he hoped to dominate the air of the Caribbean and South America: In short, what was good for Pan American was good for America. In this view he was sustained by Postmaster General Walter Folger Brown, who was in fact more interested in building an efficient air mail operation to Latin America than in favoring Pan American. It just so happened that Trippe's characteristic "go getting," to use a contemporary term, placed Pan American in the position to fulfill Brown's interests as much as vice versa. This "impartial favoritism" contributed greatly to Trippe's "peaceful conquest" to the south and helped immeasurably in eliminating a number of Pan American's rivals. When these hapless, and sometimes struggling, pioneers submitted bids to the U. S. Government for airmail lines in South America they were disconcerted to learn that Pan American, with unerring acumen, had already sewn up the landing rights at the various points and, worse, was awarded the mail contract despite the fact that it was not the lowest bidder for the route. The Post Office

Department got around this technicality with another: by quoting the rather broad regulations of the Foreign Air Mail Act, which authorized the Postmaster General to issue contracts to "the lowest *responsible* bidders that can *satisfactorily* perform the service required to *the best advantage of the government.*" Note the added emphasis, for these generalities made it possible for Postmaster General Brown to exclude Pan American rivals from Latin America. This was especially effective in dealing with United States-based lines.

Two of Trippe's most troublesome and toughest competitors were home-based. One was not concerned with aviation at all: W. R. Grace & Company, a great shipping combine reputed to own "practically everything on the west coast" (that is, the Pacific coast) of South America. An airborne invasion into Grace territory was not regarded with equanimity. Nor was Grace & Company a simple one-pilot airline; it was a complex organization with interests in banking, import, and export as well as shipping. Already solidly entrenched Grace could muster formidable resistance to Trippe's aerial adventuring. But Trippe too had more than a few stratagems at his command. One, of course, was that bottleneck he had secured at Havana, which blocked Grace's plans, if any, for its own international airline. Another was the purchase of a small airline in Peru and establishing another—but only on paper—in Chile; both in the very heart of Grace territory.

What actually resulted, to mix metaphors a bit, was a Mexican standoff. Pan American could not actually operate an airline on the Pacific coast without the cooperation of Grace, particularly without the advantages that might be furnished by the radios of its ships. On the other hand, even though Grace held the coasts of Peru and Chile, it did not have any air privileges inland; these belonged to the fast-stepping and

An early S-38 in Pan American colors and in its proper if secondary element. (Pan American)

fast-thinking Juan Trippe. Nimble and alert though he was, and firmly entrenched as Grace was, there was ultimately no solution to their standoff but compromise, a solution that contributed nothing to the harmonious bliss of either.

The result of this unhappy marriage, made in February 1929, was Pan American-Grace Airways, better known as Panagra. However infelicitous, the marriage did establish Pan American along the South American west coast. The two companies split the ownership of the Peruvian and Chilean Airways exactly in half, and Panagra was in business. But, as phrased by Henry Ladd Smith, it was true that "As a small child, Panagra grew up in a broken home. Both parents fought for custody of the offspring, but since each had exactly equal rights and privileges under the law, neither could win control. Panagra grew up to be an important airline but its full development was always hampered by the family squabbling." One of the bitter fruits of this bickering was that eventually (and outside the chronology of this story) Panagra lost out on the chance of operating a trunk line between the Pacific coast of South America and the mainland of the United States. Following the Second World War, in the postwar reshuffling, Panagra and Pan American found their contentious air invaded by another line, Braniff International Airways (which eventually bought out Panagra).

With the west coast sewed up, Trippe turned his gaze to the east (momentarily setting aside the problem of Peter Paul von Bauer's SCADTA in between), and he did not like what he saw. A near counterpart to Pan American, namely with American financial backing and a zest for planning ahead, had been formed almost simultaneously with the name of New York, Rio, and Buenos Aires Line, Inc., or more simply as NYRBA—and heavy handedly as "Near Beer."

Behind this upstart rival, this mote in the eye of Juan Trippe, were a goodly number of money men, among them James H. Rand (of Remington-Rand), W. B. Mayo (of the Ford Motor Company), F. C. Munson (of the Munson Steamship Lines), Reuben H. Fleet (founder of Consolidated Aircraft Company) and, among impressive others, Lewis Pierson of the Irving Trust Company. Obviously NYRBA was no fly-by-night gypsy airline.

There was also a touch of personal enmity in the line's makeup: the name of Pierson evoked the name of Bevier, for Richard Bevier was the son-in-law of Lewis Pierson and brother of K. M. Bevier—all now on NYRBA's board of directors and all once associated with the original Pan American Airways, Inc., which had been squeezed out of existence when Trippe's Aviation Corporation of the Americas had bottled up the exclusive landing rights in Havana.

With Richard Bevier as board chairman and J. K. Montgomery as vice president of the rival line (for the latter also had been one of the original founders of the first Pan American), Trippe could expect formidable opposition from veterans of the competitive wars. Nor was he facing amateur airmen, for associated with NYRBA was also Ralph O'Neill (who had been a

salesman for Boeing aircraft in South America and a famed pilot himself); and Reuben Fleet not only contributed his knowledge gleaned as a wartime pilot (he had even participated in the first air mail flights in 1918), but also the technical facilities of his Consolidated Aircraft Company.

Not that Fleet visualized NYRBA as a convenient outlet for Consolidated Aircraft; the company, in fact, began operations with the Ford Trimotor and the Sikorsky S-38. The aspiring airline had purchased the prototype of the Sikorskys and had begun flying it even before Pan American had put its first S-38 into service. But the most impressive plane used by NYRBA was, indeed, a product of Consolidated.

This aircraft, the first of a noble (if such a quality may be ascribed to a machine) line, had grown out of a design competition sponsored by the U. S. Navy in 1928. According to the specifications announced by Rear Admiral William A. Moffett, chief of the Navy's Bureau of

The prototype S-38, completed in June 1928; it was initially operated by the New York, Rio, and Buenos Aires Line (NYRBA), an early Pan American rival in the race for a footing in the Caribbean and South America. The plane was taken over by Pan American when it absorbed NYRBA in 1930. This first S-38 was lost a year later when it struck an underwater obstruction during a landing at Ponce Harbor, Puerto Rico. Though the plane was lost, no passenger was injured. (Sikorsky Aircraft)

Aeronautics, the required craft would have to result in a giant flying boat capable of flying nonstop from the mainland to Hawaii (and other points—Alaska, the Philippines, the Canal Zone)—in other words, a distance of some two thousand miles—dependent upon a fuel capacity of 750 gallons. Responsible for the design of this plane was Consolidated's I. M. Laddon (only recently hired away from the U. S. Army Corps' Engineering Division). Laddon's solution to the problem was a hundred-foot wing-spanned boat, the all-metal hull of which had been patterned after that of the Navy's historic NCs. The major difference was that the hull of the Consolidated boat was elongated and did not require outriggers for the small twin rudders.

The plane, officially designated the XPY-1, was ready for a test flight on January 22, 1929, when it proved itself both sea- and airworthy by taking off beautifully from the Anacostia River in Washington, D.C. Powered by two Pratt & Whitney "Wasps" (450 hp each) the slender flying boat, according to a newspaper account of the time, "roared down the river on a ten-mile wind . . . lifted easily after a 650-foot run, and climbed quickly." Captain Holden C. Richardson, who had served on the design team of the Navy's NCs and who had piloted the NC-3, was aboard for the flight and pronounced the XPY-1 "very stable. It felt good to have something solid under foot."

Also aboard for the flight was the Navy's Assistant Secretary for Aeronautics, Edward P. Warner, who spoke enthusiastically of the advent of the huge flying boat and how the Navy's nurturing of the design might contribute to its development for commercial aviation. What followed rendered his expectations ironic.

Consolidated Aircraft had produced the prototype, but it was the Glenn L. Martin Company that won the Navy's production orders. For the nine aircraft Martin had underbid Consolidated considerably and began production of their version of the plane, the P3M-1, almost immediately. This was an unsettling outcome for Consolidated, whose staff took some consolation in saying, even long after the event, that Martin "underbid us a half million and lost a million on the job."

Not that the loss of the production order daunted Consolidated as far as the XPY-1 was concerned. It had certainly proved itself. This had come around the time of the passage of the Foreign Air Mail Act and the emergence of the New York, Rio, and Buenos Aires Line. The initial explorations for the line had already been completed by Ralph O'Neill, who found as he flitted about South America that he regularly ran into Pan American, solidly entrenched, practically everywhere he went. It was not until he arrived in Argentina that O'Neill became lucky and was granted with an exclusive mail contract by the government—this, most significantly, sewed up the port of Buenos Aires on the east coast. Moving westward, O'Neill also managed (he spoke Spanish fluently) to acquire a terminal at Santiago, Chile, which happened to be the southernmost point of the Pan American-Panagra combine on the west coast.

Santiago, therefore, according to the NYRBA plan, would be linked with Buenos Aires by Ford Trimotor. The plan, then, waxed ambitious. With the new Consolidated flying boat—now called the Commodore—NYRBA would connect Buenos Aires with Rio de Janeiro, Brazil, more than twelve hundred miles to the north.

It was a conception worthy of Juan Terry Trippe himself, and he did not delight in the compliment. Even so, NYRBA proceeded with its plans, and on October 3, 1929, the first Commodore flying boat was christened the *Buenos Aires* by the President's wife, Mrs. Herbert Hoover, at the Naval Air Station in Washington, D.C. By

Martin P3M, which won a production contest over Consolidated's XPY-1 from the U. S. Navy. The XPY-1 was then converted into the Commodore. The close resemblance between the two craft is not accidental: It was the type the Navy wanted; Martin merely underbid on it. (Martin Company)

early 1930 four Commodores were operating in South America and ten more were on order for the ambitious new line. Trippe's offers to buy out the partners of NYRBA fell upon deaf ears; this was hard to take. Worse: NYRBA's mail rate was half that charged in South America by Pan American.

By the spring of 1930 Pan American suffered from a number of sore spots: one was in its lower western extremity at Santiago, where it shared a terminal with NYRBA; the other was along the eastern coast, especially in Brazil, where NYRBA had chosen to ply its Commodores over waters that Trippe coveted. Not that they were alone, for the two American-based airlines challenged the already entrenched French (Lignes Latécoère) and German (Sindicato Condor and Viaçao Aérea Rio Grandense) lines along the eastern coast. These more established operators, though wary, remained aloof from the "air war" (as it was called) between the battling upstarts.

Generally the "war" was fought on the

A NYRBA Commodore dips a wing over New York Harbor early in 1930; the plane was a refined version of the XPY-1 Admiral. NYRBA, in 1929, operating the then longest airline (nine thousand miles) by a single company, ordered fourteen Commodores. The flying boat accommodated up to thirty-two passengers. (General Dynamics/Convair)

management level in New York, or politically in Washington (where in fact the outcome would be decided), but rarely among the rival flight crews. For a time actually there was a friendly give-and-take between the Pan American and NYRBA crews. This was especially advantageous to the Pan American men, for south of their bases in Paramaribo in Dutch Guiana, there were no Pan American radio stations or bases. As Pan American proceeded with survey flights southward into NYRBA's territory during the summer of 1930 an occasional problem, such as engine trouble or a fuel shortage, meant that the survey plane could set down upon a NYRBA-manned base and be welcomed. But by summer the ill will that smoldered at the management level had filtered down to the field. From New York came an order to "Discontinue render any and all services to Pan American pilots . . ."

The immediate result was the bloodless skirmish that came to be called the "Battle of Lake Montenegro." It erupted one day during a Pan American survey flight along the coast of Brazil. To the dismay and surprise of the pilot the Sikorsky engines began sputtering at an inopportune moment and he realized that for some reason they had begun to run low on fuel. Luckily he spotted Lake Montenegro, just inland from the ocean, and set the plane down. He knew that NYRBA had an emergency station on the lake; what he did not know was that the order had come down to deny "any and all services" to the likes of him.

Pleased with his good fortune, the pilot taxied toward the NYRBA station where he expected, as before, to take on fuel. To his chagrin he found himself greeted by a surly group of NYRBA employees armed with monkey wrenches, clubs, and an invitation to leave the premises. He was not even permitted to use the radio to inform the outside world of his fate. So he and

his crew were driven off into the jungle to make their own way home afoot.

For three days no word came from the crew of the "lost" S-38; search parties were formed, and a certain dismay filled some Pan American hearts. Finally on the fourth day the lost crew, having stumbled its way through the jungle from Lake Montenegro into a town, reported in to Pan American headquarters and cabled for instructions. Their mood, after four days and three nights in the Brazilian wilds, was anything but pacific. For their next flight to Lake Montenegro an S-38 fitted with bomb racks rather than survey equipment seemed appropriate to this frame of mind.

Surprisingly the reply to their contentious cable was a plea for peace—Pan American had all but acquired NYRBA. Negotiations had reached a point at which it would only be a matter of time; NYRBA, in fact, was not doing well financially, which fact Trippe used in dealing with the NYRBA high command: "Your company is losing money every day. Every day the settlement is delayed means that it is worth so much less to us."

James Rand, who was the largest backer, later admitted, "If the argument had run a week longer I would have given Trippe our company for nothing."

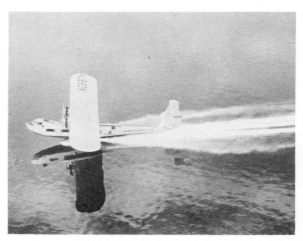

A Commodore on the step just before lifting off the water. (Pan American)

There were two other factors, besides Trippe himself, that contributed to this sad state. One, of course, was the Depression that had afflicted the United States and that tightened the money situation. The other was the Post Office Department, which favored Pan American as its sole representative in Latin America. Although NYRBA had the eastern coast nicely sewed up, had its contracts with South American governments, it did not have any agreement with the United States. In other words, once the mail left Rio in the Commodores for Miami it traveled free over the most lucrative stretch of the line. Or there was no mail at all going south. And Postmaster General Brown made it clear to NYRBA that there was no mail contract forthcoming.

That NYRBA had spoiled the balance of payments with its low rates in South America (thus complicating the Post Office Department's relations with the foreign governments already under contract to Pan American) did not help its situation. And then Argentina began to press for the delivery of its mail within seven days to the United States as its agreement with NYRBA stipulated (actually it was requiring eight or nine days); to meet this demand—which had not arisen until Pan American representatives had arrived on the scene—an elaborate and expensive system was devised by Captain O'Neill using both the Commodore and a fast little landplane, a Consolidated Fleetster, to follow up (and overtake the Commodore) with the late mail. This sped up the mail, but it placed NYRBA deeper in a financial hole.

When Postmaster Brown made it clear that NYRBA would not receive a mail contract, the company threw in the towel. The day after the merger of Pan American and NYRBA was announced the Post Office advertised for bids on the new route joining Paramaribo (which happened to be Pan American's then southernmost terminal on

the northeast coast of South America) with Rio, Montevideo, and Buenos Aires on the east coast. This happened to be the precise route for which NYRBA had petitioned so fruitlessly. The only bidder, it is almost unnecessary to say, was Pan American—and it was to Pan American that the route was awarded, to no one's surprise. Trippe now had air tracks running down both coasts of South America, a crosscontinental line joining Buenos Aires (east) and Santiago (west), as well as the entire Caribbean encircled.

But one eyesore remained on his map: the Sociedad Colombo-Alemana de Transportes Aéreos of wily Dr. Peter Paul von Bauer in Colombia. Bauer was in a good position—in Colombia. The government was suspicious of all Americans, having never forgiven the United States for its role

A SCADTA Junkers floatplane flies over a South American river in December 1925, almost three years before the advent of what would become Pan American Airways. The presence of the nominally German-controlled airline disturbed Trippe's business senses as well as the U. S. Army, with the Panama Canal within easy flying distance of SCADTA's planes. (U. S. Air Force)

in the revolution of 1903, which led to the loss of the isthmus of Panama—as well as to the completion of the Panama Canal. Bauer's SCADTA had been in operation for nearly a decade when Trippe came on the scene.

Trippe's motivations were neither patriotic nor, in any sense, military; it was a simple matter of business. Trippe's fervent dream was to build a great aerial empire; that this dream more or less coincided with certain commercial and military realities was incidental. But Trippe was not so much the dreamer that he could not exploit the coincidence. For all his vision, he was a sharp dealer, in the most traditional Yankee sense, or in the neat phrase of Henry Ladd Smith, ". . . no one ever got back too much change from Mr. Trippe."

But as in the case of Grace & Company, Trippe was confronted with a solidly entrenched adversary in Bauer's SCADTA. On the other hand, Bauer found himself hemmed in by Pan American's lines to the east, west, and south. It was obvious that he wasn't going anywhere, but then neither was Trippe as far as points directly below the Panama Canal were concerned. There was only one solution: negotiation and its concomitant, money. In secret talks Trippe offered Bauer more than a million dollars for his little airline and the latter, no fool, accepted.

It was a curious deal, for Pan American owned the controlling interest in SCADTA, but because of the citizenship proviso of Colombian law, Bauer remained at the head of the line as president in more than nominal charge. Although Pan American

Symbol of victory: an ex-NYRBA Commodore in the colors of Pan American. NYRBA had proved to be Juan Trippe's most serious home-based rival on the South American scene. With the fall of NYRBA, Pan American planes dominated the skies over the Caribbean and South America (although slightly besmirched by a few foreign wings). (Pan American)

owned over 84 percent of the stock, it was Bauer—to keep up appearances—who held the vote in the company's corporate meetings. In other words, SCADTA continued operating within Colombia, but Pan American had acquired operating privileges in Colombia's major port city on the Caribbean at Barranquilla as well as other stops on the Pacific side, particularly Buenaventura. With the acquisition of these ports Trippe had succeeded in closing his South American circle—Pan American wings dominated the skies of the Caribbean and South America.

Trippe's victory, such as it was, required one further touch: the hand of officialdom. Despite the fact that Trippe and Bauer had come to an agreement, it did not follow that Colombia warmed up to the "Colossus of the North." The United States State Department entered into a special air treaty, known as the Kellogg-Olaya Pact (1929), which had been drawn up one afternoon in Washington by Francis White, of the State Department, and Juan Trippe.

According to the terms of the pact the United States and Colombia exchanged flying rights. This, of course, opened up Colombia officially to Pan American. At the same time it opened up the entire American coastline—Atlantic, Pacific, and the Gulf of Mexico—to Colombia. There being no threat of any Colombian civil airlines at the moment, this concession seemed of little importance. In fact, Colombia was satisfied with the right to fly one of its planes over the Canal Zone. This gesture soothed to some degree its official animosity toward the United States, and all seemed fine indeed. (The Kellogg-Olaya Pact, though it solved a problem at the time, would surface to haunt Trippe and the United States after the Second World War. With the postwar growth of airlines, and the emergence of South America as a great air complex, Colombia found itself the signatory to one of the most generous and valuable international air agreements in existence).

With Colombia appeased, with SCADTA within the fold, Trippe had rounded out his Latin American empire by 1931. Having explored the potential of his ideas in the Caribbean and having acquired the aircraft that would realize his dreams, the Sikorsky amphibian, he had only to demonstrate the practicality of his dream of empire. While he had been occupied in the corporate warfare that had swallowed up such rivals as NYRBA and several smaller lines, that had boxed up Grace & Company and contained SCADTA, Pan American pilots and their aircraft had been making aviation history.

3: Caribbean Laboratory

If Juan Terry Trippe, in his own quiet, deceptively ingenuous but deadly manner, proved himself to be a master of the business wars, he also revealed an equally adroit skill in selecting those men who would attend to the main business of Pan American, flying. Trippe's heart was primarily that of an airman; unlike most businessmen he understood flying, aircraft, and the men devoted to both. If his personal drive was to create the world's greatest airline, he was no less driven to acquire the best in those elements, men and machines, to fulfill his obsession.

The quality of his planning was evident in the caliber of the men grouped around Trippe—whether on his board of directors, "in the field," or on Pan American's pilot roster. One of the first pilots hired after the formation of Pan American was Edwin C. Musick, a veteran airman and expert in navigation over water. An ex-Army and Marine pilot, Musick had acquired much of his Caribbean experience as chief pilot for the defunct pioneer line, Aeromarine West Indies Airways (formed in 1919 by Inglis M. Uppercu; the line floundered in 1924). Musick flew the run between Havana and Nassau, which later came into the Pan American sphere. He was a veteran of airline operations as well as a master pilot of seagoing aircraft.

Another early Pan American pilot was the colorful L. R. "Dinty" Moore, a one-time U. S. Navy airman who had served aboard the NC-3 as engineer. Two first-rate pilots were acquired by Pan American during its swallowing-up phase in the Caribbean and points south: from West Indian Air Express came Basil L. Rowe, who had flown the route between Port Au Prince, Haiti, and San Juan, Puerto Rico; and from NYRBA came its chief pilot, William S. Grooch, who had gained his first flying experiences in the U. S. Navy. These were but a handful of the many Pan American pioneers who flew the early routes in the Caribbean and South America.

Trippe depended upon the solid abilities of these senior pilots to initiate operations, but he also, as was typical of him, planned for the future. Pan American, having recognized the efficacy of flying boats (or, to be more precise at this point: amphibians), would have to train very special crews. As part of his training to become a Pan American pilot a young airman passed through many degrees of proficiency, attained to some extent through correspondence courses, examinations and, of course, practice. Even an apprentice pilot (the lowest degree) was required to have a university degree or a degree in aeronautical engineering and be already a pilot. The extent of Pan American's operations required certain special skills having to do with maritime law, radio operation, international law, and a speaking knowledge of Spanish. These were not essential to a pilot for a domestic airline.

The operation of an aircraft from water was a special skill in itself. Taking off, for example, was not the same as with a land-plane: with the latter, takeoff procedure required pushing forward on the stick to raise the tail before leaving the ground. Taking off a seaborne plane was just the opposite; the stick was pulled back to raise the nose out of the water, then forward to lift the tail, provided the plane had the power to come unstuck from the water. Landing in the water was its own little adventure; the chief problem to avoid was porpoising, as already mentioned. Pan American, therefore, evolved an early system of special pilot training that produced a high level of airman.

By early 1929 Pan American had engaged the most celebrated pilot on earth and in the air when it was announced that Charles A. Lindbergh was to be technical adviser to the company. Upon his triumphant return from Europe after his epochal transatlantic solo flight, Lindbergh revealed that he was no mere stunt pilot on the make. He declined offers that would have exploited his feat—and him—and that

Two powerful minds behind the early growth of Pan American Airways: Juan Terry Trippe and Charles Lindbergh. Lindbergh joined Pan American in 1929 as technical adviser; photo was taken on January 9, 1929, at the dedication of Pan American's 36th Street Airport in Miami. (Pan American)

would have made him instantly rich. His flight, of course, immediately stimulated a somewhat dormant interest in aviation.

When he spoke, Lindbergh also revealed a concern for the future of American aviation. "All Europe looks on our air mail service with reverence," he told the National Press Club. "But, whereas we have airlines, they have passenger lines. All Europe is covered with a network of lines carrying passengers between all the big cities. Now it is up to us to create and develop passenger lines that compare with our mail routes . . ."

Although he rejected various avenues that might have led to personal success (including the inevitable offer of a movie career), Lindbergh had no doubts about advancing the cause of aviation. He toured the country, stopping in each of the forty-eight states, under the auspices of the Daniel Guggenheim Fund for the Promotion of Aeronautics. Late in 1927 and early in 1928 he made an extensive good will tour of Mexico, Central America, and the Caribbean in his *Spirit of St. Louis,* leaving behind him everywhere a great, almost overwhelming affection for Lindbergh the shy, poised, and youthful airman, and a growing enthusiasm for aviation.

Shortly after his return to the United States Lindbergh was appointed chairman of the technical committee of the newly formed Transcontinental Air Transport, for which he surveyed and organized one of the pioneer transcontinental airlines (now TWA). Having created what was called "The Lindbergh Line," the youthful airman was ready to turn to Pan American's ambitious plans for international lines.

As Pan American's technical adviser it was not Lindbergh's job, of course, to fly the mails and passengers. He would survey routes, fly them himself, test out equipment, make suggestions to aircraft manufacturers as to the design of aircraft and, not the

least, lend the magic of his name to Pan American's growing ambitions.

"When Lindbergh flies, the world watches," stated, with candor, an editorial in the company's house organ *Pan American Air Ways.* "Quite naturally then, if we need call the attention of Old Man Public to an air mail service, and any new service does need this attention, an obvious way is by having our own technical adviser pilot the opening flight.

"He did and the whole world now knows that letters go surely and safely in a week from the great North American cities south and from the great South American cities north via Pan American Airways System."

Lindbergh's first official flight for Pan American began at Miami, Florida, on February 4, 1929, when he inaugurated Foreign Air Mail Route 5, connecting Miami with Cristobal, in the Canal Zone, via Havana, Belize (British Honduras), Managua (Nicaragua) and Punta Arenas in Costa Rica. The projected flight plan would cover a distance of more than twenty-three hundred miles.

With a large crowd assembled at the Miami airport in the early morning of the fourth, Lindbergh attended to the last-minute checks of the Sikorsky, to the loading of some five hundred pounds of mail, and to the keeping of the eager crowd (some members of which were dressed in evening clothes, it being barely five in the morning) away from the S-38's propellers. His copilot for the flight was Trippe's old flying friend John Hambleton, who was also vice president of Pan American; rounding out the crew was Henry L. Buskey, serving as flight engineer and radio operator. As special passenger on the first leg of the flight (Miami to Havana) was Trippe himself. There were no other passengers, as the inaugural flight was dedicated to getting the mails from Miami to Cristobal and to surveying the future possibilities of such a mail/passenger route.

Charles Lindbergh, with Pan American's Vice President John Hambleton in the co-
pilot's seat to his right, prepares to take off from Miami in his first flight for Pan
American, inaugurating Foreign Air Mail Route 5, joining Florida by air with Panama.
(Pan American)

Lindbergh lifted the S-38 (NC-8000, the second S-38 built) off the runway a few minutes after six o'clock in the morning and flew the amphibian into a rather overcast sky. Coincidentally, the date just happened to be Lindbergh's twenty-seventh birthday.

The flight across the Straits of Florida to Cuba was made without incident; at Havana a large crowd had assembled at the airport to greet the plane—and, of course, to see Lindbergh—to hear welcoming speeches from high officials, and to hear Trippe say that the "flight is but a forerunner of air mail and passenger service that will go to Valparaiso [Chile] by April first." Refuel-ing the Sikorsky for the next leg of the flight took about as much time as the trip from Florida to Havana, a little over an hour.

By nine twenty-five in the morning the S-38, minus passenger Trippe but with additional mail, took off bound for Belize, British Honduras. Another fuel stop was made at Le Fe, Cuba, shortly after noon prior to heading out over the Yucatan Channel, the longest overwater stretch of the flight. Making landfall on the northeastern tip of the Yucatan Peninsula, Lindbergh then guided the Sikorsky in a southerly direction, with the Yucatan to his right and the Caribbean Sea on the left, until after some nine hours and forty-seven minutes of flying time since leaving Miami, he brought the plane down into the bay at Belize. It was 2:55 P.M.

A special ramp had been built into the bay from the beach—it was twenty feet wide and jutted out nearly two hundred feet into the water. Lindbergh guided the plane onto the ramp, the wheels touched the wooden structure (at a depth at around four feet), and the S-38 rose out of the water and headed for the shore and a large square platform where it was to rest until takeoff time the next morning. The entire process went as smoothly as the rest of the flight, but for some reason, the plane moved off the edge of the platform and the wheels sank into the sand of the beach. This small mishap did not mar the gala reception awaiting Lindbergh and his crew, although as soon as the governor, Sir John Burdon, had concluded his welcoming speech Lindbergh slipped away from the reception to see to the condition of the Sikorsky.

Relieved to find that there had been no damage, Lindbergh lent a hand in preparing the plane for the next morning's takeoff. The wheels were dug out of the sand, planks were laid down, and a tractor pulled the Sikorsky onto solid ground. Satisfied that the plane was ready, Lindbergh could return to the celebrations in honor of the crew. As his own contribution, combining business with pleasure, he treated Governor Burdon and a few friends to a flight in the S-38. As he toured the area Lindbergh studied it in terms of future airport possibilities.

The day was topped off with a dinner reception at Government House and a party at the Polo Club, where speeches were made by the governor and Lindbergh. For the latter it was his second visit at Belize, having landed there in the *Spirit of St. Louis* in December 1930—"the first man to land a plane in the British Honduras," as underscored by Governor Burdon. He also noted that it was Lindbergh's birthday, which prompted the guests to cheer and applaud. Lindbergh accepted the honors with customary dignity, diffidence, and self-effacement. He spoke briefly; his greatest pleasure obviously was in the fact that Belize was now linked with the United States and South America. "I hope," he concluded, "that before long these planes will not only land here once in two weeks but once each day, and I think I can assure you that before many months will have passed that that will be realized."

The next morning Lindbergh and crew were off for Managua, the next major stop in their flight, some five hundred miles away from Belize over a short stretch of sea (the Gulf of Honduras) before a refueling stop at Tela, Honduras. Lindbergh did not traverse the shortest distance between the two points; since they were making a survey flight as well as carrying the mail, he guided the Sikorsky in a roundabout flight plan marking various sites that might serve in the future development of the route. He also treated the townspeople of a number of cities in Honduras and Nicaragua to what to many may have been their first sight of an airplane.

Over Tegucigalpa, capital of Honduras, he spent a few minutes circling and dipping the wings of the Sikorsky, which brought out enthusiastic observers, who cheered him from the streets and rooftops. Despite his excursions, Lindbergh brought the plane into Managua at three in the afternoon—two hours ahead of his scheduled arrival. The flight, including sightseeing, had taken a little less than six hours.

The final leg began the following morning, February 6, 1929, at six-thirty when Lindbergh flew the S-38 off the waters of Lake Nicaragua and, after three refueling stops at San José and Punta Arenas, Costa Rica, and at David, Panama, arrived at their destination, France Field, near Cristobal, at four in the afternoon. Flying time for the seven hundred miles was just fifteen minutes short of seven hours.

A crowd of about two thousand people was on hand to greet the Pan American plane. Over Gatun Lake Navy planes met the Sikorsky to furnish official escort; some high-spirited pilots contributed to the festivities by stunting over and around the formation as it approached France Field. As the S-38 taxied toward a hangar the exuberant crowd spilled onto the runway, causing anxious moments as the plane was moving; the swirling propellers were always a danger to unreasoning crowds. The police finally cleared a path through the human thicket, enabling Lindbergh to get the plane inside and out of danger to all concerned. Characteristically he set about the business he was upon, even ignoring a plea from a newsreel cameraman, who asked him to turn around. Instead, Lindbergh checked the mailbags, turned them over to G. D. Bliss, Postmaster of Cristobal, signed various official papers, and conferred with medical authorities. There was a general air of excitement for, for the first time in history, the air mail had come from the United States to the Canal Zone, a distance of nearly two thousand miles, in twenty-one hours and twenty-seven minutes of flying time.

During the next four days Lindbergh rested, fished, flew, and generally flitted in and out of the limelight. A celebrity who craved seclusion, he managed to find some of that aboard the carrier *Saratoga,* which stood some seventy miles off Panama away from the adulators and newspapermen. After nearly two days of relaxation he was again in the public eye: the New York *Times* (among other papers) reported that on the morning of February 8 Lindbergh had become the first Army pilot to make a carrier takeoff. Leaving the *Saratoga,* Lindbergh flew the little Navy fighter plane and landed at Albrook Field, near Balboa. Then began the preparations for the return

to Miami—and the pressures of being observed constantly by public and press.

Actually not until that day was it certain that there would be a flight back. Not until Congress agreed to the reciprocal contracts would it be possible for the mails to be flown to the United States from those points at which it had been left on the flight in. However, it would have been most intractable (and apathetic to the public relations import of the flight of Lindbergh and Hambleton) to have spoiled the mission at the halfway mark. To the surprise of no one, Congress approved the return mail. That the political cliff-hanging impressed few was obvious in the fact that all the special air mail stamps for the flight were sold out and that some fifty thousand letters (weighing a fraction over eight hundred pounds) were ready for the flight to Miami. To assist in transporting this heavy load, plus whatever would be picked up at Managua, Belize, and Havana, an additional S-38 was placed in service.

It was still dark when preparations for the return flight got under way around five-thirty in the morning of February 11, 1929. Although the return would be as trouble-free as the flight to Panama, being in a sense a reverse but with pretty much the same type of greetings, speeches, and state dinners, there were a number of incidents.

The first occurred before the Sikorskys got off the ground. As Postmaster Bliss turned over various papers to Lindbergh (receipts for the mail, etc.), prop wash from the engines caught them and blew them all over France Field. Bliss and a handful of volunteers who had arrived to see Lindbergh off ran around the runway retrieving the papers as Lindbergh pointed them out with the beam of his flashlight. The documents duly, if indecorously, recovered, both Sikorskys had left Cristobal by six.

The next mishap, an insignificant one, was a flat tire that Lindbergh noticed on the second Sikorsky when it landed at Belize.

Lindbergh and Hambleton deliver the first air mail to the Canal Zone: this photograph was taken on the day of their return flight, February 13, 1929. Hambleton, hands on knees, observes. Not long after, Hambleton died in the crash of a private plane he was piloting. (Pan American)

However, this day was brightened and made newsworthy when, in Mexico City, Ambassador and Mrs. Dwight W. Morrow announced the engagement of their daughter Anne to Charles Lindbergh. This added a further romantic note to the return flight—and removed the glamorous airman's name from the list of the world's most eligible bachelors. The announcement was followed by the flight's few moments of suspense. Lindbergh had consistently arrived early on the return—over three hours before he was expected at Managua and a full twenty-four hours early at Belize (by cutting off a fuel stop at Tela); but on February 13 he was hours overdue at Havana.

He had swung the S-38 in and around the eastern coast of the Yucatan Peninsula, checking on possible future landing spots, and then decided to refuel at the island of Cozumel. The chore, which generally consumed an hour, stretched out to more than four in the choppy waters. Both the amphibian and the little refueling vessel bobbed

and tossed in the heavy seas, making the process a lengthy and delicate one. It was not until they finally arrived at Le Fe, Cuba, to take on fuel for the last lap to Havana (about 180 miles to the east) that word was flashed out that Lindbergh and his crew were safe. The companion S-38 had already arrived at Havana, but Lindbergh did not arrive until evening, after dark. As he circled the field ground crews improvised landing lights to enable a night landing. Lindbergh brought the plane in for a gentle landing. The next day he completed the circle, arriving in Miami—greeted by a cheering mob of an estimated three thousand. The short flight across the Straits of Florida was a mere hop compared to the rest of the segments. It seemed a matter of simple routine to cross the 260 miles of water; but the fact of history was that for the first time Miami and Cristobal had been linked by air.

In September (1929) additional linkage and good will were introduced when, following their marriage, the Lindberghs joined the Trippes blazing an air trail from Havana eastward along the outer edges of the Caribbean through the Leeward and Windward Islands to the northern coast of South America, at Paramaribo, Dutch Guiana. Again the Sikorsky amphibian was used, with Basil Rowe along to serve as Lindbergh's copilot. This flight, like Lindbergh's first for Pan American, was highly successful—perhaps even more successful, for it included the presence of glamor in the persons of Anne Morrow Lindbergh and Elizabeth Stettinius Trippe (both of whose fathers were connected with J. P. Morgan & Company).

Wherever they landed—at St. Thomas, St. Johns, St. Kitts, St. Lucia, Port of Spain (Trinidad), Georgetown (British Guiana), and Paramaribo—the two attractive couples were greeted warmly with bouquets, welcoming speeches, and gala banquets in the evenings. There was an aura about the entire flight that was more festive than fiscal. Although, in fact, they were pioneering what was Foreign Air Mail Routes 2 and 3, the flight had all the romantic aspects of an exotic honeymoon for the Lindberghs.

The Lindberghs withdrew from the flight at Trinidad, leaving Rowe, with copilot Charles Lober, to attend to the return trip. The Lindberghs then swung around the northern coast of South America and returned to Miami via Central America, with an excursion to the ancient Mayan ruins in the Yucatan.

For Trippe there were some distractions —the burgeoning battle with NYRBA (which he won by the summer of the following year) and some mumblings in the American business community that their European rivals had the advantage over them because it was possible to send airmail faster from, say, Paris via Compagnie Générale Aéropostale (using a system of ship and aircraft: flying the mail to Dakar in French West Africa, crossing the South Atlantic at its narrowest point by ship to Natal,

Brazil, where it took to the air again) to important South American cities. Aéropostale could make this trip in eight days between Paris and Buenos Aires—by ship alone it took sixteen days. The New York to Buenos Aires mail ship took twenty days. Obviously the solution lay in Pan American's air mail routes.

Trippe believed that Pan American's eight-day connection between points in the United States and Buenos Aires could be cut by a full day, thus justifying the American businessman's trust in Pan American. One means of accomplishing this was to cut some time out of the "Lindbergh Circle" route between Miami and Cristobal, Canal Zone. Instead of stopping in the Yucatan, in Honduras, and in Costa Rica, the idea was to cross the Caribbean from Havana to Puerto Cabezas, Nicaragua, refuel, and then proceed directly to Cristobal. The cross-Caribbean flight would establish the world's longest scheduled over-water crossing; the total distance was 1294 miles, which cut two hundred miles off the original route.

Once again Lindbergh would act as the pilot, with Basil Rowe (who actually knew the route, having surveyed it on April 11,

Bert Denicke, radio operator, Charles Lindbergh, and Basil Rowe, pilots, the crew of the Sikorsky S-38 in which a cross-Caribbean route was inaugurated in April 1930. Rowe had already surveyed the route two weeks before. Photo was taken in Miami prior to takeoff. (Pan American)

1930) as co-pilot and Bert Denicke as radio operator. The inaugural flight, set for April 26, would carry only mail. The plane, in fact, was stripped down in order to make room for necessities. As recollected by Rowe shortly after the flight, "Every possible ounce of surplus weight had been removed from the NC142M, including the floor. . . . Two large cabin gasoline tanks of one hundred gallons capacity each had been installed to allow enough gasoline to assure us of getting across the Caribbean in case we ran into bad weather or headwinds. This was in addition to the usual four eighty-gallon gasoline tanks in the upper wings of the Sikorsky, giving us a total gas capacity of 520 gallons. As the Department of Commerce limits these machines to a gross weight of 10,480 pounds, we could only carry 120 gallons in the cabin tanks after loading our mail [weight: 249 pounds]. The usual twenty gallons of oil was increased to twenty-four gallons.

"As we left Miami at 3:29 P.M. on the first leg of our journey to Havana we carried only a hundred gallons in the cabin tanks and 220 gallons in the tanks upstairs. We only had a flight of 261 miles ahead of us and we would fill our tanks to the 440 gallons allowed capacity at Havana.

"Flying a corrected compass course of 205° from Miami to the south end of the Florida mainland carried us a few miles west of our course. Altering our course 3° to the east, we passed directly over Marathon, midway down the Florida Keys, which was directly on our course for Havana, at four-nineteen. As we left the mainland I raised the wheels of the landing gear in case we had to land in the water.

"After checking our speed and position as we passed Marathon, Lindbergh sent our position to Havana, stating that we would arrive at five thirty-five. As we passed over the Gulf Stream leaving the Keys behind, we saw many steamers bound in all directions. The Florida Straits is a much-traveled

waterway, and we were seldom out of sight of one or more boats during the time we were over the water between Marathon and Havana."

Visibility was good, though some cloud could be seen in the southwest. The twin "Wasps" sang in throaty unison as they cruised along easily; Denicke received a message from an approaching Pan American Fokker F-10, which had left Havana at three o'clock bound for Miami. Pilot Roy Keeler informed the men aboard the S-38 that he was about midway between his terminals and that the weather was good except for local showers. Forty-seven minutes later the two planes passed each other—the Fokker about five hundred feet above the Sikorsky. Lindbergh radioed Miami of the meeting and continued toward Havana.

Around five the radio crackled again, informing them that the San Juan Fokker, delayed by weather, was still at the Havana loading platform. Lindbergh was asked to delay his arrival ten minutes to give the Fokker time to take off and get away. Complying, Lindbergh throttled down the Sikorsky; Havana was already in sight. Lazily the great aircraft winged over the Cuban capital until they were informed that the Fokker had taken off. Soon the trimotor appeared, and the two planes waggled wings in the traditional greeting of airmen. Lindbergh then banked the Sikorsky and set down on the airstrip at Camp Colombia; they were just two minutes later than Lindbergh's original estimate.

When Lindbergh emerged from the cockpit a great cheer went up and the usual round of official greeting began, initiated by no less than a Cuban State Department attaché, with an added title of Introducer of Ministers, one Señor Enrique Soler y Baro. A veteran of the post-landing banquet circuit, Lindbergh asked that all social festivities that might have been planned for Rowe, Denicke, and himself be canceled so that

Lindbergh observes while ground crew goes over S-38 NC-142M during a stopover on the cross-Caribbean flight. (Pan American)

the airmen could get some rest and take off at first light in the morning.

"The day broke fair and clear," Rowe continued in his narrative, "and at five-twenty we were starting the motors. The night had been cool so we warmed them thoroughly, as we could not have a motor falter taking off while it was still dark, with our heavy load [444 gallons of fuel, twenty-four gallons of oil for the expected flight of nine hours], from a field that is none too good and surrounded by many obstructions.

"At five-thirty, the wheel chocks were yanked from in front of the wheels and we started to taxi toward the northwest corner of the field as we were taking off into a light southwest breeze. It was still quite dark, but dawn was breaking fast as Lindbergh shoved both throttles wide open and we gradually gained flying speed. After bump-

ing along over the uneven ground about six hundred feet we could gradually feel the load being taken from the wheels as the speed picked up and the lift of the wings increased, and we were in the air. After making a couple of turns to avoid high obstructions he set it on our course for Puerto Cabezas."

The overwater hop from Havana to Puerto Cabezas would be the longest of the flight, about 630 miles. This was a lonely, empty stretch and should trouble occur, might have proved troublesome. It had been arranged, before they left Havana, to have the U. S. Coast Guard cutter *Cassin* ply the approximate course of the Sikorsky below, just in case of trouble. Although ship and plane were in contact by radio, neither actually saw the other. (In fact, during the entire course of this long leg, the crew of the S-38 sighted only two ships, neither of which they identified; even so, as Rowe put it, they "were most welcome sights in that vast sea of water.")

Lindbergh gave up trying to locate the *Cassin,* deciding the cutter was off its course. Rowe's comment was laconic: "No one ever hears of an aviator being off his course unless he is lost, and he always hits his landfall 'on the nose.' That is, if you let the aviator tell it himself, but they often go wandering around trying to orient themselves endeavoring to locate their objective 'on the nose.' "

Another checkpoint, a stationary one, was tiny Swan Island, just off the northeastern tip of Nicaragua, but that too proved to be elusive. "As we approached Caxones [their first landfall in the approach to Nicaragua]," Rowe noted, "the colonel passed the controls to me and climbed over the gasoline tanks for another shot at the sun. At 10:46 [A.M.] he sent the following message: 'Dead reckoning position 83°08' West Longitude, 15°55' North Latitude at twelve twenty-three. Observed position two miles west of D.R. position.' I thought we were farther west than either of these, but I never use anything but dead reckoning, which means that unless you reckon correctly you are dead. In either case there is plenty of chance for error. But what is a few miles more or less of water when there is plenty out there for everybody and altogether too much for me?

"At exactly 11:00 A.M. we passed Cape Gracias a Dios on the farthermost northeast tip of Nicaragua. As the colonel was flying, at the time I wrote out the position and passed it to him to sign, since position messages are sent out by the senior pilot. As Cape Gracias a Dios translates into English as Cape Thank God I merely wrote: 'Thank God at 11:00 A.M.'

"I gathered from the questioning look on his face that he did not get the translation, so I explained it. I guess he thought some-one would take it just as I wrote it, so he said he thought the position in Spanish would sound better. I destroyed that masterpiece and wrote 'Cape Gracias a Dios at 11:00 A.M.,' which he signed."

Within a half hour they were on the approach to their next stop, Byrd Field (a Marine base) at Puerto Cabezas. The few remaining Marines were on hand (for the post was being evacuated, the troubles in Nicaragua having lessened) to keep the excited townspeople away from the chopping propellers of the plane when it landed. This was always a serious concern to pilots landing in spots where the airplane was an unfamiliar object of curiosity. With the added celebrity of Lindbergh the problem was magnified—and whirling propellers were difficult to see.

"After dragging the field a couple of times at a low altitude to look it over and get an idea of the best part to land on, the colonel made a splendid three-point landing at exactly eleven-forty after being in the air six hours and four minutes from Havana, during which time we had flown a distance of 638 miles," Rowe observed. "Not a record for speed or endurance by any means, but I believe it to be a record for a regularly established overwater air mail route."

They only remained on the ground long enough to take on additional fuel. There was a touchy moment during the takeoff of the now heavier craft; their run toward the north end of the field was pointed directly at some telephone lines, which festooned the edge of Byrd Field. The Sikorsky lumbered and bounced as the wires thickened and loomed more and more menacing in Rowe's eyes. Their craft was "getting too close for comfort," but they "passed over them at a safe margin" because, as Rowe dryly put it, "I held myself up by pulling on the bottom of the seat."

The final leg of the flight, Puerto Cabezas to Cristobal, covered an overwater distance of 395 miles. They had taken off at twelve-fifteen, and Lindbergh estimated they would arrive at about 4:15 P.M. With the aid of a tailwind, they were there ten minutes early. The time in the air was routine except for one small incident, which newspaper writers attempted to magnify. As he passed through the cockpit into the plane's cabin Lindbergh snagged his sleeve on some obstruction or other and ripped it quite badly. Not wishing to arrive in Cristobal with a dangling cuff, he borrowed Rowe's jackknife and, as Rowe put it, "amputated the sleeve just below the elbow. I suggested that he remove the other sleeve to match, but he didn't. That shirt with the jagged sleeve caused all sorts of comments, questions, and speculation for a possible story among the newspaper reporters. They tried their damndest to make a thrilling incident of the manner in which he lost his sleeve. They tried in many ways to put words into my mouth—that he caught it in a propeller and came close to being killed. I wouldn't care for all his fame if I had to accept all the side dishes that accompany it."

The tattered sleeve was nothing compared to the situation over Cristobal. "As we approached to within fifty knots of Cristobal heavy black showers appeared ahead extending across the entire horizon, so there was nothing to do but stick our nose into it." The S-38 and the tropical storm arrived over the field simultaneously. "Flying low over the field to get the wind direction, the colonel set us down squarely in the middle of a large water puddle on the second turn around, and it seemed that all the water in the ocean came over us.

"It was raining so hard that he could only see to land by opening the top of the cockpit and half standing on the rudder pedals to enable him to peer over the top, as the rain was building up on our windshield like a flood and it was impossible to see a thing through them. There is some advantage in having long legs."

It was Sunday, April 27, 1930. The return flight was not scheduled until the following Thursday. The layover was set in order to await the arrival of the northbound mail on Wednesday afternoon by the redoubtable "Dinty" Moore, in a Sikorsky, "Red" Williams and Fred Robinson in Ford trimotors (for the over-Andes flight). Moore's flight, from Talara, Peru to Cristobal, was no less than 1355 miles. Williams' flight, from Santiago de Chile to Buenos Aires, achieved an altitude record when it passed over the Andes at twenty thousand feet.

Boarding another Sikorsky (the same one in which Rowe had surveyed their route two weeks before), the trio of Lindbergh, Rowe, and Denicke took off from France Field at 7:58 A.M. on Thursday, May 1, 1930. Their objective was, of course, Puerto Cabezas, but they had decided, what with the changing weather situation, to set their course so that they would skirt the Marine base at Bluefields (Nicaragua) just in case their objective was weathered in.

They had just passed their "point of no return" out of Cristobal when the Sikorsky began to vibrate wildly. As the amphibian bounced and shuddered, Lindbergh pulled back on the throttles. That appeared to dampen the vibration, but at a cost: The S-38 barely maintained flying speed. Together he and Rowe attempted to isolate the cause of the problem. They cut the power to the engines (one at a time) and, while the oscillation decreased, it came up again as soon as the power was increased.

Rowe told of what followed: "It [the trouble] seemed to originate from the rear, so Lindbergh passed the controls to me and crawled through the windowless hole separating the cockpit from the cabin. Opening the rear hatch, he stuck his head out into the slipstream and soon determined the cause of the trouble. Yelling to me to keep her in the air, he crawled out the open hatch while I reduced power and speed to

Cristobal, May 1, 1930: Surrounded by Pan American employees and officials, Lindbergh and, to his left, Rowe and Denicke, are ready to begin the flight back to Miami. (Pan American)

a minimum. Then I saw what he was after. The horizontal member between the 'V' struts that supported the tail structure and carried the wind-driven generator had broken in flight, and the two ends were flailing wildly in the slipstream.

"That was one time I was glad Lindbergh was tall and had a long reach. With his toes hooked on the rear edge of the hatch, he slid along the afterdeck, and with his hands bent the two broken ends down against the 'V' struts, which prevented further waving of the tail section. Fortunately the base of the clouds was high, which permitted us to cruise at higher than normal altitude at the time it happened, or we would have been in the rough sea before he could complete his mission and that might easily have been a sad, wet story.

"It was easy enough for him to slide down the afterdeck with the push of the slipstream, but bucking it on the return trip wasn't so easy. But that was old stuff to Lindbergh, with his background of wing walking and parachute jumping. All the time Slim was stretched out there on the afterdeck I had been studying the heavy seas and trying to decide whether I should parallel the large swells and land crosswind and take the chance of a huge wave swamping us or try to slide the keel down the rear side of a wave into the wind at the greatly reduced speed. It was a great relief to hear Slim yell 'Pour it on' as his feet hit the stringers that now answered as the cabin floor. We still had a little altitude, but it was fast disappearing. Since we had lost our generator we had no radio for the balance of the trip, which caused considerable suspense and worry for the ground forces."

Nothing was said about the incident at Puerto Cabezas, although the broken strut was removed (it served, they found, no truly critical function), not wishing the problem to be enlarged into a near crash in newspaper headlines.

After spending the night in Puerto Cabezas, the trio took off for Havana early the following morning (May 2, 1930), and made that leg in just under seven hours; they waited around for two hours, and in the early afternoon left for Miami. Except for some storm threat on the leg to Havana, the remainder of their flight was uneventful. They landed in Miami at 5:00 P.M., "completing the schedule," as Rowe observed, "from Buenos Aires exactly on time and cutting one whole day from the original schedule. . . . At Miami we saw the same crowd that we had left only six days before, yet mail had gone to Buenos Aires and back in this short elapsed time and had done it on schedule. A lot we are asking of aeroplanes these days to fly through all sorts of weather, across all kinds of oceans, swamps, jungles, plains, mountains, and snow-capped peaks; through rain, haze, fog, and snow; from hottest tropical sunshine to coldest atmosphere at twenty thousand feet altitude and do it on schedule."

Rowe gave credit where it was additionally due—to the network of ship's radios and weather stations that had supplied them with weather reports; to the superb radio complex of Pan American itself; and to the Coast Guard cutter, although unseen, which stood by throughout to render assistance if that had been needed. "All very fine," he concluded, "but how about the air mail pilots who will be making the run every week? Will you ever hear their names mentioned as they carry out their routine work of flying this route all in a day's work?"

Once a route was inaugurated with a maximum of fanfare, the routine was taken up by other airmen, lesser celebrities than Lindbergh. While he endured the limelight gracefully, Lindbergh would have been happier simply flying and not engaging in pub-

Historic aircraft: NC-9776, an S-38B (early model, prior to sloped windshield) that was used by Rowe to survey the cross-Caribbean route and by Lindbergh and crew for the return flight to Miami. This was a standard aircraft, similar to those used on regular routes. (Pan American)

lic relations, though he recognized its value in the popularization of aviation.

However, even the lesser names were accorded due recognition, for, in fact, their work was not always "routine." Flights into underdeveloped countries were always potentially adventurous. They were pioneers, in their own way, however routine their flights had become. They even put new names on the map—for maps of the Caribbean and much of South America in Pan American's laboratory days were hardly better than those one might find in a high school geography book.

One newly coined place name that Basil Rowe remembered was known as "Spook-Gear Landing." This existed as a reminder to a certain new pilot of a curious mishap. This pilot—called Harrison in Rowe's book, *Under My Wings*—came upon the scene and quickly alienated everyone with annoying insinuations. He could not understand, Harrison maintained, how any pilot could be so stupid as to forget to lower the wheels of a Sikorsky before coming in to land on the ground. Harrison, accustomed to land planes, answered his own question one day on his first flight in an S-38 when he came in with wheels cranked up under the wings (they were not truly retractable in the modern sense yet), landing beautifully on the field. Except for the fact that he had forgotten to lower the gear, it might have been a very good landing. But there he was on the ground, skidding along on hull-bottom, until the Sikorsky struck something that caused it to flip over onto its back.

As the astonished Rowe watched, he saw the wheels being lowered skyward (since the plane had turned turtle). Harrison made certain to lower his wheels before he prepared his story—that he had hit something on the runway that caused the plane to tumble, and pointing out that, at least, the wheels were down.

Pilots had to learn their planes as much as they had to learn their routes. Being pilots, they now and then enjoyed their little pranks. One, William Fuller, noted that his co-pilot one day had fallen asleep and just thought he might give the sleeper a little turn. They were flying in from Nassau to Miami, a fairly uncomplicated hop. To relieve the monotony of the routine, Fuller spotted a calm little bay that would serve his droll, he thought, design. As the innocent co-pilot snoozed, his captain eased the Sikorsky down to the water. His plan was to bump the plane into the bay, knowing that the jarring boom would have, for him at least, a most gratifying effect.

"It did," Rowe sardonically noted. "It also sucked the bottom off the boat as if it had been taken off with a chisel. Fuller fought the ship back to Nassau, looking down between his legs at the water." The bay he had selected for his little *jeu d'esprit* was known forever after among his peers as "Fuller's Folly."

Within a year after the Lindbergh-Rowe inaugural flight to Cristobal, Pan American could announce that it had shifted its southern base in the Caribbean from Panama, eastward, to Barranquilla, Colombia—this thanks to the acquisition of the troublesome Bauer's SCADTA in the spring of 1931. This coup cut an additional 170 miles off the overwater flight and put Barranquilla "within two and a half days of New York with a mail and passenger service twice weekly." This eliminated a day from the old schedule. Pan American further elaborated that departures "from Miami over the new route will be made Tuesdays and Fridays with arrivals at Barranquilla and Cristobal on Wednesdays and Saturdays. The Tuesday plane will proceed from Barranquilla to Maracaibo [Venezuela], arriving at the city each Wednesday.

"Northbound mail will depart from Cristobal and Barranquilla on Sundays and Wednesdays, arriving at Miami on Mondays and Thursdays. The Sunday plane carries the northbound Maracaibo mail.

"With a base at Barranquilla it will be possible for passengers to make direct connections for Bogotá, capital of Colombia, twice a week.

"This new route to Barranquilla," Pan American's announcement concluded, "makes the fare $165 against $329 formerly charged to this city via Cristobal."

Within his Caribbean laboratory Trippe was shifting and expanding his holdings. On April 12, 1931 it was also announced that a direct service had been opened to San José, Costa Rica, a move that linked all of the capitals of Central America by air. It was pointed out that "it is possible for a person in the Canal Zone to fly to San José, transact business, and be back in Cristobal for supper."

The significance of these experiments in the laboratory was noted editorially in the house organ, *Pan American Air Ways:* "It is this type of improvement along with schedule performance that is constantly building up in the mind of the public a greater faith in air travel."

With this very idea in mind two newsmen, Ward Morehouse of the New York *Sun* and Leo Kieran of the New York *Times,* accompanied by the airline's public relations director, W. I. Van Dusen, made an extensive air tour of the Caribbean and South America. In 17½ airborne days they visited twenty Latin American countries, traversing some eighteen thousand miles of the Pan American Airways system. "It was a tour that left me somewhat bewildered," Morehouse said, "by the swiftness and vastness of it all and has also left me with the largest and fanciest collection of hotel luggage stickers this side of the China Sea." Their flight, all but one hour of it accomplished in daylight, took them over spectacular vistas—"over two great oceans, desert, jungle, the highest peaks in the Western Hemisphere, the rolling Pampa of the Argentine . . ."

Responding to the wonder of the air age, the newsmen rhapsodized lyrically: "I don't think I'll soon forget Rio from the air, or the chocolate brown of the Rio Plata, or the swarms of old rose flamingoes along the coasts of the three Guianas, or the splendor of the snow-splotched Aconcagua Peak, or the pools of rose water in Chile.

"I'll remember, too, the grapes the size of hen's eggs at Mendoza, the purple-and-red squares on the cultivated Argentine pampas, the placidity of the Dutch Guiana town called Paramaribo, the Balieff-like smile of the floor waiter in Rio, the burnished mountain peak jutting through the clouds at Ovalle, the jungle villages in Brazil, the crumbling Inca temples in Peru, and the Panama Canal from the legalized fifteen hundred feet." This last was a reference to the regulation that provided that aircraft could not fly below the altitude of fifteen hundred feet over the strategic Panama Canal.

Morehouse jotted a few vivid impressions: "Four miles in the air, ten degrees below zero, the highest peak in the two Americas [Aconcagua] to our left, a glacier just ahead, and snow all about us . . . that was how we flew over the Andes today to climax our 830-mile jump from Buenos Aires. And before a provincial New Yorker, transported from Georgia, goes into ecstasies over the experience, let it be said that for the pilot, C. K. Travis, it was the 112th time he has flown the Andes. To this big blond Texan, who was Lindbergh's roommate at Kelly Field, Texas, in 1924, it may be old stuff, but to the average John Public it's a whole lifetime in one brief hour."

Crossing over the Andes, especially, quickened the bard who skulks inside the newsman. "In soaring over the Cordillera de los Andes we reached an altitude of nineteen thousand feet as we swept past snow-enshrouded Aconcagua, the daddy peak of the Andes and the highest point of land in the Western Hemisphere. We

Christ of the Andes, which stands on the Chilean-Argentine border. (Braniff International)

zoomed over gaunt and bald-topped ridges, beautiful emerald lakes, crazily zigzagged rivers, and passed within sight of the figure of Christ of the Andes, which forms the Chilean-Argentine border . . .

"To our left was Maipo, a snowy peak of a mere 17,500 feet and on ahead, to the right, was the majesty of Aconcagua, rearing itself 22,850 feet. Aconcagua is awesome and enthralling in its sheer lonely loftiness, and it was the sight of it that caused a mechanic on his first Andes flight to remark that it made Pike's Peak look like a sunken garden."

The Good Life, too, inspired lyrical economic comment. "Quite a place, the Country Club de Lima. Airplanes forever in the sky, golf courses on all sides, guests taking swims before breakfast, the New York papers and magazines and Swiss maids, valets, waiters . . . eggs a cent apiece . . . luscious pears five cents a dozen . . . avocados four cents each . . . excellent Chilean wine twenty-four cents a quart." It was as if, given certain advantages, that it seemed possible even to escape the Depression in the air age.

Nor were the more statistical realities slighted. "On our eighteen-thousand-mile air jaunt we used ten planes: two Fokkers, three Commodores, one Lockheed, two Fords, and two Sikorsky amphibians. There were nine pilots—and their names stick in my memory: Swinson, Dewey, Bill Grooch, Toomey, Travis, Colliver, Farris, Moore, and Sullivan. Some of them picturesque fellows, all of them good men in strenuous jobs—particularly those in the West Coast service."

"The accomplishment of this great setup that covers in all more than twenty-two thousand miles of Central America and Mexico, in addition to the routes covered by this party, requires more than seventy-eight multimotored passenger transport planes, each with two pilots and a radio operator, plus an auxiliary equipment of twenty-three fast single-engined mail planes, forty-five ground radio stations scattered along the routes, and a great army of mechanics and other overalled workers who are busy night and day." This elicited deserved glorification of the men on the ground, ". . . these pioneers of a winged generation . . . the tingling history of this peaceful army of young Americans in overalls, scattered through a score of strange lands thousands of miles from home, who blazed these trails across tropic jungles, over ice-capped mountains and open sea . . . is a story that has never been told.

"In many of the countries along the way they have accomplished practical miracles. In a matter of months they have blasted away barriers of time and distance that for ages have separated the American nations from each other and from the world. In the highly modernized civilization in which we live here in the United States the airplane is still a novel and subordinate factor. But in many of these lands to the south it is accepted, if not entirely understood, as an active and dynamic force in their lives."

It remained for Van Dusen to note one of the most striking statistics of all. In slightly less than four years Pan American's total international system had flowered from the little 110-mile route between Key West and Havana to a great network two hundred times greater than the initial route. Juan Terry Trippe had won his first empire.

Perhaps a deeper meaning to the phrase that referred to the aircraft in Latin America as "an active and dynamic force" in the lives of people could not be better exemplified than by the function of aircraft in times of distress. Even as the ecstatic newsmen toured the twenty South American countries, disaster came to Nicaragua in Central America.

Early in the morning of March 31, 1931, word was flashed from Managua that the city had been stricken by a severe earthquake, that the wreckage was being swept by uncontrollable fires, that water mains had burst in the quake and that water was in short supply, that food and medical supplies were running out—and then silence. No news came out of the city and, because the roads and railroad were impassable, it was impossible to get into Managua. The silence from the area was ominous.

As soon as word had come from the city, New York's Pan American office radioed an airborne Sikorsky, somewhere between Miami and San Salvador, to "Drop passengers [there were four] at San Lorenzo and proceed to Managua. On arrival offer facilities to government officials."

Within two hours—it was by then around seven in the evening of March 31—the amphibian set down in the waters of Managua Bay. The crew was appalled at the sight of the burning city in the twilight. But with their radio Managua once again had communication with the outside world. Harry Rammer, a traveling airport manager for Pan American, sent details of the calamity (he wrote by candlelight late in the evening of the first day): "The earthquake which occurred at Managua today, came at 10:19 A.M., C.S.T. and, although it lasted only a few seconds, was of such severity that no building escaped damage. The worst damage was done in the business section of the city where the buildings are

tallest. Fire broke out immediately afterward, and owing to the lack of water supply, soon spread over the entire business section. The U. S. Marines are making attempts to check the fire by use of dynamite and it is apparently under control, although still burning. We are still experiencing tremors at about half-hour intervals."

Pan American's office was totally destroyed by the tremor and fire, as were the various living quarters of personnel in the town. Rammer moved out to the airfield, where he set up cots (borrowed from the Marines) for himself, passengers, and other Pan American refugees. The injured were cared for in the Marine hospital, which had escaped serious damage. By evening it was estimated that "there are about four hundred known dead and about one thousand injured," Rammer reported. "These figures do not include those buried under the debris."

From the field Rammer could see the city still aflame—"we have just received word that the entire city will probably be destroyed by fire"—and made preparations for the evacuation, under the direction of Pan American's division manager, Erwin Balluder, for the evacuation of the refugees from Managua—mainly women and children—by air.

From the air Managua presented a spectacle of desolation.

From every direction, thanks to aircraft, help poured in. As soon as the Sikorsky had settled into Managua Bay and activated its radio, requests went out for relief, describing the situation so that these requests could be intelligently filled. From Mexico, Cristobal, and Miami, Pan American planes took to the air with medicine, food, doctors, nurses, and a variety of supplies. The governments of the United States, Mexico, the various Central American countries, and the Canal Zone availed themselves of Pan American's facilities to assist in the relief. President Herbert

Hoover dispatched Ernest J. Swift, director of the American Red Cross, to Managua to direct relief proceedings. When Swift arrived in Miami, he found an S-38 waiting to fly him down to Nicaragua. At the same time supplies were flown in from Panama and Salvador.

Evacuation from the disaster zone was carried out by air also. By noon of the first day (April 1, 1931) planes had carried ninety-eight passengers—American women and children—out of Managua to Corinto to the north. By the next day the total had reached 119 persons. The four passengers who had been "bumped" from the S-38 at San Lorenzo when the quake had struck, were flown the next morning to their proper destination, Cristobal. The entire operation had been carried out with exemplary efficiency; by the second day, no less than six planes were carrying refugees between Managua and Corinto. There were small delays and interruptions, such as that of the four passengers to Cristobal, but no serious disruptions. The mail was delayed a day to make room for Red Cross director Swift, and reserve planes that might have carried mail in Central America were shunted off on relief missions. Basil Rowe flew dozens of such missions in NC-9151; after he had attended to immediate medical needs he earned the nickname of "The Flying Baker," as he spent several days delivering bread into Managua picked up by plane at neighboring cities and towns.

Such missions were not unique, and had happened before; they would happen again. It was a policy of Pan American to avail its aircraft for relief in the event of such disasters. In September of the same year as the Managua earthquake, Belize, in British Honduras, was smashed by a vicious hurricane that destroyed much of the city and wreaked havoc among the people. Rowe found himself again at the controls of an S-38 flying in supplies, medicine, and medical personnel to assist in the relief of the city. This was but another in a series of such "mercy missions" flown by Rowe and other pilots of Pan American when a natural disaster struck.

Manmade disasters, too, figured in the story of Pan American's Caribbean laboratory epoch. Latin America seethed with social disturbance, which from time to time erupted into revolution and the overthrow of government.

It occurred to one Walter Voss, a German living in Brazil, that he might realize a little profit if he could put his hands on one of Pan American's S-38s and sell it to some band of dissidents or other. With three others, one of them an aviation mechanic apparently with delusions of grandeur, Voss stole up one night on the Pan American base near Rio de Janeiro. There, in a placid lake, rested the Sikorsky NC-113M, at anchor. This plane, which had been transferred from the now defunct NYRBA to Pan American at a cost of more than fifty thousand dollars, was a prize indeed. Voss and his henchmen subdued the night watchman, took him prisoner, and placed him aboard the Sikorsky. Voss, in his more or less carefully laid plans, had apparently arranged for a mechanic and a night watchman—but no pilot. The mechanic, who according to one report had been drinking, claimed this position by virtue of his familiarity with aircraft.

Quite a bit of noise accompanied the boarding of the S-38 by the foursome. The engines were started, and the S-38 went splashing through the water; within seconds it was airborne and headed southward in the early morning light. What actually occurred in the plane is not known, but after it had flown about fifteen miles, it was observed flying erratically, then it whipped into a sudden dive, continued diving "crazily," as reported in the New York *Times,* and crashed into the ground near Merity. When the plane was reached by a search party it was a total wreck, had

NYRBA's S-38, NC-113M, which later went to Pan American and operated from Rio. It was this plane that was stolen by a group of men who hoped to sell it to Brazilian revolutionaries. The plane took off under the hand of an untrained pilot and crashed, killing all aboard. (Sikorsky Aircraft)

burned, and all five passengers were dead.

In Cuba, too, the dictator President Machado was having his problems with insurrectionists. His regime, begun in 1925 with high promises for social reform and a liberal outlook, had degenerated into a virtual police state by the early thirties. It had been Machado who had, in 1927, signed an exclusive landing rights agreement with Juan Trippe. This was the foundation, in fact, upon which all of Pan American's vast Latin American empire had been based. With Havana denied them, no other airline could hope to invade Trippe's domain.

Although he may not have been popular at home, Machado was regarded with favor by the *gringo*. In his honor one of the giant Fokker F-7s was named *General Machado*. The event was marked with appropriate ceremony in an atmosphere of mutual affection. Then one sad day the *General Machado* fell into the sea. Machado, upset and undoubtedly reading the handwriting in the sky, took the symbolism of this accident seriously; he also took to his bed for a few days.

He had interpreted truly. By 1933 there was an uprising in Cuba led by Sergeant Fulgencio Batista and Army insurgents, backed by the Cuban people and with some aid from the United States. Machado was tumbled from office (only to be succeeded by another dictator, Ramón Grau San Martín, who was in turn overthrown by Batista) and given permission by the Batista-Grau forces to leave the country.

The long-suffering Cuban people, however, did not concur; they were out for blood. So much of theirs had been spilled during Machado's dictatorship that only his would assuage them. The general, accompanied by a couple of other unpopular officials, fled to Pan American's Havana terminal, where they hurriedly boarded a chartered Sikorsky amphibian. Their plans had been formulated so precipitantly that they spent the next hour and a half perspiring freely, awaiting the proper clearance for takeoff. This was, of course, neatly ironic; for this delay they could thank their own penchant for obstacle and red tape (one of the nervous passengers was the deposed chief of the vicious National Police).

Pilot Al McCullough was himself uncomfortable in the cockpit of the S-38. His wary eye noted a great mob approaching down the runway; it was no time to comply with the arbitrary regulations of a defunct regime—most of which he had in the cabin behind him. With a howling mob rushing toward the S-38, McCullough gunned the engines, waddled the plane down the runway, pushed the throttles wide open, and climbed into the safety of the air. It had been a close thing.

After landing at Vanadero Beach to snatch Machado's family out of danger also, McCullough flew on to Miami, where Machado and company sought asylum in the United States, where he lived out the rest of his life living off the fat of his people's land. There was something curiously Biblical in his deliverance: He had cast his bread upon the waters and had found it after many days—by air.

4: "Ugly Duckling"

The S-38 was literally Sikorsky's best seller. Its appearance and performance brought orders from a number of sources, ranging from the U. S. Navy and Army, airlines other than Pan American, as well as private purchasers in search of aerial adventure. The S-38 was the tenth Sikorsky design; the first nine produced only ten aircraft. The single tenth design resulted in 120 S-38s. It was Sikorsky's wish to coin a new term for this plane; instead of calling it an "amphibian"—which would have placed it among the beasts—he called it an "amphibion," which would have placed it in a class by itself. Although widely used in Sikorsky's own publications, brochures,

and advertising, the term never caught on and the plane was called, among other things, amphibian.

The rash of orders placed a strain upon the Sikorsky facility at College Point, on Long Island, New York, so that Sikorsky began seeking out more capacious sitings to accommodate the business upswing. After searching for just the right location, which would have to be on deep water, he selected a spot in the town of Stratford, on the Housatonic River, Connecticut. This was in the spring of 1929—a year that was destined to end disastrously for many businesses. However, Sikorsky made another move—this time a business one—when he

The bustling Sikorsky factory at College Point, Long Island, New York. S-38 in left foreground is NC-9753, the first of the S-38Bs, being built for Chicago Tribune *publisher, R. R. McCormick, in 1929. The plane was eventually christened 'Untin' Bowler and came to grief in Newfoundland. (Sikorsky Aircraft)*

A Duckling being readied for Pan American taxies onto the Sikorsky ramp at College Point. (Sikorsky Aircraft)

Interior of Sikorsky's new plant at Stratford, Connecticut, 1930. Five S-38s are under construction on the line. (Sikorsky Aircraft)

elected to become a subsidiary of the great aviation combine, United Aircraft and Transport Corporation. This was a wise move for, despite the great number of S-38 orders that began coming in in the summer of 1928, it is unlikely that Sikorsky would have survived the Depression alone. Within the workings of the giant corporation, which viewed the Sikorsky operation with a mingling of benevolence and fiscal dismay, the aviation pioneer and mystic continued to operate the company like a one-man business as of yore.

A great number of Sikorsky's factory hands were, like himself, Russian refugees, some of them once of the aristocracy. Visiting Russian dignitaries appearing at the plant would upset production for the day as greetings were exchanged and gossip passed back and forth, and little work was done. Whenever any cultural event of a Russian caste took place, be it the opera or ballet, culture invariably took precedence over commerce. As reported by Frank J. Delear in his biography of Sikorsky, such curiously loose business methods inspired United Aircraft's president, Frederick B. Rentschler, to say, "There is a limit to the contribution United Aircraft can make to Russian Relief."

But Sikorsky prevailed, and the S-38 rolled off the assembly lines in Stratford. Above the noise of the plant, the ungainly-looking craft snorted and waddled into the water and took to the air. One wag described the plane as "a collection of airplane parts flying in formation." Captain Charles Elliott, chief pilot of Inter-Island Airways (now Hawaiian Airlines), affectionately called the S-38 "the flying tadpole." He summed a consensus when he told S-38 historian Mitch Mayborn that "There may have been better land planes and better flying boats, but none that combined the two half so well."

Elliott, who had acquired his sea wings as an enlisted Navy pilot, joined Inter-Island

Airways, its first employee, as chief pilot. The first Sikorskys arrived, via ship and in crates, in October 1929. Following assembly and christening, *Hawaii* and *Maui,* the amphibians began operating on a regularly scheduled airline—the first in Hawaii—on November 11, 1929. Thus began a relatively trouble-free series of flights over spectacular Hawaiian terrain. Elliott recalls flying varied cargoes in the S-38, from photographers snapping the eruption of Mauna Loa to scattering grass seed on the mountain's sides between the lava flows.

In all, Inter-Island owned four S-38s, the other two being named *Kauai* and *Molokai,* which were used for passenger and freight service as well as for training. The *Kauai* probably enjoyed the more colorful history. In addition to being used as a training ship, it was equipped with radio devices for training pilots in the use of blind flying techniques. When the Japanese attacked Pearl Harbor, the *Kauai* was the only Inter-Island craft to escape damage in the bombing. During the war the plane was used to fly fresh meat into Honolulu from Molokai, hauling in, at the same time, various supplies, from food to sawdust, to Molokai. The aircraft was retired after more than a decade of service.

An Inter-Island Airways S-38, the Kauai, *flies over an extinct volcano in Hawaii. This plane was the third of four Ducklings operated by Inter-Island. (Sikorsky Aircraft)*

Although most of the Ugly Ducklings—the most prevalent nickname for the S-38—were acquired by Pan American Airways and its various affiliates, others went to such smaller operators as Colonial Western Airways (New York), Western Air Express (Avalon, California) and Curtiss Flying Service, Garden City, New York. These Sikorskys were used in charter service, transporting both passengers and freight as the need arose.

The concept of the executive plane came into being with the S-38 as its kind proliferated. The Grigsby-Gurnow Company, of Chicago, manufacturers of the Majestic radio, owned one of the dependable amphibians for a time and used it for carrying its own personnel as well as for promotional flights. Standard Oil, Hughes Products, and the Chicago *Tribune* owned S-38s. The *Tribune*'s publisher, Robert McCormick, evidently hoped to exploit the general public interest in aviation after Lindbergh. He bought an S-38 that he named *'Untin' Bowler,* dialect from the hunting cap worn by fox hunters, with which he hoped to glorify the name of the *Tribune* by sponsoring a transatlantic flight. The pilot of the craft was Robert Gast, the navigator-radio operator was Parker Cramer, and the passenger

was aviation editor Robert Wood. McCormick preferred his thrills vicariously and would be happy just reading about the flight in the *Tribune*.

Starting out on July 3, 1929, the plane got as far as Cape Chidley, Newfoundland, where it was fogged in for several days. When the wind came up to clear the air, it also blew the icebergs into the little plane's haven. The *'Untin' Bowler* was crushed by the chunks of ice and sank into the freezing water before the crew could get it out of danger. That ended their flight plans right there. McCormick, shortly after, acquired another Sikorsky again folksily named *Arf Pint*. But he seems not to have attempted any further armchair flying, and the plane was eventually bought by others.

It might be noted that several of the S-38s passed through many hands before they were retired, junked, or suffered accidents. For example, Margery Durant, daughter of the then president of General Motors, bought one for sport flying from her home in Old Westbury, Long Island. After three or four years, and the erosion of the novelty, she sold the plane to two barnstorming pilots who were based in Stockholm, Sweden. It then passed into a Swedish charter airline and eventually faded from view when it was purchased by a French firm for use in Africa. These were sturdy and reliable planes, for all their unlovely, but memorable, aspects.

The Sikorsky saw service in the U. S. Navy as experimental craft, the official designation being XPS-2 (of which only two were acquired). There was also a later PS-3, of which a half dozen were used. Navy pilots had few problems with the Sikorskys, accustomed as they were to water operations, and the amphibians were used as patrol boats (although unarmed) prior to the advent of the big flying boats that would appear with regularity in the 1930s.

The Army Air Corps purchased no less

An unusual view of an S-38 in flight over Long Island, New York, which was operated by the Curtiss Flying Service in the early thirties. (Sikorsky Aircraft)

An S-38 coming unstuck—a perfect takeoff. In the first photo the plane is skimming on the step for the moment before leaving the *water. The nose rides high to eliminate porpoising. (Sikorsky Aircraft)*

than eleven S-38s for use as cargo and transport planes. The first was officially designated C-6 and an additional ten, slightly modified, were C-6As, which went into operation in the early thirties. To the landlubbering Army pilots, the ducklings proved a nearly insuperable enigma.

At the root of the problem was the technique of landing on water. Nor, for that matter, were normal landings on the ground always successful. The landing gear of the S-38, not too well adjusted to absorbing shock, required fairly sophisticated technique in setting the plane down. So it was that not long after delivery of the C-6As the filing of Army Air Corps accident reports became rather common.

Although the pilots chosen to fly the Sikorsky were given special instructions in handling the plane, few seemed able to master the problem of porpoising—and the bouncing and bumping that resulted did little good to the structure of the aircraft. In analyzing a series of such accidents Basil Rowe, veteran S-38 pilot and of thousands of water landings, attributed the problem primarily to "gross amateur piloting from landlubber pilots. . . . No ship can porpoise if the nose is held sufficiently high. As soon as the speeding hull shows a tendency to porpoise, lift the nose a little higher and it will disappear." This last is a point to keep in mind when reading excerpts from

the official accident reports that follow. Rowe also concluded that "The S-38 had excellent hydrodynamic qualities.

"Some of them were Jonahs and were always having trouble of one kind or another while others were ladies with the most complacent dispositions that one could imagine. They were temperamental hunks of metal and linen and each and every one required special treatment."

This is not what they received, apparently, from the hapless Air Corps pilots, some of whom blamed their accidents on weak engine mounts and other "peculiarities of this type of plane." A report by a now anonymous pilot of aircraft No. 30–402 based at Nichols Field in the Philippines is typical. The plane suffered two accidents, one a rough ground landing that split a landing gear strut and caused some small damage to a wingtip; the other is described by the pilot who "glided down and the hull struck the water in a normal manner but the plane rebounded. I opened both throttles full but could not keep the plane in the air and the hull struck again with such force that the glass in the windshield and windows in the pilot's compartment were broken. This accident is believed to have been caused by a combination of the poor hydrodynamic qualities of the C-6A airplane and lack of experience of the pilot in landing this type of plane on the water."

U. S. Army Sikorskys (C-6As) in flight over land—wheels are in down position for operation over land. (U. S. Air Force)

As can be gleaned from these reports, pilots were instructed to correct for porpoising by "pushing the wheel all the way forward to get the nose of the plane into the water," while Rowe's solution was just the opposite: raise the nose. The pilot of aircraft No. 30–400 apparently followed instructions and came to grief, despite this—or rather, because of it. He had come in for a water landing in a normal glide, though with the tail low. The plane bounced. "On next impact with water he failed to keep wheel forward and the plane bounced again into the air. After several bad bounces he opened the throttles and made another circle and attempted another landing, with the same results as the first.

"He opened the throttles and attempted another landing but again bounced and plane came down right wing low and almost stalled. Plane struck water, the windshield was splintered and it was later discovered that the hull was sprung. Plane was taken

in for overhaul. Other pilots found difficulty making smooth landings on the water with the plane, evidently due to the characteristics of the hull, but by following best method closely smooth landings could be made."

Army C-6A in flight over water; a few of these craft were based in the Philippines and Hawaii, where they were used as rescue craft and for target towing—and most came to untimely ends because of hard landings on the sea and ground. (U. S. Air Force)

The entire Army C-6A program came to an end on July 25, 1933, when a Sikorsky, based at March Field, California, took off in the morning for a practice flight. The pilot was Second Lieutenant Carl H. Murray of the 64th Service Squadron; he carried six passengers. The plane was aircraft No. 30–399, the second of the C-6As acquired by the Air Corps in 1930; in its nearly three years of service the Sikorsky had been flown, "almost entirely from land fields," in the phrase of historian Mitch Mayborn, by a number of different pilots. Although it had not been subjected to the doubtful thrills of porpoising, it had, in its more than eleven hundred hours of flight time, been bounced to earth in many a hard landing. Apparently the shocks of these, as well as the normal wear and tear of flight, weakened the craft's structure. The landing gear shock impact was absorbed by the main gear and, to some extent, was dissipated into the hull and wing. The pounding of repeated rough landings could only have been detrimental to what is called "the integrity of the aircraft."

Murray had taken off from March Field shortly after eleven o'clock that morning with his six passengers aboard. They were Sergeant Archie W. Snodgrass, Sergeant Bonnell L. Herrick, Corporal Walter T. Taylor, and Privates Stanley Book, Albert Overend, and Vincent J. Galdis. All occupants of the plane wore parachutes. About an hour after Murray had taken off he was cruising at about an altitude of two to three thousand feet heading for Rockwell Field. They were over Oceanside, California, when without warning the right wing panel ripped away at the engine station. Within moments the craft fell spinning and rolling end over end, the occupants being trapped inside because the wing had folded against the cockpit door. It smashed to earth killing everyone aboard. The investigation that followed did not reveal the exact cause of the accident, although the plane had endured a series of rough landings and it was

discovered that a nut was missing on one of the bolts that held the wing panel to the wing center section. Either might have contributed to the crash. But the accident, added to the others, led to the scrapping of the battered aircraft that remained. The Air Corps turned again to the employment of the Atlantic (the American-built Fokker) for cargo and transport. Through no fault of its own the Ugly Duckling's brief Army career had not been very glorious.

Not that its story lacked romance. Consider the Pan American adventures in the Caribbean and South America, the flights of Captain Elliott over the lush and volcanic Hawaiian Islands—even the escape of such a scoundrel as Dictator Machado from Cuba. It remained for adventurer-explorer-moviemaker Martin Johnson to bring a new dimension to the African safari.

Johnson, who began his career in Kansas as a young itinerant photographer, initiated his adventuring as a bad cook on Jack London's *Snark* on a cruise to the glamorous South Seas. This gave him a taste for exotic peoples, places, and things and, in company with his pert, diminutive wife Osa, began exploring such exotica during the First World War. During the twenties and thirties the filmic record of his explorations were fulfillment of every red-blooded American boy's dream, the very titles of which conjure up the magic of strange, distant, perhaps Depression-free, places: *Cannibals of the South Seas, Congorilla, Simba*.

By the spring of 1932, after several successful excursions to Borneo and Africa, Johnson had decided that the one piece of equipment he lacked was an aircraft. "I suppose a person in a plane over Africa could see quite a lot," he musingly told his wife one day. He admitted at the same time that he really did not care for flying, but the opportunity for reaching spots otherwise inaccessible to him overcame this one chink in his armor.

Both Johnsons learned to fly with a local

SIKORSKY AMPHIBIO

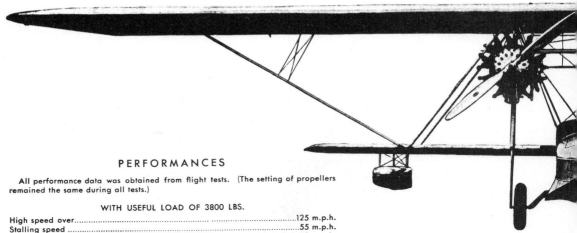

PERFORMANCES

All performance data was obtained from flight tests. (The setting of propellers remained the same during all tests.)

WITH USEFUL LOAD OF 3800 LBS.

High speed over...125 m.p.h.
Stalling speed ....55 m.p.h.
Cruising speed at sea level at 1750 r.p.m....................................110 m.p.h.
Initial climb ....750 ft. p.m.
Ceiling ....18,000 ft.
Takeoff time from land...12 sec.
Takeoff time from water...18 sec.

DISTRIBUTION OF LOAD FOR A FLYING RANGE OF ABOUT 600 MILES

Ship empty ....6500 lbs.
Gas for 6 hours at cruising speed—264 gals. ....1584 lbs.
Oil for 6 hours at cruising speed—16 gals ....120 lbs.
Eight passengers }
Two crew   } ....1700 lbs.
Standard and extra equipment of boat and passenger luggage ....576 lbs.

GROSS WEIGHT AS PER DEPARTMENT OF COMMERCE
CERTIFICATE No. 126...10,480 lbs.

IMPROVEMENTS IN 1930 MODEL

Slanting Windshield; Higher Cabin; Improved Stabilizer; Positive Hydraulic Brakes; Steel Compression Struts; All Metal Pontoons; General refinement throughout.

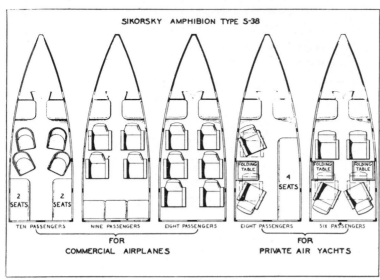

CABIN SEATING ARRANGEMENTS

STAND...

2—Wheels with Brakes
2—Propellers, Hamilton Met...
2—Hand Inertia Starters
1—Magnetic Compass
1—Altimeter
1—Air Speed Indicator
1—Bank and Turn Indicator
2—Oil Pressure Gauges
2—L. G. Oil Pressure Gauge...
2—Oil Thermometers
1—Inclimeter
1—8-Day Clock
2—Tachometers
2—Magnetic Fuel Gauges
1—Set (3) Navigation Lights
1—Riding Light
5—Light Switches for Instru...
    Board
1—Master Switch
2—Scintilla Engine Switches
2—Hot Shot Batteries
2—Hand Fire Extinguisher...
    Cockpit
2—Hand Fire Extinguisher...
    Cabin
2—Windshield Wipers
8—Passenger Seats
2—Pilot's Seats with Cushion...
8—Passenger Safety Belts

The centerfold from the Sikorsky S-38 brochure of 1930; a close reading of the "Standard Equipment" columns is interesting, containing as it does such items as Ash Receivers in Cabin, Portable Bilge Pump, Canvas Water Bucket, and a Raw Hide Bow Fender, among other nauticalia. (Sikorsky Aircraft)

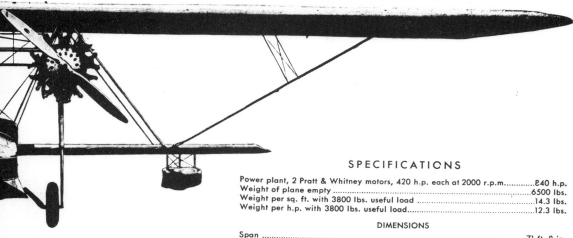

UIPMENT

—Pilot's Safety Belts
—Dome Lights in Cabin
—Ash Receivers in Cabin
Aerokit
Seat Cushion (extra)
Toilet
Anchor
' Manila Floating Rope
Heaving Line
Portable Bilge Pump
TB Boat Hook
—Canvas Fenders
Raw Hide Bow Fender
Canvas Water Bucket
Towing Sling
Mooring Sling
Hand Stroke Air Pump
Tire Valve Extension
Toolbox, with Tools
Toolkit
Engine Instruction Book
Toolkit   } In Package
Engine Instruc- } for Ground
tion Book   } Service Only
Airplane Instruction Book
Engine Log Books in Bag
Airplane Log Book
Engine Covers
Two-piece Hull Cover

SPECIFICATIONS

Power plant, 2 Pratt & Whitney motors, 420 h.p. each at 2000 r.p.m.............840 h.p.
Weight of plane empty ....6500 lbs.
Weight per sq. ft. with 3800 lbs. useful load ....14.3 lbs.
Weight per h.p. with 3800 lbs. useful load..12.3 lbs.

DIMENSIONS

Span ....71 ft. 8 in.
Length overall ....40 ft. 3 in.
Height ....13 ft. 10 in.
Width of tread...9 ft. 8½ in.
Span upper wing ....71 ft. 8 in.
Span lower wing ....36 ft. 0 in.
Chord upper wing ....100 in.
Chord lower wing ....59 in.
Dihedral upper wing ....0°
Dihedral lower wing...1°
Gap..95.3 in.
Stagger..4.5°
Area upper wing (including 42.2 sq. ft. for ailerons)..................................574 sq. ft.
Area lower wing ....146 sq. ft.
Total wing area...720 sq. ft.
Area stabilizer ....51.4 sq. ft.
Area elevator ....35.5 sq. ft.
Area fins ....15 sq. ft.
Area rudders ....20 sq. ft.

U. S. GOVERNMENT CERTIFICATION

Complies with Department of Commerce regulations for landplanes and seaplanes.

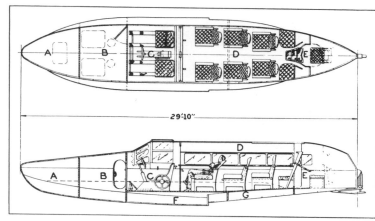

INTERIOR ARRANGEMENT OF THE HULL

Compartment A, 2400 lbs., marine equipment; B, 6300 lbs., luggage, mail and radio; C and D, 11,000 lbs., pilot's cockpit and passenger compartment; E, 3600 lbs., lavatory; F and G, 2800 and 1000 lbs., respectively, underfloor watertight compartments.

NOTE: Weights given indicate submerged displacement.

(Chanute, Kansas) airman of considerable reputation, Vern Carstens. Johnson, despite his reservations about flying, soloed first. Osa Johnson proved a slightly less apt pupil, and during her solo flight had trouble landing, bouncing down and up again several times before the plane stayed on the ground (". . . I was lucky to get down at all."). Carstens greeted her with a lecture

on coming into a field with "your tail in the trees and just missing the telephone wires!

"What was the matter with you anyhow?" he demanded of the still shaking Osa Johnson. "I thought we were going to have to shoot you down!"

Having acquired a degree of aerial proficiency, the Johnsons visited the Sikorsky plant at Stratford, ostensibly only to look

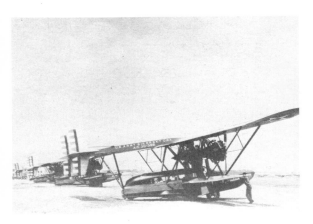

Sikorskys of the 64th Service Squadron lined up on March Field, California. Plane in foreground is the one in which seven men were killed when the plane crashed; this brought an end to the use of the S-38s by the Army. (Sikorsky Aircraft)

Control column and instrument panel of the S-38. Column could be shifted from pilot's position (as here) to copilot's seat by simply removing the pin that held it in place. (Sikorsky Aircraft)

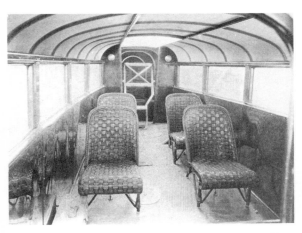

Interior view of S-38 cabin, aft from cockpit. Wicker seats were light in weight. Ladder descends from entry in cabin top. Getting in and out of a Duckling was its own little adventure, especially for the ladies. (Sikorsky Aircraft)

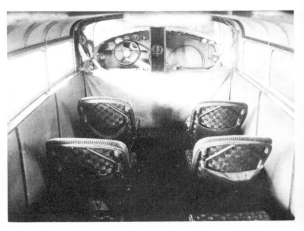

Passenger's view of the S-38 flight deck. Instrument on center divider is an altimeter, in the event the passenger liked to know how high was up. (Sikorsky Aircraft)

at the only type of plane that would serve them in Africa, an amphibian. Before they left, however, they had acquired two planes —an S-38 and a single-engined S-39 (a scaled-down S-38 with a wingspan of fifty-two feet, about twenty feet less than that of the original design). The larger craft was decorated with zebra stripes and named *Osa's Ark* and specially converted for use in Africa. Since it would be operated more than six thousand feet above sea level it was fitted with supercharged Pratt & Whitney "Wasp" engines. New wings were fitted also, and the original seats were replaced by "Two light-framed but comfortably upholstered sleeping bunks. . . . We had a tiny washroom, a little gasoline stove with two burners and an oven, a compact outfit of pots and pans, a set of dishes that nested into an extremely small space, and a supply of food staples. Every inch of space was used for storage, of course—under the bunks and seats and overhead . . . ," Osa Johnson wrote in *I Married Adventure*.

"One unipod camera mounting specially designed by Martin was installed to facilitate his aerial photography, and I designed a very complete typewriter desk . . ." The nose compartment, forward of the cockpit, was used for baggage and other equipment. Another precaution: The Johnsons hired their teacher, Vern Carstens, to serve as their official pilot.

"We shipped out of New York New Year's Eve 1932," he has written, destination Capetown, South Africa—this in order to miss European winter weather. In order to get the two aircraft to our headquarters city of Nairobi, Boris Sergievsky went along and then returned to the States immediately afterward of our arrival in Nairobi."

Besides pilots Carstens and Sergievsky (lent by Sikorsky), the Johnsons were accompanied by Sikorsky mechanic Al Morway, two film sound experts, Arthur Sanial and Robert Moreno, and Johnson's assistant, Hugh Davis.

The Martin Johnsons in Africa posed before Osa's Ark: *Osa and Martin Johnson, Vern Carstens (pilot), and Robert Moreno, sound man. Assistants are seated on the ground; all seem to be wearing the official footgear of the Johnson expedition—Keds. (Vern Carstens)*

"Our adventures were many as we were pioneering the use of aircraft as safari equipment," Carstens recalls. "There were no precedents and we were on our own: no weather reporting stations, very poor and inaccurate maps, no radio aids. We built seven different runways, sometimes under very trying conditions. . . . But the use of aircraft allowed much greater areas to be covered in the search for interesting things and people . . .

"The S-38 was really a workhorse, had seven hours' fuel capacity if needed, and could carry tremendous loads from all altitudes. We operated from runways and lakes from fifty-five hundred feet to seven thousand feet above sea level, and most always overloaded. We carried our own Tetra Ethel of Lead so that we could mix gasoline to the proper octane rating for our supercharged motors. This was necessary for both planes. . . . The S-39 had only 3½ to four hours of fuel, so it was mostly used for the shorter, smaller jobs.

"I think we were the first ones to operate both aircraft off of water at altitudes of sixty-five hundred feet above sea level. . . ."

Gassing up Osa's Ark. *The Johnson expedition carried its own special aviation fuel for high-altitude operations. (Sikorsky Aircraft)*

The S-39, decorated in giraffe spots, was named *Spirit of Africa;* both aircraft, by the time the Johnsons returned to New York, had logged some sixty thousand miles.

Johnson had been right, they saw Africa as never before: "Mountains, jungle, plain were a vast panorama beneath us; great elephant migrations, herds of thousands, also great flocks of white herons and countless giraffe and plains game were spotted one moment from the air and the next

moment were being recorded by our cameras. We were able to land in ordinarily inaccessible places where white man had never been, and here saw natives of strange, remote tribes."

Tribesmen, seeing an aircraft for the first time, were remarkably sophisticated about it. They seemed to be more impressed with the amount of shade thrown by the wings of the Sikorsky than by the fact that it traveled through the sky. Obviously they reasoned it was a machine made to travel through the sky; if so, that is what it was supposed to do. The Johnsons treated some tribesmen to flights. One, a member of the Turkana tribe, revealed a curious reaction to the air age.

As they passed over a village a cow was pointed out to him. His reply was, "That is not a cow, a cow has legs." When he was shown a tree, the Turkana replied, not without a slight note of disdainfulness, "That is not a tree. You look up to see a tree, and you can walk under a tree. That is not a tree."

It would have been interesting to get his

Visitors study a lashed down Spirit of Africa, *Osa Johnson is in the foreground. (Culver Pictures)*

impressions upon seeing, at nearly eye level, the first views of Mount Kenya and Mount Kilimanjaro. The vista was spectacular as Carstens brought *Osa's Ark* over Mount Kenya (which rises 17,040 feet above sea level): "Great snow fields lay beneath us and slow-moving glaciers," Osa Johnson wrote. "We looked down into deep craters and yawning crevices, while steep, barren peaks seemed within reach of my hand. It was piercingly cold."

Kilimanjaro, Africa's highest peak (19,-565 feet), was, however, another problem. Carstens doubted the wisdom of flying over it, for the danger of downdrafts over the ice fields was considerable. Instead he did agree to take the Johnsons above the clouds to enable them to film "for the first time the glittering snow-capped crest." This was to be their final African exploit; for reasons of health Osa Johnson was forced to return to the United States. Upon her recovery, the Johnsons decided to return to Borneo, where they had shared their earliest adventures. For this trip they only took their S-39, the name expanded to *Spirit of Africa and Borneo,* with them and hired James Laneri as pilot. Carstens returned to Kansas and eventually became chief test pilot for Beech Aircraft.

The Borneo trip was, in fact, the Johnsons' last exploration by air and camera. Upon their return they embarked on a lecture tour, crossing the country by plane. In January 1937 the airliner in which they were traveling crashed and Martin Johnson died; although injured, Osa Johnson survived. The death of her husband closed a unique career in African exploration and one in which the utilization of aircraft, particularly the amphibian—and specifically the S-38—in discovery and filming was dramatized.

Another flying family made a name, of sorts, for itself in the popular Ugly Duckling. George Hutchinson, his very attractive wife Blanche, and their two young daughters,

*A Duckling—*Osa's Ark—*at rest sixty-five hundred feet above sea level on the dappled surface of Lake Naivasha, northeast of Nairobi. (Vern Carstens)*

Spirit of Africa, *the Johnsons' Sikorsky S-39, and* Osa's Ark *in the clouds over Africa. (Sikorsky Aircraft)*

"UGLY DUCKLING"   73

Blanche Kathryn (who was eight) and Janet (who was six at the time of their most memorable flight), had gained a small reputation as an airborne family in the early thirties. Their "act" consisted of flights to all the states in the Union, where they appeared in costumes that might be called the cartoonist's conception of what the well-heeled sportsman explorer would wear. The most conspicuous of this were the riding breeches worn by the entire family (father donned dashing tall boots), including the girls—and their dolls. To heighten the effect, the Hutchinsons carried a lion cub with them for their appearances.

It was some time in 1932 that George Hutchinson decided that the "Flying Hutchinsons" would cross the Atlantic *en famille,* an idea undoubtedly inspired by the flight in May by Amelia Earhart. She had been the first woman to solo the Atlantic; the Hutchinsons would become the first family. Hutchinson acquired an S-38 that he named *City of Richmond* (where he had spent his boyhood; he was a resident of Baltimore in 1932). He even designed a coat of arms with the legend *Familia Volans* inscribed on the prow of the hull. He would be the pilot; he hired Peter Redpath to serve as navigator; Gerald Altissish was radio operator; Joseph Ruff was the engineer-mechanic, and Norman Alley came along as cameraman. Filling out the crew, of course, were Mrs. Hutchinson and the two girls.

There was trouble right from the beginning. Newspapers picking up the story began upbraiding a man who was willing to risk the lives of his children in a silly stunt flight. Hutchinson argued that it was no mere stunt and that flying was no more hazardous than driving. More official criticism came from the government of Denmark, which refused to issue Hutchinson a permit to fly over Greenland or even to land anywhere on the Greenland coast. Despite this Hutchinson and party took

off from Floyd Bennett Field on August 23, 1932, and headed northward. Their first leg, a hop of 511 miles, brought them to Saint John, New Brunswick. It was here, since the rest of the flight would be over water, that the wheels of the Sikorsky were removed. This would reduce weight and increase their fuel capacity for the longer cross-Atlantic flight. The following day the Hutchinsons flew to Port Menier, Anticosti Island (in the Gulf of St. Lawrence), where they sat out a period of impossible flying weather for six days. On August 30, they were off again and succeeded in arriving at Hopedale, on the Labrador coast. So far, so good; but their next stop would have to be in Greenland and the Danes had not, in the interim, relented.

Still undismayed, Hutchinson set off on September 2 from Hopedale, crossed the more than six hundred miles of cold Atlantic waters, and blithely set the *City of Richmond* down in the waters of Godthaab, the capital of Greenland. They were not greeted with open arms. Danish officials imposed a fine on Hutchinson for illegal entry (which made him liable to payment of 5000 *kroner* for each of the eight members of the party). For some reason, only a token fine of 1000 *korner* (about $180) was exacted, and the Danes no longer seemed determined to deter the Flying Hutchinsons. They had, after all, flown a considerable distance and demonstrated no mean abilities in piloting and navigation.

Having won that hard-earned blessing, Hutchinson and Redpath decided that rather than traverse the vast Greenland icecap, they would, to some extent, backtrack southward to Julianehaab (near the southernmost tip of Greenland), then swing northward for Angmagssalik on the eastern shoreline. From there they could then hop to Iceland and across the Atlantic.

By September 7 they had landed in Julianehaab (about three hundred miles

George Hutchinson's City of Richmond *taking on supplies at St. John, New Brunswick. Wheels have been removed from the plane. Hutchinson appears in lower left-hand part of picture. (Sikorsky Aircraft)*

south of Godthaab), and on the eleventh they were under way again. They skirted the tip of Greenland at Cape Farewell and headed north for Angmagssalik. It was at this point of the flight that a larger hand than that of the Danish government placed obstacles in the path of the *City of Richmond*. A deep, woolly fog enshrouded them as they flew toward Angmagssalik. Soon they could see neither land nor sea. Further misfortune arrived at this critical point; they might have been able to turn around and return to Julianehaab, but one of the fuel tanks was found to have sprung a bad leak, and all too soon it was obvious that they could reach neither port. Hutchinson turned the Sikorsky seaward to get out of the fog bank and thick ice floes. Attempting to land close to land harbored the possibility of striking a peak or iceberg.

So he bounced the plane into the tossing water, then began warily, for there were heavy waves and the ice floes to elude, taxiing for shore.

This was the last word heard radioed by the Hutchinsons to the outside world on their voyage. Altissish had been able to radio an SOS, giving their approximate position some thirty miles or so short of

Angmagssalik, in the general vicinity of Iterusak Fjord. Then the radio went silent (because of the heavily charged atmosphere of this area).

Immediate search efforts were put into motion, ranging in vessels from Danish naval ships to Eskimo kayaks. This was done despite the forlorn hope held for the Hutchinsons. The very nature of the coastal terrain—indented, ice- and fog-filled, rough and dangerous—made the enterprise a doubtful one from the beginning. There were literally hundreds of fjords, the searching of which might consume days; in the freezing weather, not to mention the fact that their plane may have already been sunk in the deadly water, the Hutchinsons did not have that much time. The *City of Richmond* had become a winged needle in an icy haystack.

While these undoubtedly fruitless searches went on, a British fishing trawler, the *Lord Talbot,* out of Aberdeen, made its way into Greenland waters. So did the hapless *City of Richmond*. It pitched dangerously in the heavy seas, water poured into the cabin, and ice floes smashed against the hull, threatening to sink the battered aircraft. The party managed to work up a modicum

The City of Richmond *down in the sea battering against a tiny (and lucky) rock island as male crew members salvage supplies. (Sikorsky Aircraft)*

of warmth by bailing out their cabin as Hutchinson, dodging the floes as much as possible, continued for shore. It was slow, tortuous, and freezing going.

As they approached the shore, dimly showing through the fog, a small island of rock revealed itself in their path. Hutchinson set the nose of the plane against the island and his family, the crew and, finally himself, scrambled ashore. It was a barren, uninhabited pile of rock, but it was solid ground. The waves and ice pummeled the *City of Richmond,* which could not be brought up the steep incline of shore. The men went to work salvaging as much as possible from the plane. There was little food, and worse, no clothing suitable for enduring the Arctic weather.

When the *Lord Talbot* received word of the emergency landing of the *City of Richmond,* it began working its way along the coast in search of some sign of the plane and its party. Its skipper, one Captain Watson, hugged the rugged shoreline as close, or even closer, than was safely possible. Word had come on September 11; by the thirteenth no one had yet sighted the Hutchinsons. After two freezing days and a night it seemed improbable that they could have survived.

Captain Watson was about to give up that night when he spotted a small flicker of light off shore. He ordered a message in Morse code flashed at the source of light, asking that if they were the Hutchinsons to flash a second light (it could have very readily been an Eskimo campfire). Then a second light flashed. The *Talbot* had found the Hutchinsons!

Interestingly, although it was in fact the Hutchinson party, they were not aware of having been found. No one had seen the Morse message; their rescue had come about by accident. They had, in fact, lighted some film hoping to attract attention from the sea, just in the event that there were search parties out. They were unaware of the presence of the *Talbot*. The second flare spotted by Captain Watson was nothing more than someone lighting up a second length of movie film. Except for this, the *Talbot* would have continued upon its cruise along the coast.

A boat was put over the side and fought its way through the waves to the rocky resting place of the by now hopelessly battered *City of Richmond* (which was ultimately destroyed in the surf). Although suffering from exposure and hunger, the eight former passengers of the doomed Sikorsky were taken off their tiny haven in reasonably good health. The *Talbot* took them to Scotland; then they proceeded to London, where they were received as heroes. Their reception in New York was not quite so triumphant, their own countrymen not being quite so taken with the fate of the underdog as the British. Hutchinson was attacked again by newspapers, and the whole enterprise was condemned as foolish and pointless. The Danes immediately instituted an emergency bond of 10,-000 *kroner,* payable before any future airman attempted a flight over Greenland in the future (it was not rescinded until the outbreak of the Second World War, when flights over Greenland became common).

Hutchinson, undaunted, could not let the press coverage (however unfavorable) go to waste. He formed up a vaudeville act, appositely named "The Flying Hutchinsons," which was booked into a Brook-

"And as our ship sinks slowly in the west . . ." Blanche Hutchinson and daughters Blanche Kathryn and Janet Lee watch the City of Richmond *being ground up in the surf. (Sikorsky Aircraft)*

lyn theater. But the Brooklyn Children's Society intervened and the act was canceled; when he was forbidden to appear also in Manhattan (the objection was specifically to the employment of the two children; but undoubtedly the true reaction was to Hutchinson's having taken them on the aborted flight). Soon after, the Flying Hutchinsons faded out of the history of aviation and show businesses.

The Sikorsky "Duckling," too, was approaching the close of its career. While it proved to be Igor Sikorsky's most profitable product, his restless, inquisitive mind sought to create variations on his original theme. The first of these was the S-39, and even this craft appeared in variant form: the S-39A (with two engines) and the S-39B (with a single engine). The design was obviously based on the S-38, complete with typical hull, high wing, and the twin booms. The wingspan stretched fifty-two feet (compared to the S-38's seventy-one feet, eight inches). It was hoped that with the boom in aviation and the American economy, the smaller version of Pan American's (and others') airliner would prove popular with wealthy sportsman fliers.

But the plane arrived at the wrong time —1929—and the Depression canceled out

Igor Sikorsky at the controls of his S-38 in 1931 during a flight to Panama. (Sikorsky Aircraft)

The S-39B (single-engine) variant of the S-38. Although twin outrigger was retained, this design featured a single tail. Intended for the sportsman flier, the plane arrived during the Depression, when there was a decided paucity of sportsmen. (Sikorsky Aircraft)

An S-39 aboard the yacht Lotusland—*the epitome of Depression-time luxury. (Sikorsky Aircraft)*

many a potential sale. As noted, the Martin Johnsons acquired one for their photographic explorations of Africa and Borneo (it was later used as a rescue craft during the Second World War and was lost). Another purchaser of an S-39 was Colonel Edward A. Deeds, a member of the board of directors of Pratt & Whitney Aircraft. His was an S-39B, which was stowed aboard his yacht *Lotusland*. The craft was raised from and lowered into the water by means of a sling—it did not operate from the ship itself. Deeds, in fact, owned two S-39s, one of them being lost when the sling broke during a raising, dropping it into the water in an inverted position. The plane sank. The pilot, a youthful Air Corps Second Lieutenant named Elwood R. Quesada, managed to extricate himself from the damp cabin and went on to become a leading general during the Second World War as commander of the Ninth Air Force and later director of the Federal Aviation Agency.

There were not, however, very many such purchasers as Deeds, the Johnsons, and the small Varney Speed Lines, among others, and only twenty-three of these amphibians were built before the Depression forced their production to be cut back (with a resultant reduction in the workforce at the Sikorsky factory). Several of these rugged little planes eventually ended up in Alaska as bush planes, and others served in the Civil Air Patrol during the Second World War; but very few ever functioned in their original role as a luxury craft. They had simply been born at the wrong time.

Incidentally, even as production of the S-39 ended, work on filling the orders for the S-38 continued. Sikorsky next produced another variant, which he hoped would be an improvement on the original—the S-41 (which actually appeared before the S-40) of 1930. The refinements, however, did not necessarily lead to performance improvement. The wingspan was increased by eight feet, one inch over that of the S-38, to seventy-nine feet, nine inches. The size of the hull was increased so that the plane could carry from nine to fourteen passengers (as compared to the S-38's ten) plus a crew of two.

The S-41, in fact, was not an improved S-38, as had been hoped. Only seven were built: three went to the U. S. Navy; Colonel Deeds acquired one; SCADTA bought one, and Pan American bought two. It was not a very popular plane. Captain Basil Rowe, who flew it, tells why: "This was a very delicate ship to handle because of the badly located step (too far forward), which caused wild porpoising unless the pilot stayed awake and ahead of the brute by anticipating the porpoising before it started."

But this was not the only problem. Rowe found it "even worse in the air during the [landing] approach. When the power was cut the nose would drop in a steep dive, which was impossible to correct with the elevator control alone. This required rapid work on the stabilizer control. And then, if power was required to drag into a field, the damn ship sat on its tail and required even faster manipulation of the stabilizer wheel to avoid a stall.

"At the time I flew the acceptance tests of our first S-41, the NR41V, at Bridgeport on August 30, 1930, I suggested that the elevator area be increased so that the ship could be controlled with the elevator alone without the required assist from the stabilizer, but that involved too great a change, so we flew them as they were. It was a tricky devil on the approach—otherwise it was a good ship and had what we needed so badly—a surplus of power to get off the water with an overload. Of course this was illegal, but the CAA seldom inspected our operation, as they had too much to do with the domestic operators."

Another S-38 variant, the S-41, which, because of meager sales, was never developed to the point where it might have proved to be an improvement over the Duckling, as had been hoped. This is one of the three that were used by the U. S. Navy. (Sikorsky Aircraft)

The modifications that might have made the S-41 an outstanding plane were impossible in light of the few sales of the ship and the economic stringencies of the Depression. It was easier to stop production on the plane.

But ideas continued to flow from Sikor-

A Sikorsky one-of-a-kind, the XP2S-1, completed in March of 1932, hopefully for purchase by the Navy—which rejected the biplane, tandem-engined, amphibian. This departure from typical Sikorsky configuration was a small anomaly until the next flying boat appeared. (Sikorsky Aircraft)

sky's active mind and, despite disappointments, he continued to produce new aircraft. One design, of about this same period, which suffered the same fate of the S-41—only more drastically, for only one was built—was the XP2S-1. This was a bid for a Navy contract in the patrol boat category; it was one of the last of the biplane patrol aircraft designs in the evolution of the Navy's big boat series. Sikorsky's design, however, was supplanted by those of Consolidated and Martin. It was, at the same time, an interesting configuration, a notable feature of which was its twin engines mounted in tandem between the wings; another departure for Sikorsky at the time was the single tail. The fact that the XP2S-1 had been rejected by the Navy was a disappointment, as were the cutbacks in S-39 production and the bugs that afflicted the S-41. But there were other ideas where those had come from: Stirring in Sikorsky's mind was the wish to produce the world's largest amphibian. Of this same mind were Juan Trippe and Charles Lindbergh of Pan American Airways.

5: American Clipper

When Pan American approached Igor Sikorsky with the idea of producing an aircraft for their Caribbean runs that would in every way be an advance over the S-38 —greater range, better performance, greater payload capacity—he was a happy man, indeed.

Ever since his earliest years as an embryo aircraft designer in Russia it had been Sikorsky's most persistent, and fondest, dream to build giant aircraft. There had been some fleeting fulfillment with the advent of the giant four-engined *Grand* (1913) and the even larger *Ilia Mourometz* (with a wingspan of 102 feet, ten more than that of the *Grand*), which followed the next year. The earlier plane was the world's first four-engined aircraft—and it flew (although it was destroyed on the ground when it was struck by an engine that had fallen off another plane flying overhead). The *Ilia Mourometz* was the first "heavy bomber," of which more than seventy were built during the First World War.

Since those hectic days, of course, two things had occurred: The Revolution had driven Sikorsky out of Russia to the United

States, and engines had developed greatly. With the Pan American request for an improved amphibian, it was possible for Sikorsky to indulge his youthful dream, exploit the knowledge he had acquired as designer of giant aircraft, and take full advantage of the advance in power plant design.

Not that he had dismissed his trust in intuition and instinct. When preliminary studies for the hull design for the new plane, assigned the designation S-40, began, it was an exercise in characteristic pragmatism. Various hull shapes were tested on the Housatonic by towing them from a boom attached to a speedboat. The wooden models were about six feet long and were submitted to around two thousand runs (at about 30 mph) in some two hundred hours of testing. Sikorsky preferred this form of testing the seaworthiness of the several different designs to the purely mathematical approach.

During the planning stages Sikorsky made the short trip from Stratford to New York, where Pan American had its headquarters, for conferences with Lindbergh, Preister of the engineering department, and Trippe. When he first saw the design for the new plane Lindbergh was disappointed; it appeared to be little more than an enlarged S-38 (including the boatlike hull slung under the wing and the twin tail booms), except for the four Pratt & Whitney "Hornets," which were also suspended from the wing. One source of disappointment to Lindbergh was the multitude of struts, at variance with the more recent designs with their streamlined, cowled fuselages and cantilevered wings. Lindbergh found himself referring to the S-40 as the "flying forest."

But Sikorsky's view prevailed. Since they were making a step forward, it was best to remain with a tested design—besides, there was some urgency, in that Pan American wanted to have an improvement over the S-38 as quickly as possible. Any radical approach would consume time. Priester, a born conservative, agreed, and Sikorsky returned to Stratford feeling that Lindbergh's criticisms were well taken and that his suggestions were sound. One of Lindbergh's suggestions was absorbed into the design of the hull. As a pilot, he thought the pilots' compartment belonged about one-third of the distance between the bow and the leading edge of the wing; in other words, well forward to afford the pilot good visibility. One immediate effect it would have was the elimination of the water spray that afflicted the takeoff and landings of the S-38.

Sikorsky has written, "It was exciting to watch the huge spars, the ribs, and finally the great wing being assembled, as well as the roomy boat hull gradually taking shape." It was with a deep sense of gratification that Sikorsky and his employees—for he invariably included them in his projects—observed "one more ambitious dream materialized." By early spring 1931, the great ship had been completed and was proudly towed out of the factory hangar. To Sikorsky it was a thing of joy and beauty: Its very size to its designer was thrilling. The wing stretched 114 feet (and was no less than sixteen feet wide); from the tip of the hull to the tip of tail it was

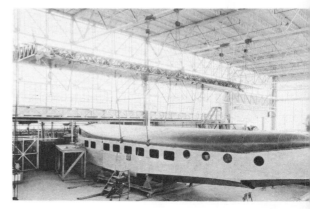

The hull of the S-40 takes shape in the Sikorsky factory; suggestions made by Lindbergh in the design were heeded by Sikorsky, particularly in cockpit location. (Sikorsky Aircraft)

Rollout of the S-40, spring 1931. (Sikorsky Aircraft)

nearly seventy-seven feet long and, as it stood on its great wheels—which were nearly as tall as a man—the wing towered more than twenty-three feet from the ground. The tiny "Hornets," with their equally diminutive propellers, seemed dwarfed by the craft's impressive dimensions. Empty it weighed 24,748 pounds; when loaded gross weight came up to thirty-four thousand pounds—seventeen tons (as compared with the little S-39's two tons). To absorb the shock of landing, it was necessary to search afield for the springs for the landing gear. Unable to use either the standard aviation springs nor automobile shock absorbers, Sikorsky found what he wanted in a railroad yard. Thus the springs used in the S-40 were the same as those employed in a medium-sized railroad car. It was for its time "a lot of airplane," indeed.

The craft was eased into the waters of Long Island Sound for test runs by Boris Sergievsky. Following some tentative taxiing Sergievsky, with a tense Sikorsky ob-

serving from a nearby motorboat, throttled the plane up and lifted it gracefully off the water. Despite its size, the ship quickly revealed itself to have fine qualities, and a series of test flights ensued in order to comb out the few "bugs" bound to crop up in any new aircraft. The S-40, having passed its tests, returned to the factory where it was finished in Pan American's colors, and the interior was finished in the luxurious style of the period.

On September 25, Basil Rowe arrived at the factory with a crew to test the plane officially for Pan American. "We requested a number of changes," he has written, "the most critical of which was the lateral control, which was exceptionally heavy. We discussed several corrective measures and finally decided upon a greater gear ratio. This was far from the ideal solution, but it was the best we could do at that stage of completion. The trouble with our compromise was constant winding of the wheel, but it was better than doubtful control in rough conditions." Captain Rowe's final evaluation was that the "S-40 was perhaps one of the best and most serviceable of any that Sikorsky built and had no bad habits or faults except the excessive wheeling to keep her wings level."

On October 10, 1931, Rowe and the Pan American crew "flew down to Washington and landed at the Anacostia Naval Air Station, where it had been arranged for Mrs. [Herbert] Hoover to christen the ship the *American Clipper,* midst the usual fanfare that accompanies such an event when the wife of the President takes part." This was the first of the flying clippers, and the idea of naming them so was Juan Trippe's. After Mrs. Hoover smashed the bottle of water from the Caribbean on the nose of the ship, Trippe called it a "flagship," and "the first American example of the great airliner of tomorrow that will speed trade and good will among the nations."

Ceremony appropriately attended to, Rowe flew the plane back to Stratford "for more minor changes and made publicity flights, as it was 'THE SHIP' of the period. On the trip down the coast we stopped at all the larger cities for more publicity flights: Norfolk, Savannah, Charleston, Jacksonville, Palm Beach. Arrived Miami Beach Oct. 25 [1931], which was a big day in Miami aviation."

The S-40 was the first in a long line of Pan American's clippers, and just as the big amphibian was a dream come true for Sikorsky, so was it a realization of the aerial-nautical dream of Trippe. All aboard the liner was shipshape, complete to cabin-like passenger compartments and even small, but functional (if needed), life preservers. The pilot was called the captain and the co-pilot the first officer; time aboard the plane was measured in bells and speed in knots. Trippe had ushered in a second Clipper Ship era. While the new aircraft would continue to ply the Caribbean waters (as would its two sister ships), Trippe had already set his eyes on the dis-

tant horizons. The "American Clipper" was a step in that direction, but was not yet the solution. It was still capable of longer overwater flights than any other aircraft then in operation.

The inaugural flight took place on November 19, 1931, with Lindbergh as captain and Rowe as first officer; among the thirty-two passengers aboard (of a possible forty) was Igor Sikorsky. The flight plan initiated at Miami, with stops at Kingston in Jamaica, Barranquilla (Colombia), and then on to Cristobal in the Canal Zone. Since the plane was not loaded to capacity (this was in order to facilitate a certain freedom of movement and left the lounge free), it was possible during the flight, with the capable Rowe at the controls, for Lindbergh and Sikorsky to discuss, even sketch out, ideas for the next clipper—hopefully a transoceanic flying boat. (Eventually the S-40 was modified from amphibian to boat by the removal of the wheels, thus eliminating a good deal of dead weight, and operated only from water.)

The flight was remarkably trouble-free, although not without an incident or two. One occurred after they had completed the first leg at Kingston. Since flying was done only by day, there was a layover in Jamaica. Lindbergh was principal speaker at a dinner the first evening and would address a mixed audience of British and Americans. Just as he was about to rise to speak, a waiter passing behind him spilled a tray he was carrying and Lindbergh suffered the indignity of having a pitcher of cream spilled all over him. With some slight tartness he recalled the incident and told Frank Delear that "The English ignored the incident, and the Americans laughed. It seemed so typical of the two nationalities." Despite this, Lindbergh with a display of that personal dignity so characteristic of him, spoke at length, his subject being the importance of Jamaica as an aerial crossroads between the two great American continents. When

Igor Sikorsky with test pilot Boris Sergievsky. (Sikorsky Aircraft)

The S-40 (wingspan: 114 feet) dwarfs the little S-39 (wingspan: fifty-two feet). Cowlings have been added to Hornet engines since the rollout. This shot confirms Lindbergh's "flying forest" nickname. (Sikorsky Aircraft)

Basil Rowe flies the S-40 to Washington for christening ceremonies. (Pan American)

Mrs. Herbert Hoover, wife of the President, christens the American Clipper, *the first Pan American plane to bear the name. The event, occurring during Prohibition, was marked with the breaking of a bottle of water from the Caribbean instead of the traditional champagne. (Pan American)*

American Clipper *over Manhattan, with Basil Rowe, pilot, during the barnstorming period of this aircraft before its official inaugural flight. (Pan American)*

Charles Lindbergh at the controls of the American Clipper on its inaugural flight, November 19, 1931, over the Caribbean. (Sikorsky Aircraft)

he had finished both nationalities joined in generous applause.

At Barranquilla, the following day, another incident of much greater gravity (and of the worst possible consequences) occurred. The "American Clipper" was docked and being refueled as Lindbergh stood atop the wing observing the operation. There was a sudden overflow of fuel, which ran down the wing and into the water adjacent to the pier. Lindbergh noted that several people on the pier were smoking cigarettes.

"Stop smoking!" he shouted from his perch on the wing. Then to his dismay he

Arrival at Barranquilla, Colombia, on the inaugural flight of the American Clipper. *It was here that the flight nearly went up in smoke. Basil Rowe continued from this point, while Lindbergh relaxed until the return flight, when he again became first pilot. (Pan American)*

saw all the smokers reacting in the most natural manner: to extinguish their cigarettes, they simply tossed them into the water from the pier—and into the gasolined water. "Luckily there was no fire," Lindbergh told Delear, "but the trip could have ended there."

For Lindbergh, in fact, it did. He remained in Barranquilla while Rowe, with Charles Lorber as co-pilot, took the clipper to the Canal Zone and back. Then Lindbergh again took up the role of ship's captain for the return to Miami. It was at this point that a slight hitch occurred. There was a short delay in the takeoff from Kingston so that Lindbergh had to make a choice: the possibility of arriving at Miami at dusk and making a landing in darkened waters, or stopping somewhere midway and landing in some convenient lagoon before darkness set in. This last would mean that the passengers might have to spend some hours in an isolated spot without facilities or risking a night water landing.

Banking on the chance of arriving at Miami before it became too dark, Lindbergh decided to push on to Miami. But upon arrival he was a little disconcerted to see that darkness had indeed fallen and that he would be forced to set the plane down into the water with no idea of the direction of the wind. There were no night flying instruments in the "American Clipper."

Lindbergh came in smoothly, touched water, there was a little porpoising and then a sudden swerve to the left. A couple of passengers who had neglected fastening their seat belts were tossed from their seats, although no one was injured, nor was there any damage to the plane. Later that night at dinner, Sikorsky was uneasy and finally said, "Charles, I want to claim part of the credit for that bouncy landing."

"You can take it all," Lindbergh replied with a gleam in his eye.

Sikorsky then admitted that he had made

an error in the design of the hull and that landing the giant plane demanded the most absolutely delicate landing technique. "The point I want to make," he told his biographer, Frank Delear, "is that it was I who made the blunder, not Lindbergh."

Lindbergh laughed when he heard that Sikorsky took "credit" for the landing and said, "That's quite typical of Igor—to take the blame himself and never blame the other fellow. Actually, it was not his fault. At the time he built the S-40, a great deal remained to be learned about hull design. He and [designer-engineer] Michael Gluhareff used to put a scale model of a hull on the end of a stick and test it at the side of a launch on the river near the plant in Stratford. This method did not of course provide the accuracy obtained later with elaborate instruments and test basins. So it was not surprising that the S-40 and even the S-42 hulls were not ideal. This sort of thing applied not only to seaplanes but to landplanes also—in the design of landing gears, tail skids, and other parts. The knowledge was just not there at that time in aviation history. Igor had done a good engineering job, and it was the pilot's job to handle the airplane properly. True, the hull could have been better, but the knowledge just wasn't there."

Passengers boarding the S-40. (Pan American)

Sikorsky more than compensated for the then limited technical mastery with a mother hen's attention to details. In a literal sense this was revealed during one of his flights with Basil Rowe as pilot. Knowing the designer was aboard the flight, Rowe turned the controls of the big plane over to his co-pilot and went aft to speak to Sikorsky. To his surprise he found the otherwise poised and dignified little man "down on his knees in the aisle, feeling around the floor and the sides of the ship, with the passengers looking on in alarm."

Rowe inquired as to the nature of Sikorsky's search.

"I keep hearing a peep, peep, squeak, squeak," he was told.

Rowe smiled, then suggested that he not be concerned about it.

"I'll get a mechanic to check it when we arrive in Kingston," Rowe assured him. They were then flying over Cuba on their way south.

But Sikorsky was not so easily put off. If the strange sound annoyed him, it was bound to annoy the passengers, but him more than the passengers, for Sikorsky did not wish to have his name attached to a squeaky aircraft. He returned to the kneeling position in the aisle, checking for some mechanical flaw. Rowe returned to the pilot's compartment, chuckling. They arrived at Kingston, attended to the usual details, and took off again. Airborne again and with the plane at cruising altitude, Rowe returned to the cabin.

"Well, Mr. Sikorsky," he asked, "do you still hear that peep, peep, squeak, squeak? My mechanic was supposed to take care of it in Kingston."

"No, it's gone—what was it?"

"It was a thousand baby chickens in the cargo department," Rowe informed him. "We unloaded them at Kingston."

When he returned to the cockpit Rowe could see that Sikorsky had turned to the window, laughing merrily at his own inability to trace the source of the "peep, peep, squeak, squeak." A gentleman with a sense of humor, one thing Igor Sikorsky had never done was raise chickens.

One of the strangest flights made by Basil Rowe in the "American Clipper"—to continue briefly in the live stock vein—was to race the great craft with an ox-drawn cart. The idea was to dramatize the fastest means of transportation of the day by pitting it against one of the most ancient—an old Cuban high-wheeled cane cart. Both vehicles were to start at the same time from Havana. Rowe was supposed to estimate the distance the oxen could cover in the time it would take the clipper to fly to Miami. His guess was that the oxen would travel at about a rate of four miles an hour.

As it proved, Rowe was off a bit in his estimate, for three good reasons: "The first and foremost was the method used by the Cubans in handling oxen: goading them along with a nail in the end of a pole. The second factor was a northeaster I had to buck. The third was the Cuban himself and his inherent love of gambling."

The great day dawned in a flurry of excitement and holiday spirit. "The oxen had a police escort and a cheering throng soaked in Bacardi to speed them on their way." The crowd was large and enthusiastic—and the betting reflected it accordingly. Practically everyone was putting his money on the nose of the oxen and had "started to push the cart and pull the oxen until the poor beasts were doing about ten miles an hour and gaining on me as I battled the northeaster out over the Gulf Stream."

Rowe was kept informed of the progress of the speedy oxcart and, as he nosed the big plane into the wind, realized that he might very well lose the race. That would be ignominious. "I couldn't louse up the publicity. Besides, the Cubans had been two-timing me all the way. I didn't have anyone sticking a nail into the tail of my

clipper." The redoubtable Rowe grew crafty; he would win the race on the theory that it was the winning of the race that counted, not the running of it.

He was barely more than halfway to Miami (the oxen were a mile and a half from their finish line) when he selected a glassy stretch of calm water in the lee of the Keys. He set the big clipper down and radioed, with a modicum of verity, "Just landed." He then "planed along on the step for a half mile or so, then pulled up and continued the flight. It was a dirty trick, but so is sticking nails in oxen. When I was declared the winner, there was such a riot among the oxen fans that the next day I was transferred to another route. Pan American didn't want to lose a pilot."

Although only three S-40s were built, a thousand flights were accumulated by them in the Caribbean from that first flight by Lindbergh in November 1931 through January 1934, with an on-time arrival record of 99 percent. After being retired from Pan American service the clippers were employed in charter operations and later, during the war, served as training ships for U. S. Navy pilots. Theirs was a remarkably trouble-free record, and during the years of their

Passenger luxury aboard the American Clipper, *aplomb being the keynote. On right, as demonstration of the smooth flight characteristics, two men assemble a jigsaw puzzle, one of the fads of the thirties. (Pan American)*

The Sikorsky S-40 in flight over the Caribbean, over which it logged millions of miles and carried thousands of passengers. (Sikorsky Aircraft)

service logged an estimated ten million miles of flight.

Long before the S-40s had flown their millions of miles, Igor Sikorsky had begun work on his next large clipper. In fact, it was during the inaugural flight of the "American Clipper" that he had begun discussing an improved aircraft with Lindbergh in the ship's lounge, making preliminary sketches on the menu. Having taken the step from the S-38 to the S-40, the designer believed they, meaning himself and his company, were ready for "as large a step forward as we could in refinement of design." Behind this decision was Pan American's request for the next clipper, the requirements of which were most ambitious. In the words of Sikorsky, "These included a lifting capacity that would permit carrying fuel for a twenty-five-hundred-mile nonstop flight against a thirty-mile wind, at a cruising

speed far in excess of the average operating speed of any flying boat at that time—a difficult problem."

Obviously Juan Terry Trippe had cast his eyes upon the oceans.

In order to provide him with the aircraft for such aspirations, Sikorsky realized that he too would have to aspire, to reach, and to excel. The solution to their major problem—long range and high speed—Sikorsky and his colleagues realized lay in higher wing loading. Each square foot of the proposed aircraft's wing would be required to lift more weight than any wing then being used—about thirty pounds per square foot, double the standard wing loading of the period. The design of the wing was done under the direction of Michael Gluhareff, who introduced several innovations, among them an entirely new wing shape for Sikorsky. Instead of the conventional slabby wing

Charles Lindbergh and Igor Sikorsky on wing of S-42, the innovational Sikorsky flying boat of 1934. (Sikorsky Aircraft)

with rounded tips, the new wing tapered at each tip (also rounded). Although the span was four feet longer than that of the S-40, the area of the new plane totaled 1330 square feet, as against the 1875 square feet of the S-40. Top speed of the latter was 134.7 miles per hour (cruising speed: 115), while the top speed of the S-42 would be 180 mph, with crusing speed 160. Both aircraft landed at a speed of 65 mph. This was made possible in the S-42 by designing a new wingflap into the trailing edge of the rectangular panel of the wing. This provided additional lift for the takeoff and a braking action for landing.

The four engines, Pratt & Whitney Hornets, did not dangle from the wing as did the powerplants of the earlier Sikorskys. Instead they were installed directly into the leading edge of the wing. These engines (the work of George Mead and Andrew Willgoos) supplied the power to lift the great flying boat (with a gross weight of 38,000 pounds, compared to the S-40's 34,000; payload of the latter was 5902 pounds, compared with the S42's 8060).

Another contributing factor was the Hamilton controllable pitch propeller (the brainchild of Frank Caldwell), which enabled the pilot to manipulate the pitch of the propellers even while the plane was in flight, to attain highest efficiency under takeoff and cruise conditions. For takeoffs the blade was set at a flattish angle (relative to leading edge of the wing) for full power. When the plane reached cruising altitude the blades could be set at a greater angle in order to reduce fuel consumption. This single contribution was decisive in the high performance of the S-42 (as well as subsequent outstanding aircraft) and won the Collier Trophy for Caldwell in 1934.

Because the engines had been faired into the wing, the necessity for the multiplicity of struts, which had been so characteristic of the earlier Sikorskys, was eliminated. The wing itself was faired into the fuselage also, by means of a low pylon. Not all external struts had been eliminated, of course, but those that remained were constructed of streamlined Duralumin. Gone, however, was the twin boom configuration (although the duo rudder remained), which had been so typical a feature of the Sikorsky design. In the S-42 the tail members were attached directly to the after hull, which was a beautifully sleek design in itself (one friend of Sikorsky's likened it to the form of the whale he had seen suspended from the ceiling of New York's Museum of Natural History).

The design of the S-42, regarded as the most beautiful aircraft of its time, and one that performed in a manner ahead of its time, was in fact a committee product. Besides Sikorsky and his staff, Pan American contributed the ideas of Charles Lindbergh and doughty and doubting André Priester, whose very conservatism was ever a valuable quality. Priester's major concern was

The S-42, "the most beautiful aircraft of its time," on a takeoff run. NACA-cowled engines are faired into wing and fewer struts interfere with streamlining, as on earlier Sikorskys. (Pan American)

passenger safety, followed by efficiency and trouble-free operation; payload and spectacular performance were considered, but in Priester's book they came down near the bottom. While he might drive a designer to near distraction, Priester's reasoning was always sound.

Another contributor to the design of the S-42 was the National Advisory Committee for Aeronautics (NACA, now NASA), a repository of aeronautical facts and figures freely available to anyone interested. A mass of technical, scientific, and theoretical thinking had combined to produce the S-42— the first true flying boat designed in the United States.

Work on the design of the plane had begun late in 1931, construction was started in 1932, and by Christmas of 1933 the aircraft was completed. The iced-over Housatonic precluded any launching until the end of March 1934. The new boat was turned over to Boris Sergievsky, with Sikorsky in

The delivery of the first S-42 (Brazilian, later Colombian Clipper) on June 5, 1934. From left to right: Edwin G. Musick, chief pilot of Pan American; André Priester, vice president and chief engineer of Pan American; Charles Lindbergh; Juan T. Trippe; Igor Sikorsky; E. L. Vidal, director of U. S. Air Commerce Department; F. R. Neilson, President of Sikorsky Aircraft. (Sikorsky Aircraft)

S-42 in flight; this shot shows the wing flap in the center trailing edge of the wing to increase efficiency of wing in takeoff and landing. (Pan American)

the co-pilot's seat, for water testing, which was first on the agenda. The lightly loaded plane did indeed maneuver through the water like a graceful whale. Its response to various throttle settings was noted. Then it was decided to bring the ship up on the step at accelerated power. The clipper, in the words of Sikorsky, "went on the step almost immediately and continued to run nicely and to accelerate in spite of the fact that the throttle was again reduced to some 45 or 50 percent of the power. From my seat in the cockpit it was easy to see how quickly and easily the large ship was gaining speed."

Sergievsky "did not have an opportunity to make many of the tests while running on the step, because a moment later we were in the air. This was a grand feeling, but a flight was not on the program for that day . . ."

The following day, March 30, 1934, Sergievsky took the plane up for its scheduled flight test. After these various tests, all data were scrutinized and discussed and the final adjustments and modifications made—the

Interior of the S-42, looking forward into cockpit. Small metal plates over archway read (on left): "Compartment 'B'—No Smoking" (in English and Spanish). Right plate: "Life Jackets under Floor" in English, Spanish, and Portuguese. (Sikorsky Aircraft)

most important was relocating the step farther back on the hull to improve handling of the flying boat in the water. Another improvement was in an engine change: more powerful "Hornets" had evolved (from a 700-hp capability to 750, which added eight miles per hour to the top speed, bringing it up to 188 mph). The various modifications increased the weight of the S-42 by two tons. But it did not restrict its performance, obviously.

Beginning on April 26, the S-42 began a spree of record-breaking flights in several international categories: payload, altitude, and speed (with various payloads). The series culminated on August 1, 1934, when no less than eight world records were established. There was a banner crew aboard, among them Sergievsky, Lindbergh, and Pan American's chief pilot, Captain Edwin Musick. When the day's flying came to a close the United States led the world in the number of flight performance records, seventeen compared with France's sixteen. Of the seventeen, the S-42 held ten.

Almost simultaneously with the emergence of the big flying boat, Sikorsky designed and produced yet another aircraft of S-38 lineage. This was the S-43, which evidenced genetic kindred to both the old Ugly Duckling and the new S-42. It was an "amphibion," to use Sikorsky's word; it was a twin-engined craft, carried a maximum of eighteen passengers (with a crew of four), and was employed generally in the Caribbean as a replacement for the aging S-38.

Sikorsky S-43, designed to replace the old S-38 in the smaller "amphibion" class. This is an example of the later model, with twin rudder. Early S-43 had single rudder. Its impact on aviation was not as great as either that of the S-38 or S-42. (Pan American)

It was also placed in operation by Inter-Island Airways, besides Pan American's affiliates, Panagra and Panair do Brazil, as well as the U. S. Army (five) and Navy (seventeen). A total of fifty-three S-43s were built (it also proved to be a record-breaking aircraft). The S-43 represented the ultimate in the evolution of the two-engined amphibion, from the S-38 of 1928 to the streamlined 1935 new craft.

Unlike the S-42, the first great flying boat, the S-43 was not innovational but the end result of several innovations. It remained for its larger sister to play a greater role in the events in aviation to come.

Even before the S-42 had accumulated its ten records it was officially delivered to Pan American (on June 5, 1934), the first of ten of these craft that would be used by the airline. On August 15 the ship was launched on its inaugural flight to Argentina; in Rio de Janeiro the wife of President-Dictator Getulia Vargas christened the NC 822M the *Brazilian Clipper*. The great boat then proceeded on its traversal of some fifteen thousand miles and twelve South American countries, proving itself as a superior aircraft in the beginning of a long and fruitful flying career.

With the advent of the formidable S-42 it was obvious that Juan Terry Trippe had been presented with a flying oceanliner.

All he lacked, for the moment, were oceans.

The Brazilian Clipper *en route to South America. It was in this plane that Boris Sergievsky set ten world's records in 1934. Later, in August, the plane made a fifteen hundred-mile tour, most of it over South America. (Pan American)*

6: The Great Circle, or The Big Runaround

Trippe's eye naturally fell on the Atlantic. As early as December of 1929 he initiated discussions with British officials proposing a cooperative transatlantic venture, with emphasis on the northern route between the United States and Europe but touching lightly on the possibility of Bermuda as a stopover point slightly to the south. With the French Trippe then went into the potential of the southern route (Lisbon-Azores). Neither of the European airlines (Imperial Airways, Ltd. and Aéropostale) had aircraft that boasted the range for making these crossings (neither did Trippe, for that matter, but he was getting there with his Sikorsky series). What they—the British and French—did have were the absolutely indispensable refueling points. They also enjoyed official governmental blessings and backing (Trippe, of course, had at least the former) and, as it eventuated, an obstructive national pride. As the talks proceeded, generally in secret, the British particularly became more and more jealous of their ocean. Although he came to recognize this sentiment as the negotiations proceeded—and what it meant to his plans—Trippe had already taken preliminary steps just in the event that all should go well.

In the summer of 1933 the Lindberghs began to survey the three major airways over the North Atlantic in their specially built Lockheed Sirius, later named *Ting-missartoq* (an Eskimo word meaning "the one who flies like a big bird"). The routes covered by the Lindberghs were designated by the airman as the northern "Greenland Route," the southern "Azores Route" and the "Great Circle Route" between. The latter, defined as the shortest surface distance between two points on a sphere, roughly paralleled that over which the "Flying Hutchinsons" had made their transatlantic attempt the year before.

Taking off from Flushing Bay, New York, on July 9, 1933, the Lindberghs flew northward in their Lockheed in carefully planned stages. They were not seeking adventure and took no risks; if visibility turned poor, they remained on the ground. Besides a meticulously equipped aircraft, they also had a supply ship that accompanied them along the way. This was the S.S. *Jelling,* which had been commissioned by Pan American. Lindbergh, with customary attention to detail, had measured to the very ounce every piece of equipment carried in the plane. These ranged from a quarter-inch Allen wrench ("1 oz") through a package of needles ("½ oz") and personal clothing and equipment ("18 lbs each"). In order to facilitate an especially delicate takeoff on the return flight home, the bulk of the equipment was left behind—this included, for example, the Allen wrench, but not the needles, and all but twelve ounces of the personal clothing and equipment.

By the time the Lindberghs returned to Flushing Bay, on December 19, they had flown more than thirty thousand miles and had explored various points in the North and Central Atlantic as future bases for airline operations. They made their leisurely way to Copenhagen via Newfoundland, Labrador, Greenland, and Iceland. This route combined the northern and Great Circle approaches to Europe—and achieved this without depending upon landing rights that belonged to Great Britain. Trippe evi-dently was already considering the British defection from his scheme for a joint Atlantic operation. The key, however, lay with Newfoundland (a separate British Dominion and then not part of Canada), which because of its status could grant Trippe his landing rights without interference from London. The same, of course, applied to Canada.

After some weeks of European travel, the Lindberghs returned to the United States via the South Atlantic. They flew down to Africa and took off (after stripping their plane of much equipment) from Bathurst, Gambia, and after nearly sixteen hours in the air, landed at Natal, Brazil (some of the details of this flight are poetically related in Anne Lindbergh's beautiful book, *Listen! the Wind*). When they put down finally in Flushing Bay they brought with them a mass of information about sites, weather, and other essential data necessary to the plotting of air routes across the Atlantic.

But, for the moment, it was not to be. Within a few months Newfoundland had suffered a deep economic crisis, there were riots, and its Dominion status was canceled. When Newfoundland became a Crown Colony, and therefore directly under the control of the British government, Trippe's landing rights agreement was canceled also. The British had taken back the Atlantic Ocean.

This setback, plus others—for the French, with whom Trippe had an agreement also on the Azores route, simply lost their franchise by default, and Portugal seemed inclined to favor the British—did not discourage Juan Trippe. He merely set aside his Atlantic plans momentarily and turned to another that had engaged him some years before. He revealed his intentions, according to company legend, at a Pan American board meeting when he quietly announced, "We are now getting ready to fly the Pacific."

In truth, Trippe had characteristically

The Lindberghs' Lockheed Sirius at the finish of their North Atlantic survey, December 1933. Opposition from British airlines canceled Trippe's hopes for a Pan American track over the Atlantic, which turned his attentions to the Pacific. In this same aircraft the Lindberghs had, in 1931, also surveyed a Great Circle Route to the Orient. (Pan American: J. E. Jacks)

been "getting ready" for quite some time. In the summer of 1931, even before the Atlantic Surveys the Lindberghs had made an exploratory flight across the Arctic "Great Circle" route linking Alaska with Japan and China. The aircraft used was the same Lockheed Sirius that they would use in the 1933 Atlantic survey; this story was told in Mrs. Lindbergh's book, *North to the Orient*. Their flight, while successful, came to grief at Hankow when their plane was capsized in the swollen Yangtze River. The plane, still fastened to the British aircraft carrier *Hermes* by a cable, was damaged, but the Lindberghs escaped without harm. The Sirius was retrieved from the river and taken aboard the *Hermes* to Shanghai, where it was crated and shipped to Lockheed for repairs. A new engine was installed and the plane was ready for the Atlantic surveys.

By the time he had switched his attentions from the Atlantic to the Pacific, Trippe had also abandoned the idea of a "North to the Orient" route. He was not at all encouraged in his dealings with the Russians by the U. S. State Department, although the Russians appeared to be remarkably cooperative. The State Department frowned upon such benevolence, interpreting it as a bid for certain reciprocation. At the same time diplomatic relations between Japan and the United States were not terribly cozy. Japan had already, in 1931, begun its military adventures in the Pacific.

Trippe would have to find another—and longer—airway to the Orient. He chose a route through the Central Pacific, the first leg of which, between California and Hawaii, stretched over no less than twenty-three hundred miles of empty sea. It was this barrier that inspired the letter dated June 26, 1931, in which Trippe stated that the "Pan American Airways System will presently require additional flying equipment for long-distance, high-speed, over-water air mail transportation. . . . The aircraft will be a multimotored flying boat, having a cruising range of twenty-five hundred miles and providing accommodations for a crew of four with at least three hundred pounds of air mail and twelve passengers. . . ."

This was, for its time, an extremely large order to fulfill and of all the aircraft manufacturers to which copies of the letter had been sent, only two answered. One was, of course, Sikorsky, who provided the S-42 eventually in compliance with the gist of the letter. The other answer came from

Glenn L. Martin, whose answer materialized a year after Sikorsky's in the form of the M-130.

If producing the aircraft capable of sustained overwater flight was a challenge, arranging for the berthing of such planes once they had made such flights provided its own form of headache. Having been blocked in Russia and Japan, Trippe turned to China. In order to acquire a foothold, Pan American bought out an ailing, partly American owned airline known as China National Aviation Corporation. North American Aviation (a subsidiary of Curtiss-Wright) owned 45 percent of the corporation and the Chinese government owned the controlling interest. This was the common practice, not merely an anti-American activity. The Chinese government owned two-thirds of Eurasia Aviation Corporation, the other third being held by Germany's Lufthansa. The Chinese point of view was that it did not wish any foreign nation (especially Japan) to gain a dominating aerial foothold, to mix metaphors, in China.

Trippe hoped "to anchor down the opposite end of the future transpacific line" by acquiring North American Aviation's interest in China National Aviation Corporation (CNAC), which he did in March of 1933. This placed Pan American inside China and operating along the eastern coast with terminals in the south at Canton, in the north at Peking, and with Shanghai roughly centered. The line extended inland as far west as Chengtu, linking at certain points with Eurasia's terminals. Thus between them the two lines provided air service among China's major cities. These services were eventually curtailed as Japanese military aggressions increased during the early and mid-thirties.

But Trippe's problem—Japanese warmaking aside—was not truly solved. CNAC

The Douglas Dolphin, with which Pan American began a modest airline operation along the China coast in 1933. The Dolphin could carry eight passengers at an average speed of 135 miles an hour. Wingspan was sixty feet and fuselage length, forty-five feet; power was supplied by two Pratt & Whitney Wasp Jrs. Landing gear was not really retractable, but could be folded out of the way manually while the plane was in the water. (Douglas Aircraft)

operating along the China coast (using, among other planes, the Douglas Dolphin) meant only that a subsidiary of Pan American was functioning *inside* China proper. It did not mean that Pan American had the privilege of landing its aircraft *in* China if that plane had not already been there to begin with. In short, there were no Chinese landing rights granted with the purchase of CNAC. And there were more than enough vexations connected with that operation to require full-time footwork by Pan American's trouble-shooter on the scene, Harold M. Bixby. A Missourian interested in aviation (he had been one of Lindbergh's backers in the 1927 flight to Paris), Bixby received a liberal education in Oriental psychology and politics. Negotiations were carried out with great ceremony and delay. For example, when Bixby hoped to arrange for a contract to carry mail between Canton and Shanghai, he was first directed to the minister of railroads. He was then referred to the minister of communications—of which, over a period of six months, there were three, each of whom required a period of getting acquainted, protocol—and delay.

One element of Chinese dealing that Bixby hoped to avoid was "the squeeze" (which in the United States was known more bluntly as "graft"). Whenever negotiations for construction, shipping, or purchasing came up, there appeared numerous Chinese officials along the line to squeeze a few yen out of the coin of the realm. By refusing to participate in this ancient game Bixby saved himself, and Pan American, an infinity of future headaches. Meanwhile, however, he had a sufficiency. Another problem was that even if official contracts with the government were properly signed, it did not follow that they would be honored by a warlord of the interior who did not recognize the Chiang Kai-shek government as official. Or neighboring feuding warlords might complicate matters. But Bixby persisted, and progress prevailed. Wealthy Chinese merchants were convinced of the "face" value of traveling by air—after all, it was possible to fly from Chungking to Chengtu in three hours; by sedan chair it had taken three weeks.

Like South America, China was not a land of railroads—its terrain did not lend itself to overland transportation. Pan American, after its Caribbean laboratory experience, was indeed in its element. But it was not yet quite its element.

China, however appreciative of the wonders of air travel, was not so grateful as to grant a foreign power landing rights. Trippe, on his part, was as inscrutable as any warlord. Hong Kong, a British Crown Colony on the mainland, was practically next door to Canton, the southern terminus of the China National Aviation Corporation's line. But the British, with their own dream of aerial empire, were not likely to grant any landing rights to an American empire builder, especially one whose aircraft were capable of spanning oceans. Besides, it would have nettled the Chinese.

So Trippe did a quick sidestep, across the Tai Shan Bay to Macao—which happened to be a Portuguese colony in China. Negotiations with Portugal were carried out unobtrusively and, since Portugal had nothing to lose and all to gain, Pan American was granted landing rights at Macao. This was accomplished so quietly that neither the Chinese nor the British were aware of it until all the concessions had been granted to Pan American. This was, of course, good business for Macao, which had been pretty much rendered a second-rate port by the bustling presence of Hong Kong across the bay.

The uproar that followed the announcement of the agreement could be heard across the bay. Chinese and British merchants visualizing the advantages of an air link with America raised a mighty holler to the degree that British officialdom relented and, by October 1936, Trippe had his Chinese terminal, Hong Kong. Macao, having served its purpose in Trippe's grand design, returned once more to its original somnolence.

Even as the Chinese negotiations proceeded *in extenso,* Trippe had initiated preparations for the day when all would work out as he had planned from the beginning. In fact, even before Hong Kong had been ascertained, his Pan American air tracks had begun to stretch across the Pacific. As the hulls of new clipper ships were laid in the Martin Company factory at Middle River, Maryland, additional Sikorsky S-42s were being produced at Stratford. Almost simultaneously a Pan American Pacific base was established at Alameda, across the bay from San Francisco. From this base a fifteen thousand-ton steamer, the S.S. *North Haven,* set out on March 27, 1935; its mission was to establish bases for Pan American's Pacific Division on three tiny, practically unknown dots in the Pacific: Midway, Wake, and Guam Islands.

These dots were placed at Pan American's disposal thanks to the cooperation of the U. S. Navy; likewise the harbor facilities at the important first stop on any flight to the Orient—Pearl Harbor in Hawaii. Beyond Wake lay Guam, also under United States naval jurisdiction, and beyond that Manila in the Philippines. From Manila to Hong Kong was but a short air hop.

Objections to Pan American's thrust into the Pacific air were made, principally by Japan, whose militarily-minded leaders saw in Trippe's Pacific expansion something they described as a "concealed military operation."

Despite the protests and general unhappiness among certain Japanese warlords, British airline wishful thinkers, and his reluctant partners, the Chinese government, Trippe launched his Pacific undertaking as scheduled. The *North Haven* steamed out of San Francisco Harbor with, in the words of a *Fortune* writer, "five air bases in its hold, five five-ton tractors, plus radio towers, launches, lumber, food, Diesel engines, and two ten-ton electric generators—a total of

The North Haven *standing off the pier at Midway Island. Unable to approach the island directly because of the reef, the ship was unloaded and supplies transferred via rafts and launches. (Pan American)*

1,018,897 items [actually 108,897], all calculated and fitted together on paper by Pan American slide-rule wizards."

Before the *North Haven* returned to home base four months later, its crew, construction workers, and other specialists had carved two (not five, as the zealous *Fortune* writer had stated) new bases out of coral and sand. These were, of course, at Midway and Wake. Honolulu, Guam, and Manila were reasonably serviceable as clipper bases and only required refinement, not a beginning from absolute scratch as did Midway and Wake.

In charge of the work parties who were to do the carving was an ex-Navy pilot who had gained further experience with Pan American, William Grooch. Following a brief stopover at Honolulu, where he hired additional men for his construction crews, Grooch and the *North Haven* set off for Midway. One thing he learned in Hawaii, after talking with some men who knew, was that practically nothing was actually known about either Midway or Wake. The

former, at least, could furnish some small semblance to civilization, being the site of a cable station that linked Hawaii with the Philippines. Midway was an atoll—two small islets, Sand and Eastern, surrounded by coral reef.

With the *North Haven* anchored about a half mile off the reef, it was necessary to transfer tons of material from the steamer via launch through passages in the reef to the beach of Sand Island. In this lagoon a perfect base for the clippers could be built, along with a radio station and other facilities, including electricity, which provided light and refrigeration. Unloading the cargo from the larger ship into the lighters—considering that the sea at times ran to ten-foot swells—was an epic of skill and ingenuity. One of the first items lowered over the side of the *North Haven* was a tractor weighing ten tons (according to Grooch—the *Fortune* writer halved the tonnage). The trick was to gauge the movement of the *North Haven,* the lighter, and the sea. At one instant all three elements were in proper

"Tent City" — Temp. Housing for Construction Gang attached to SS North Haven. 1935 (Midway Is.)

A snapshot taken by one of the Pan American work party at Midway before it was converted into a Pan American base. (Pan American)

juxtaposition; at this moment the tractor was gently placed aboard the lighter with hardly a bump. Then a launch would tow the lighter through the reef.

This work went on for ten days, in good weather and poor until all supplies were piled on the beach, construction was under way, and the radio station was operating. As he prepared to leave, Grooch could feel he would leave behind "our first small colony—isolated but independent. They would be quite comfortable in a few weeks when the quarters were completed. They would have electric light and power, hot and cold running water, an ample cold-storage supply of fresh provisions, a library, and movies twice a week."

Wake, like Midway, was actually an atoll consisting of Wake, Wilkes, and Peale Islands, roughly horseshoe-shaped with shallow channels between each of the three islets. These were encircled by encrusted coral reefs capable of cutting the bottom off a boat. On the one spot on the chart marked "the boat landing" lay the wreckage of two Navy boats that had come to grief in the surf. The waters surrounding Wake were so deep that there was no anchorage for the *North Haven*.

After circling the islands Grooch and his party agreed that, despite its hazards, the charted "boat landing" on Wilkes Island "was the only possible spot where we could land supplies." However, it was not at all acceptable as the site for a base: the "beach was a tumbled mass of coral rock, six feet or so above sea level. About a hundred feet back from the water's edge the jungle started; queer-looking thorny stunted trees and thick brush. Clearing ground on Wilkes Island was going to be a laborious process." Almost immediately the work parties began constructing a dock on Wilkes, affording an unloading spot for the supply lighters away from the coral heads that might rip out the bottoms.

Survey parties explored Wake and Peale Islands, and after finding Wake itself unsuitable, selected Peale as the station site. It was large enough, it appeared never to have been under water, and its ocean side beach was protected by a great natural coral breakwater that had built up over the centuries. This, in turn, was protected by a reef that took the brunt of any heavy seas, which then, dissipated, was stopped by the breakwater. It was a perfect haven for the clippers.

But before it became that perfect haven it had to be handmade. Supplies came ashore on Wilkes, were then dragged across the rugged island, and then transported across the lagoon separating Wilkes and Peale. Only then could the actual building on Peale Island get under way. The supplies were initially dragged across Wilkes by sleds pulled by the tractor. Then someone realized that in the hold of the *North Haven* lay the rudiments of a primitive railroad. A two-hundred-yard roadbed was blasted out of the rocky jungle from the storage yard on Wilkes down to the lagoon. Then a rail car was fashioned using truck wheels without tires; a rail was improvised out of iron stock over which, luckily, the denuded Ford rims fitted snugly. Axles were welded directly to the wheels *in situ* on the previously laid track. Over this frame a car twelve feet long and six feet wide was constructed; it could carry a load up to about two tons. Since it ran downhill, it required no engine —only a brake to keep it from ending up in the lagoon. Empty, it was light enough for one man to push it back up the slope to the storage area. Upon completion it was named "the shortest railroad in the world."

Eventually a lighter was placed in the lagoon separating Wilkes and Peale, and the work of building the station on Peale proceeded rapidly. After thirteen days all the cargo destined for Wake was ashore except provisions and the frozen meat. Within four more days the cold-storage plant was in working order on Peale Island. Assured

Unloading supplies on Wilkes Island, one of the three islets of the Wake atoll. The North Haven *stands offshore. (Pan American)*

". . . the shortest railroad in the world . . ." The improvised track across Wilkes Island to transport supplies to Peale, which had been selected as the site for the Pan American base at Wake Island. (Pan American)

that all was well at Wake, Grooch set off for Guam on May 29.

Southernmost, largest, and most populous of the Marianas group, Guam presented no such obstacles as had Midway and Wake. A great U. S. Navy outpost since 1917 (although a U.S. possession since the Spanish-American War), Guam was practically in operating condition before the *North Haven* party had arrived. Grooch was granted the use of an abandoned Marine air base at Sumay as a base of operations. Among the many things accomplished at Guam was the taking aboard the *North Haven* of a hundred tons of sacked fertile soil for Midway. After about a week in Guam and leaving the base crew (which would man the Pan American station there) and the construction crew, Grooch proceeded on to Manila. Here, too, the establishment of a base was little more than improving an already existing facility. Grooch's major reason for the trip to Manila was for the replenishment of supplies and materials for Wake and Midway. This done, the *North Haven* steamed out of Manila on its return voyage to the United States, with stopovers at Wake and Midway, to discharge cargo and to take on those men who were to return home. After a refueling stop at Honolulu, the *North Haven* pushed off for San Francisco and on July 28, 1935, passed through the Golden Gate and berthed at Pier 22. In exactly four months the so-called *"North Haven* expedition" had blazed an air trail across more than eight thousand miles of the Pacific. (This was followed the next winter by a second *North Haven* expedition, which returned to Midway, Wake, and Guam to build hotel accommodations for clipper passengers.)

Even before the first *North Haven* crews had returned to San Francisco the first clipper had landed at Midway. In fact, even as they labored at Midway, Pan American had launched the first of the Pacific survey flights.

On April 16, 1935 the *Pan American Clipper* (an S-42) took off from Alameda (San Francisco) and headed out to sea. At the controls was veteran Pan American pilot Edwin C. Musick. The gentle, soft-spoken Musick was known as "The Sphinx of Aviation" because of a taciturnity about his aerial exploits. A solid, businesslike, quietly proficient airman, he was Pan American's chief pilot and captain of the *Pan American Clipper*. First officer was R. O. D. Sullivan; engineering officer, V. A. Wright; junior flight officer, H. R. Canaday; navigation officer, Fred J. Noonan, and the radio officer was W. T. Jarboe, Jr.

This flight inaugurated the transpacific surveys, checking out the first leg of the Pacific track from San Francisco to Honolulu—a distance of some twenty-three hundred miles. Upon setting down at Pearl Harbor eighteen hours and nine minutes

The Midway Island Hotel following the second North Haven *expedition. Gooney birds, the island's original inhabitants, decorate the imported lawn. Wake was an official U.S. bird sanctuary, and all construction had to be done without disturbing the goonies. (Pan American)*

Igor Sikorsky chatting with Captain Edwin C. Musick, Pan American's chief pilot and pioneer of the Pacific survey flights, 1935–38. (Sikorsky Aircraft)

Crew of the Sikorsky Pan American Clipper: *Captain Musick, R. O. D. Sullivan,
V. A. Wright, F. J. Noonan, H. R. Canaday, and W. T. Jarboe, Jr. (Pan American)*

later, Musick's laconic comment was a simple, "Just a routine flight." Its function was to test radio navigation equipment and weather conditions. A taste of the latter came on the return flight (April 22–23) when the *Pan American Clipper* flew into strong headwinds, besides veering from a straightline course to observe the various conditions at different altitudes. This added two hours and fifty minutes to the flight time and over four hundred miles to the distance. This flight, too, was purely routine —and satisfactory, especially in the light of the fact that since 1928, although the Pacific had been flown, it had taken the lives of nine airmen who had attempted to cross it solo. Clearly a crossing of the Pacific required preparation, teamwork, and sophisticated technical apparatus.

In June the *Pan American Clipper* was ready for a further reach into the Pacific. Again starting out from Alameda (on June 12, 1935), with the same crew, the Si-

korsky boat crossed the California–Hawaii track in exactly eighteen hours, cutting nine minutes from the first flight. Then on June 15 Musick lifted out of Pearl Harbor early in the morning to cover the 1320-mile stretch of water between Honolulu and Wake Island. The *Pan American Clipper* gracefully bounced into the lagoon at Midway just nine hours and thirteen minutes later—at the very moment that the *North Haven,* having set construction crews ashore at Guam, was approaching Manila.

The harbor facilities at Midway proved satisfactory for use by the giant clipper— as did the navigation and communications to get it there. After only two days Musick and his crew headed back for home. On this flight the crew carried out a test of instruments by flying blind, with all the windows of the cockpit blacked out. This was done successfully for several hours and was duly reported to the world, dramatizing the safety and efficiency of Pan American's operations over the great watery vastness of the once formidable Pacific.

And so the transpacific survey flights continued: In August Wake Island was reached, running on a practice schedule and with an on-time arrival. The Pacific track had proceeded 1260 miles beyond Midway. The last of the new manmade outposts, fifteen hundred miles distant from Wake, was Guam. In October the *Pan American Clipper* made the round trip from San Francisco (Alameda) to Guam with a cargo of mail. (In August the Post Office Department had advertised for bids on an airmail contract to the Philippines, which naturally was awarded to Pan American, it being the only airline capable of fulfilling it. A leg of sixteen hundred miles separated Guam from Manila.) By November Pan American would be ready to begin regular air service across the Pacific, from San Francisco to Manila, all within a period of seven

months from the day the *North Haven* crews had begun their work at Midway. This epochal event would mark the advent of an entirely new aircraft, one of the most glamorous of all flying boats, the Martin M-130, the first of which would be known as the *China Clipper*. This was a revelation of Juan Trippe's shrewd optimism, as the acquisition of landing rights at Hong Kong, the gateway to China, was still a year away.

To round out the story of the Pacific surveys—and to set aside the Martin clipper momentarily—it remains only to tell of how Trippe's Pacific plans ultimately challenged the British over their own seas.

"I counted all along," he said early in 1937, "on connecting with the rich Australasian area." His idea was to build a leg southward from Honolulu to Auckland, New Zealand. This would bring New Zealand, which lay some seventy-four hundred

The Pan American Clipper II *landing at Auckland, New Zealand, March 29, 1937, another great step in Juan Trippe's Pacific expansion. (Pan American)*

Although not officially welcome, because it represented competition with British airlines in the Pacific, the Pan American Clipper II *was greeted by great crowds of New Zealanders. (Pan American)*

miles from California, within a four-day trip by air. Australia was merely a five-hour hop to the west.

Imperial Airways, of course, took a dim view of Trippe's new adventure. The British government-subsidized Imperial linked up with the Australian-based Queensland and Northern Territory Aerial Services—or more simply QANTAS—which joined Australia, by air, with the mother country. Trippe was not at all welcome in Australia. Nor in New Zealand, for that matter, but he had already sewn up the rights thanks to the good offices of Australian navigator Harold Gatty, a Pan American technical adviser since 1934. Gatty had arranged for Pan American's entré into Auckland so that by March 17, 1937, Captain Musick, in the *Pan American Clipper II,* could once again blaze an air trail across the Pacific. This one led from San Francisco to Honolulu, then south from there to Kingman

Reef, a tiny dot in the South Pacific. From there the line veered slightly westward down to Pago Pago on the island of Tutuila, American Samoa. The next leg brought the clipper into Auckland. It was on March 29, 1937 that Musick brought the *Pan American Clipper II* into Auckland to be welcomed by Gatty and a great crowd of curious New Zealanders. The clipper was joined by the Imperial Airways' *Centaurus,* a large flying boat built by Short Brothers, which completed a survey flight for the Australia–New Zealand run.

On April 3 Musick with his six-man crew began the return flight to Hawaii and, following stops at Pago Pago and Kingman Reef, arrived in the early morning of the ninth. In truth, it was found that there were certain disadvantages to this southern route, not the least of which was the question of the "ownership" of the barren pile of coral known as Kingman Reef or (Danger Island). Another was the cramped harbor facilities at Pago Pago.

To test these disadvantages further, Musick again flew the Honolulu-to-Auckland track (December 23, 1937–January 3, 1938) in the Sikorsky *Pan American Clipper II,* now renamed the *Samoan Clipper.* This flight seemed to strengthen the view that the harbor at Pago Pago might not prove suitable for clipper ship operations. Unwilling to abandon the route as laid out, Musick was determined to make another flight to be certain in his own mind. So he set out again from Honolulu on January 9, 1938, and made his way southward to Kingman Reef and to Pago Pago, where he and the crew arrived in the *Samoan Clipper* on January 10. The next day they (Musick, First Officer C. G. Sellers, Junior Flight Officer P. S. Brunk, Navigation Officer F. J. MacLean, Radio Officer T. D. Finley, and two flight officers, J. W. Stickrod and J. A. Brooks) all set out from Pago Pago for Auckland. After about an hour of flight Finley radioed the message that the *Samoan*

Arrival at Auckland on Transpacific Survey Flight No. 2, December 27, 1937. Crew of the Samoan Clipper *(formerly Pan American* Clipper II) *is escorted by Harold Gatty, Pan American technical adviser in Australasia. Gatty made a name for himself in aviation as navigator for Wiley Post during a 'round-the-world flight in 1931. (Pan American)*

Clipper was turning back because of an oil leak from one of the engines. About fifty minutes later, when the plane was within twelve miles of Pago Pago, word came again from the clipper: Musick was jettisoning fuel in preparation for landing in the harbor. Then silence.

Anxious peering into the horizon did not help, for after much time went by it was obvious that the *Samoan Clipper* was down at sea (the first Pan American clipper ever lost at sea). Residents from a nearby island reported seeing a great column of black smoke rising from the sea. A U. S. Navy tender was sent to search for the plane and found nothing the next day except an oil slick about twelve miles west of Pago Pago. Obviously the jettisoned fuel ignited and destroyed the *Samoan Clipper* (it was a known criticism of the S-42s that the emergency fuel ejection vents were too close to the exhausts, which might very well have been the cause of the explosion; however, no wreckage was recovered, so that no final reason could be determined). Musick and his entire crew perished in the accident.

With the loss of its chief pilot, Pan American abandoned the idea of a southern Pacific route for a time. Meanwhile, Trippe considered an alternate route, hoping to skip the questionable proprietorship of Kingman Reef and the harbor at Pago Pago. So the course was shaped (or bent, to employ a nonnautical term) to the west, making its first stop at tiny Canton Island, in the Phoenix group, and another at Nouméa, in French-governed New Caledonia (this was later switched to the Fiji Islands when an agreement was reached with the British).

But Canton Island proved to be no political improvement on Kingman Reef. The legal title to Canton was quite hazy. The British, waxing wrath over the U.S.

government's denial of landing rights at Honolulu, had begun to survey various alternative sites for bases against the day that they would begin to fly the Pacific. It soon came to the attention of Juan Trippe that his British rivals were being assisted by the Royal Navy which, as early as 1937, had begun stake out claims in various never before heard of Pacific islands. Generally these reconnaissance missions were officially announced as "fishing expeditions." Soon little Canton Island became an international battleground.

What has come to be known as the "Battle for Canton Island" in aviation annals began in the spring of 1939. No one, in the past, had made any official claim to the little bird-ridden island. Pan Ameri-

The Samoan Clipper *docked at Auckland in preparation for leaving for Honolulu early in 1938. The plane was lost between Honolulu and Pago Pago on January 11, taking the entire crew, including Musick, with it. (Pan American)*

can's legal researchers had to dig into the files of at least a century before (marine litigation and the logs of the first clipper ships) to find any reference to Canton. American sailing ships had made stops there during Far Eastern journeys to take aboard *guano* (encrusted wholesale bird droppings that were used at the time in producing fertilizer). This established, according to marine law, an American claim to Canton and its protected lagoon. Trippe began to impress upon officials in the State Department, the Navy, and the Department of the Interior that, in the neat phrase of Matthew Josephson, "the sacred right of Americans to gather bird-droppings at Canton Island be preserved."

These appeals did not fall upon, in a phrase, deaf ears. The Department of Commerce dispatched a crew out of Honolulu that proceeded to erect a tiny lighthouse on Canton Island. This lent a touch of claimmanship to the developing hostilities. But this was as far as it went: No one remained on the island to further the claim, and the British continued poking around the Pacific.

The lines were drawn in May 1939, when one of Trippe's agents who kept an eye on the "fishing expeditions" of the Royal Navy flashed the word: "Our cook is leaving by boat." There was no American on Canton to dash around the island arousing the birds with a cry of "The British are coming!," but Trippe rushed to Washington. There he found that President Roosevelt was away from the helm, on a legitimate fishing trip in the Gulf of Mexico. Trippe took his alarums to the State Department and the Navy. His exact strategic suggestions are not known, but the Navy did dispatch an unarmed sub chaser from Samoa. Trippe undoubtedly would have preferred a more formidable man o' war.

At the same time, Pan American construction crews at Honolulu, awaiting the coming of clement weather, hurriedly put

to sea in the faithful *North Haven*. The ship arrived off the coast of Canton Island on May 18—a Thursday—in a driving tropical rainstorm.

"The sight that greeted them in the hot tropical rain was not a particularly inspiring one," it was noted in *Pan American Air Ways,* the company paper. "Captain Oscar Peterson had maneuvered his ship in as close as he could under the existing conditions. From that position they saw little more than a sandy white blur, low-lying, and projecting, at its highest point, less than ten feet above a heaving sea, which seemed at each moment to be threatening to swallow it. Nevertheless, it was land, and the designated objective of the expedition and excitement ran high among all of those aboard.

"The task immediately ahead of the men was to get ashore to the ghostly rain-washed island, rising so certainly out of the ocean, and then to make themselves a self-contained community thereon as quickly as possible. To do this the first task was to unload some five thousand tons of foodstuffs, building, and general supplies. The preliminary step to this objective was getting off a landing and reconnoitering party, in command of Frank McKenzie, chief airport construction engineer of the Pacific Division.

"The party made a safe landing through the reef and over the sheltered waters of the lagoon within, but the word that they brought back was not for the moment very encouraging. Abnormally strong tides were running. A check of the records carried aboard the *North Haven* showed that these were higher than any ever recorded for the island in Navy hydrographic reports. 'Unusual weather,' which seems to be the fate of every visitor to some new place, had a specially ironic twist for the men aboard the *New Haven*. This was particularly true of the heavy rain, which drenched and somewhat depressed the new arrivals. Again the conditions mocked the records, which called Canton one of the driest islands in the South Pacific and which gave the average rainfall as three inches per annum.

"But despite these things, the loading booms were unlashed and the labor of landing the cargo was begun at once. Among the first things to be put overside were the *Paniar* launch and a heavy-duty tug, which had come down lashed to the forward deck of the *North Haven*. Next over were two giant lightering scows, one of them built on the *North Haven* during the uneventful cruise to 'Down Under.' These behaved well in the heavy seas then running.

"It was still raining as the first day after the arrival dawned. . . . The greatest unloading achievement of this second day at Canton was the getting ashore of the two heavy Diesel tractors, which are assisting materially in shaping up on this desert island the latest transoceanic air station.

"While the major part of the crew was engaged in these unloading labors, the remainder went ashore and began the work of staking out sites of the more important immediately needed buildings. They took ashore with them tents in which to live, and dusk of the second day saw a considerable part of the community in camp on the island.

"Dawn of the third day, which was Sunday, it was still raining, but toward noon the rain slackened and between urgent duties on which they were needed the men split up in parties and inspected the island. The beach was thoroughly combed for relics that might have some future historic value, but little of importance was found except a wrecked lifeboat from an earlier naval expedition of undetermined date."

They found too the little lighthouse that had been erected the year before—and offshore a menacing cruiser of the Royal Australian Navy. The American sub chaser

had been anchored in the small channel leading into the lagoon, thus effectively blocking entrance to the other ship. The British put a small boat over the side and came ashore.

There were words.

The British insisted that the Americans vacate this possession of the Crown. The Americans suggested that the British get the hell off—after all they were there, encamped and provisioned. Radio messages were flashed as feelings ran high, and the Americans made it clear they would not succumb to the guns of the cruiser (with which, in fact, they were not actually threatened). Obviously the word had come from Washington to hold Canton Island. Likewise the same word came from London.

The solution was, in fact, an impasse. The Americans remained on their half (the lagoon side) of the island and the British established a solitary representative of the Crown, a postal official, in a tiny shack on the beach on the other half of the island. The stalwart Briton held the thin red line of the Empire fiercely.

Probably the most exciting skirmish occurred on the day that some Americans caught some fish off the shore of the allegedly British side of the island. The postman attacked.

" 'Ere now," he firmly said, taking a stand. "Throw that fish back into the sea. Crown property."

Meanwhile London and Washington attempted to find a solution to this small war. Canton Island, it was mutually decided, would be jointly occupied by Britain and the United States. Pan American could continue with its construction and the lone Briton was ordered to hold his territory until, according to the agreement, 1990. But, then within two years an even greater war clouded over the Pacific, and the Lone Postman became the Forgotten Man, and

Royal Navy ships were drawn into other conflicts. Neither did he receive his mail, nor did he get supplies. When his provisions eventually ran out, he was taken under the wing of Pan American. Old battles were forgotten; he had not cast their fish upon the waters in vain. (It was not until 1942 that the war-preoccupied, but no doubt grateful, government remembered the Royal postman and brought him home from Canton Island.)

The winning of the Battle for Canton Island was a triumph for Trippe. He had established his great air tracks in the Pacific.

7: China Clipper

When Juan Trippe selected Pan American as the Pacific pioneer in 1931, he took no chances with his equipment. Although he had received two affirmative responses to his letter requesting bids on "a multi-motored flying boat," he went ahead and ordered both, Sikorsky's S-42 and the Glenn L. Martin Company's M-130. Four other manufacturers elected not to participate. The Sikorsky, as already recorded, was completed first and put into service in the Caribbean and as the Pacific survey plane it would also, in July of 1937, make the initial transatlantic crossing.

Martin was no newcomer to overwater flying. In his early flying days as a barn-stormer when he was known as "The Flying Dude," and had formed his own company, he made a little history in May of 1912 by making a round-trip flight between Newport Beach, California and Catalina Island. His craft was a Martin-built plane with a large center float and one small one on each wingtip. A year later he was taking passengers up for thrill flights over Lake Michigan in another floatplane he called the *Great Lakes Tourer*. Then in the early twenties his MB-2 bombers (the tool of air strategist General William Mitchell) rang the death knell for the battleship over the waters of the Atlantic by sinking the "unsinkable" German battleship *Ostfriesland*.

The Navy, which had been defeated in this peacetime battle with Mitchell, showed no rancor toward Martin and began purchasing the Martin PM-1 in May of 1929, the first of a series of Martin flying boats used by the Navy—alternating with Martin's rivals, Sikorsky and Consolidated.

So, when the request for a bid came from Pan American for a large flying boat, there was no doubt in Martin's mind that the Martin Company was capable of producing it.

The Martin Company, which was in deep financial problems when the Trippe letter came, made its bid primarily because Glenn L. Martin himself wished to "build a large passenger-carrying flying boat even at the risk of every penny I have." This was done against the advice of business manager C. A. Van Dusen and chief engineer Lessiter Milburn. In studying Trippe's specifications Martin's more practical hands came to the conclusion (after working over no less than eight versions of the contract with Pan American) that, by cutting certain corners, three such large flying boats could be produced at a total of two million dollars. Trippe and his Hard Heads believed the figure should be closer to 1 million dollars

or less. Martin, still heedless of the advice of Van Dusen, agreed.

"You'll bankrupt the company," Van Dusen snapped at him. "We'll lose seven hundred thousand to nine hundred thousand dollars on this job!" Trippe was still not giving anybody any change, and would pay no more than $417,201 for each plane. Like Sikorsky, Martin was one of the oldtime airman, an ex-barnstormer and a visionary rather than a businessman. A humorless, pursed-mouthed bachelor (and dominated by a strong-willed mother), Martin could be as stubborn as a child. When he decided that the Martin Company would produce a large ocean-going flying boat for Trippe, even at a loss (". . . I'll be happy if Pan American will absorb three-quarters of the risk"), then the Martin Company would build a flying boat. It was, of course, this same kind of determination (part dream and partly motivated by a wish to make history) that had built the Glenn L. Martin Company. But that had been in a more romantic, more economically settled, time.

Martin money had been drained off on the development of a new bomber which, initially, had been rejected by the Army

The Martin PM-1 the first Martin flying boat ordered by the U. S. Navy in 1929 and delivered in June 1930. Span was seventy-two feet, ten inches and length, forty-nine feet. Engines were Wright Cyclones. (Martin Company)

Another view of the PM-1. A total of thirty of these boats was used by the Navy during the early thirties. (Martin Company)

Air Force. Luckily for Martin, man and company, Van Dusen and Milburn worked it over and submitted it again. It was accepted and became the B-10, an Air Force staple in the years prior to the Second World War. It was for this outstanding design that Martin was awarded the Collier Trophy in 1933.

The irony was, however, that despite the high recognition and the orders coming in, and the work progressing on the flying boat, employees of the company were having trouble cashing their payroll checks. Somehow, by scraping and making phone calls to banks, the company continued to function.

Meanwhile the flying boats had begun taking shape in the plant at Middle River (near Baltimore), Maryland. Martin appeared to forget his immediate problems by observing the progress on the Pan American order. He told his friend and one-time employee, James "Dutch" Kindleberger

(later of North American Aviation) that he believed that the future of aviation lay in the flying boat. "Great new markets will open up all over the world," he insisted, "Especially in the Orient."

The company designation was Model 130; the first was assigned the company serial number 556 (this would become the *Hawaii Clipper*); the *Philippine Clipper* (557) followed; then came number 558, the first to be delivered to Pan American, the most celebrated of the three, the *China Clipper*. In the company's books these were known as Martin Ocean Transports.

This is how the plane was described in contemporary company literature:

The MARTIN OCEAN TRANSPORT is an all-metal flying boat of 130 ft. span, powered by four Pratt & Whitney R-1830 geared, aircooled radial engines. This flying boat has luxurious accommodations for forty-six passengers [actual capacity was thirty-two] as a day transport, and is convertible into an eighteen-passenger night transport with large, comfortable berths. As a passenger plane, the transport carries a crew of five [eventually eight] consisting of pilot, co-pilot, radio operator, flight engineer, and steward. This transport is also convertible into a mail plane, upon removal of the passenger equipment, having a range of four thousand miles. The hull is subdivided into the following compartments:

a—A forward anchor compartment.

b—A control room for the pilots, including the radio operator's station, with a mail and cargo compartment beneath the flooring on the starboard side.

c—A baggage compartment on the starboard side, with an entrance hatch and galley on the port side.

d—A forward passenger compartment accommodating ten passengers.

e—A flight mechanic's station located immediately forward of the leading edge of the wing above the forward passenger compartment.

f—A lounge compartment accommodating sixteen passengers.

g—Two rear compartments accommodating ten passengers each.

h—A toilet room located on the starboard side, and a steward's office on the port side.

i—A rear entrance hatch in the deck, leading into a compartment suitable for the stowage of baggage.

The anchor compartment is equipped with a winch, operative by one man, for raising and lowering the anchor. When not in use, the anchor fits flush with the hull bottom in a compartment. A removable hatch is provided in the bow to facilitate mooring operations. Two bunks for the crew are also installed in this compartment.

The control bridge is equipped with dual flight controls and instruments. A Sperry Automatic pilot is installed in this compartment. The radio operator's station is immediately behind the pilot on the starboard side, within easy speaking distance of either pilot. A hatch is installed in the deck of the pilothouse for emergency exit and to direct mooring operations. A compartment for the stowage of mail and cargo is provided beneath the pilothouse floor.

An entrance hatch equipped with hinged doors is provided on the port side immediately aft of the pilothouse. A completely equipped galley is located adjacent to the entrance hatch on the port side.

The flight mechanic's station is located above the forward passenger compartment, in the cabane, and windows are installed to give clear vision of all engine nacelles. A complete set of power plant instruments for each of the four engines is installed at this station [which was called by engineers "the throne room of the god of gadgets"].

The passenger compartments are luxuriously furnished with large, comfortable seats, convertible into berths, and equipment such as magazine racks, tables, ashtrays, etc., are included in the passenger accommodations. Curtains for the night sleeping arrangement are installed in each compartment. The lounge is equipped with several individual chairs, in addition to the fixed seats, and is large and roomy. Emergency exists for the passenger compartments are provided by the two rear windows, one on each side, in the lounge compartment.

The passenger cabins are comfortably heated and ventilated under all conditions of flight, and are soundproofed, eliminating fatigue of passengers on long-range flights. Suitable lighting fixtures are installed to give adequate light in all passenger compartments.

A noteworthy feature of this transport is the hull and seawing combination [the term was eventually dropped in favor of the more prosaic "sponsons"]. The seawings are primarily intended to produce lateral stability on the water, which purpose they accomplish better than outboard floats. In addition to their primary function of providing lateral stability, the seawings also carry 950 gallons of fuel each, in tanks built integral with their structure. The seawings hold down the spray and water usually thrown up into the tail surfaces, and derive useful lift from the bow wave. The top surfaces and tips of the seawings are of an airfoil shape, producing an appreciable additional aerodynamic lifting area. The hull is of the two-step, deep "V" type, with a pronounced reverse curvature forward of the main step, producing high water reactions at the beginning of the takeoff run causing the boat to rise to the main step quickly.

Evolution: The Martin PM-2 of 1931; major difference between this plane and the PM-1, besides more powerful engines, was the addition of twin rudders. This design hardly intimates the innovations that would appear in the Martin 130s. (Navy Department, National Archives)

Several additional paragraphs describe the hull structure ("riveted 24ST aluminum alloy"), the wing ("braced center section and two cantilever outer panels . . . of the box girder type" of construction). The wing too was aluminum-covered, "the bottom covering is smooth stressed skin and the top covering is corrugated sheet, with corrugations parallel to the span and covered with thin smooth sheet." However, fabric covering was used on the wing from the rear beam aft; ailerons were also fabric-covered. The tail surfaces were "of the monoplane type, with single fin and rudder." Tabs were attached to rudder, elevator, and ailerons for trimming the craft while in flight.

"Particular attention has been paid to the incorporation of superior maintenance features throughout this transport," the paper concludes, noting also the structure has been carefully finished with protective coatings against corrosion. All aluminum alloy parts have been anodized and painted prior to final assembly, and steel parts have been cadmium-plated. Particular care has been taken regarding the assembly of dissimilar metals by incorporating impregnated fabric between these parts." This eliminated one of the problems encountered in the early Sikorsky S-38s: electrolysis. Where brass nuts had been used to fasten aluminum, corrosion set in almost immediately, particularly after the plane had operated from salt water.

Although Martin had notified Pan American in mid-August 1931 of his intention of tackling the problem of designing and building his giant "ocean transport," the contract was not drawn up until December of 1932.

The keel of the first boat, Number 556 (license number NC 14714), was laid in May 1933—the work being done under the direction of Lassitur Milburn, assisted by W. K. "Ken" Ebel (who was also to serve as test pilot) and Project Engineer L. D. McCarthy. In the following year a definite order was placed by Pan American for three of the ocean transports—which, of course, were already under construction.

The completed aircraft were among the most celebrated of the era and immediately captured the imagination of every air-minded boy and the layman as well. Not only was the clipper an impressive aircraft to look upon—with its 130-foot wing and ninety-foot length—it was also so gracefully beautiful that it was an aesthetic treat. And, in the deeps of the Depression, it represented the spell of distant and exotic lands. This was the time when armchair travelers delighted to the adventures of a young Richard Halliburton, or sat in movie theaters and watched such travel films as *Africa Speaks,* Frank Buck's *Bring 'Em Back Alive,* and the films of the Martin Johnsons. The Martin Clipper conjured up the mystery of the East and the gateway to adventure in jungled countrysides.

The Martin Clipper immediately became one of the classic aircraft of the time, joining such memorable planes as the Boeing F4B-4, the Lockheed *Vega,* the Douglas DC-3, the Stinson *Reliant,* and the Sikorskys, among others.

Late in the summer of 1935 the first of the flying boats was rolled out of the plant at Middle River and eased gently (all twenty-six tons) into the water for testing. This was done under Ken Ebel's direction in the unique dual role of engineer and test pilot. Many who saw the aircraft in the water were certain it was simply too big to fly; it was, in fact, the second-largest flying boat in existence (the first being the German Dornier-X, with its span of 142 feet; the Do-X, however, could hardly be called a *flying* boat). The long series of tests soon proved the Martin boat to be a step forward in the design, surpassing the Sikorsky S-42 in terms of speed (150 mph over 140 cruising), payload, and range (Martin: thirty-two hundred miles; Sikorsky: twenty-four hundred miles).

The first clipper delivered was the NC-14716—"Sweet 16"—actually the third of the group, and was christened *China Clipper.* The date was October 9, 1935, when Lassiter Milburn, acting for Martin, turned the plane over to Juan Trippe, who, in his

A Martin Ocean Transport (in this case the Hawaii Clipper) *emerges from the Martin factory to begin testing. (Martin Company)*

Martin Ocean Transport on ramp leading to the water. (Martin Company)

turn, placed it in the capable hands of Captain Edwin Musick, who had completed his first round of Pacific survey flights in the S-42. He and his crew would be responsible for delivering the *China Clipper* to Pan American's California base at Alameda in time for its scheduled first flight in late November.

Engineering Officer Victor Wright recalled that uneventful flight. "We'd picked up this first clipper at the Baltimore factory and flew her down to Miami, where we made a number of flights so that we could get acquainted with the airplane." One impression that always remained was that of size —the *China Clipper* appeared to be so huge, even after the S-42.

While in Miami two National Broadcasting Company men, William Burke Miller and Harold See, came aboard to keep the world in touch with the clipper in its flight to Alameda. After the get-acquainted period in Miami, Wright along with the rest of the crew, and the two radio newsman climbed aboard for a long hop. "Then we ferried her out to San Francisco by flying across the Gulf of Mexico and the narrow part of Mexico at the Isthmus of Tehuantepec (as the clipper was a flying boat, we had to stay as close as we could to water), and then up through Acapulco and San Diego to San Francisco."

Final checkouts were made, along with blind flying tests, on November 21; the following day, officially declared to be "Pan American Airways Day" by California governor Frank L. Merriam, was to mark the inaugural flight of the *China Clipper*. It was a time of great excitement and tension. Japan, through diplomatic channels, made it known that it was not at all pleased by this step forward in aircraft design and what it meant to cross-ocean travel. Certain American aeronautical officials were not absolutely convinced that the new fifteen-hundred-mile radio direction finders, upon

The Martin Transport afloat: The next question—will it fly? (Martin Company)

Inspection by the boss: Glenn L. Martin disembarks through the hatch of his big flying boat after finding all well. There seems to be no logical explanation for his top-hatted and parasoled companions in the boat. (Martin Company)

which so much depended, were effective. One further touch marred the preparations: The Federal Bureau of Investigation had apprehended two Japanese attempting to tamper with Pan American's Alameda direction finder.

But such unpleasantness was set aside on Friday, November 22, 1935. A crowd estimated to have been around twenty-five thousand had gathered at Alameda to be on hand for the *China Clipper's* takeoff. Nosed up against a small speaker's platform, the great plane bobbed gently on the water. For this first flight it would not carry passengers, only mail and cargo; to accommodate this payload NBC men Miller and See were bounced as were two crewmen, Second Radio Officer T. R. Runnels and Second Junior Flight Officer Max Werber. Their weight was replaced by the 110,-000 pieces of mail (which totaled 1837 pounds). This was a bitter disappointment for the four men, for they were denied what might have been their rightful place in history. Parenthetically, it might be noted that this fact of historical significance was widely broadcast, for when the Oakland *Post-Enquirer* published that day it ran a double-column admonition: SAVE THIS

NEWSPAPER. IT RECORDS REALLY
IMPORTANT HISTORY MADE HERE
TODAY!

The event was thoroughly covered by
radio—a full hour in what was prime time
in the East, 5:45 to 6:45 P.M.; it began at
2:45 P.M. in California—and was flashed
practically around the world, from Europe
to Japan. Some of the exhilaration of the
moment is captured in the words spoken at
the ceremonies. The radio announcer was
the first to speak:

We are here on the shores of historic old
San Francisco Bay, on the marine ramp of
Pan American Airways' Pacific operating
base. Around us surges a great crowd of
interested, excited people, extending as far
back over the airport as the eye can reach.
Above their heads, in the bright sunshine,
wave four flags: the territorial flag of Hawaii,
the red-and-blue banner of the newly inaugurated Commonwealth of the Philippines, the
flag of the Postmaster General of the United
States, and the Stars and Stripes.

Here on the platform are distinguished national figures who are to participate in today's ceremonies. Across the Bay one hundred thousand people are watching and lis-
tening on the shores near the Golden Gate. A
thousand miles away in Hawaii are other
thousands. Eight thousand miles across an
ocean, halfway around the world, are still
other thousands. On the five continents of
the globe are millions who by the magic
of radio are about to witness with us one
of the most dramatic events in the history
of our modern world.

In a few minutes, now, we will bring to
you the sailing of the first *China Clipper*
in eighty years, from this grand old Bay
from which the original clipper ships set
sail across the perilous Pacific. Incredibly
we realize that, since time began, this vast
Pacific Ocean at our feet stood as an un-
conquerable barrier between the East and
the West. Now at long last, this barrier is
to be no more.

And it is America, whose dynamic energy
and courage to pioneer, whose aeronautical
genius, whose far-sighted government, has
alone of all nations on the face of the earth,
made this tremendous achievement possible.

What will be called the Hawaii Clipper *during
a water test, taking off and in flight. (Martin
Company)*

The China Clipper *docked in Alameda, California, before the inaugural flight, November 1935. (Smithsonian Institution, National Air and Space Museum)*

Within a few feet of our platform the *China Clipper,* studded with powerful engines, her great glistening whalelike hull resting gently in the water, stands ready.

"What drama is packed into the hold of this tremendous airliner," he continued, waxing more dramatic as he was caught up in the sound of his own enthusiasms, ". . . this tremendous airliner, the largest ever developed in America where the airplane was born, most outstanding aircraft ever developed in the world! What years of pioneering have proceeded her!" And so on until it was time for the distinguished guests to contribute their few thousand words. These included Frank L. Merriam, governor of California, Manuel L. Quezon, President of the Commonwealth of the Philippines, Joseph P. Poindexter, governor of the Territory of Hawaii—the latter two, "by the magic of radio," speaking from their respective capitals—assorted California, Post Office, and governmental officials and, of course, Juan Terry Trippe.

Postmaster General James A. Farley opened his talk with a message from President Roosevelt, who referred to himself as "an air-minded sailor," and presented the President's thoughts with remarkable brevity. "Even at this distance I thrill to the wonder of it all," he said in part. "They tell me that the inauguration of the trans-pacific sky mail also celebrates the one-hundredth anniversary of the first clipper ship in San Francisco. The years between the two events mark a century of progress that is without parallel, and it is our just pride that America and Americans have played no minor part in blazing of new trails. There can be no higher hope than that this heritage of courage, daring, initiative, and enterprise will be conserved and intensified." It was a message pertinent not

A fraction of the crowd and the speaker's platform, plus China Clipper, *Alameda, November 22, 1935. (Pan American)*

only to the "sailing" of the *China Clipper,* but also one of hope to a nation still in the depths of the Great Depression. The very fact that American industry could produce such a craft, that its men could take on such an enterprise and its airmen could dare to set off on such an unprecedented adventure was a reason for pride and hope.

The other speeches were in the same vein, though each with its own special touch—Quezon spoke of "the dawning of a new day in the history of their [the peoples of the East] relations with the Western world"; Poindexter of Hawaii saluted the entire enterprise, but also took the opportunity to put in a bid for Hawaiian statehood. Even the usually unwordy Trippe spoke at some length—his opening remarks being a pithy history of Pan American Airways.

The radio announcer returned from time to time to color up the proceedings whenever the semipolitical speeches palled. His introduction of the crew is worth repeating in full as it came over the airwaves:

All eyes now are on the *China Clipper,* riding at anchor just beyond our platform. What a thrilling sight she is! So confident, so sturdy. Her gleaming hull and wings glistening in the sunshine, her great engines ready to speed her on her way!

Along a catwalk, now, seven uniformed figures—in navy blue, with white-vizored caps —Pan American's colors—are moving along the narrow catwalk to the front hatch of the giant airliner. There is little excitement about them. They are the flight officers of the *China Clipper*—the winged pioneers about to set out on an ocean's conquest. I want to try, in a short minute here, to give you their names as they go aboard. In just a minute, now, the *China Clipper* will move to her mooring and await the order to cast off. Here they are:

The first to go aboard is R. O. D. Sullivan, who, as first officer, made the first flights to Hawaii and Midway Islands and, as captain of the *Pan American Clipper,* made the initial flights to Wake Island and Guam.

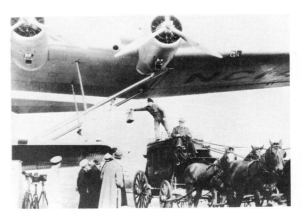

New and old: a symbolic delivery of a sack of mail by stagecoach to the China Clipper. *(Pan American)*

Captain Sullivan is first officer of the *China Clipper.*

Right behind him is another old-timer—a product of the old square-riggers and veteran of all Pan American's Pacific flights—Fred Noonan, navigation officer of the *China Clipper.*

Now George King, ocean pilot-in-training on his first actual Pacific crossing. He is second officer. Certainly the *China Clipper* can't go wrong on the engineering department. Both engineering officers, now going aboard, are Wright!: First Engineering Officer C. D. Wright and Second Engineering Officer Victor Wright. They are not brothers, by the way.

Right behind them goes William [actually Wilson] Jarboe, Jr., radio officer, another veteran of the Pacific survey flights.

The last to step aboard is Pan American's veteran, Edwin C. Musick, captain of the *China Clipper.*

On platform Captain Musick, with First Officer R. O. D. Sullivan below, awaits the loading of the transpacific mail. Postmaster General James Farley (facing camera, behind mail sacks) and Pan American's Juan Trippe (hatless, second from right) await the final word for loading. (Pan American)

Seven men in the crew. And what a crew! Five of those seven are transport pilots. Three of them are registered aeronautical engineers. Three of them are licensed radio officers. Two of them are master mariners, and two others have their navigator's papers. That will give you some idea of the preparation behind America's conquest of an ocean!

As the hour drew to a close it was, indeed, time for the *China Clipper* to set off on that ocean crossing. The exchange between the aircraft and Trippe was terse and businesslike.

Trippe: *China Clipper,* are you ready?
Musick: Pan American Airways' *China Clipper,* Captain Musick. Standing by for orders, sir.
Trippe: Stand by, Captain Musick, for station reports.

This was followed by a crackling as, one by one, the Pan American bases sprinkled across the Pacific reported in: KNBF (Honolulu), KNBH (Midway), KNBI (Wake), KNBG (Guam) and from Manila KZBQ: "Pan American Airways Transpacific Air Terminal, Manila, Commonwealth of the Philippines. Ready and standing by, sir."

Trippe: Stand by all stations. Postmaster General Farley, I have the honor to report, sir, that the transpacific airway is ready to inaugurate air mail service of the United States Post Office from the mainland across the Pacific to the Philippines, by way of Hawaii, Midway, Wake, and Guam Islands.
Farley: Mr. Trippe, it is an honor and a privilege for me, as postmaster general of the United States of America, to hereby order the inauguration of the first scheduled service on Foreign Air Mail Route No. 14 at 3:28 P.M., Pacific Standard Time, on this day which will forever mark a new chapter in the glorious history of our nation, a new era in world transportation, a new and binding bond that will link, for the first time in history, the peoples of the East and the West.

Trippe: Captain Musick, you have your sailing orders. Cast off and depart for Manila in accordance therewith.

The loudspeakers in millions of living rooms reverberated to the rumble of engines as Musick began moving the *China Clipper* carefully out into San Francisco Bay. A band burst into the strains of "The Star-Spangled Banner." The sounds of the music and the engines mixed in a thrilling concatenation. Aboard the aircraft the men went about business as usual, although, for some seconds, it might have proved the opposite.

"Our departure from Alameda was spectacular, though we didn't plan it that way," Victor Wright recalled some years later. "After leaving the waterfront ramp Captain Edwin C. Musick circled on the water a few times to warm up the engines and then headed up the bay toward the looping wires of the San Francisco-Oakland Bay Bridge, then being built. As we left the water a convoy of escorting planes closed in behind us.

"It had been our intention to fly over the bridge, but Musick quickly saw that with the engine cowl flaps open he wouldn't be

Clipper-eye view of the crowd gathered at Alameda to see the China Clipper *off to Manila. Outboard propeller is turning as the ship works it way out into the bay for takeoff. (Pan American)*

The China Clipper *on the step, an instant before lifting off the water, San Francisco Bay. (Pan American)*

The China Clipper, *with the Golden Gate under construction in the background, sets out on its inaugural flight across the Pacific. (Pan American)*

able to get up enough speed to clear the wires, so he nosed the Clipper down at the last moment and went under the bridge cables, threading his way through the construction wires. We all ducked and held our breaths until we were in the clear. I think the little planes must have been as surprised as we were, but they all followed us through." The implications of this incident are chilling, considering the international fanfare, the speeches, the massed crowds of witnesses, and the great expectancy connected with the takeoff of the *China Clipper.*

Official time of takeoff, San Francisco time, was 3:46 P.M. The entire crew cooperated on keeping a log of the historic flight, much of it written in a kind of poetry only airman are capable of, some of it in the matter-of-fact tone of the trained technician, all of it temptingly (at this late date) quotable; the first entry is marked, Friday, November 22:

"Before we were beyond sight of San Francisco Bay's holiday dress in honor of our departure, a great mass of clouds, the close companions of our now veteran Pacific airmen, covered the entire horizon. The constantly arriving weather reports from our ocean stations turned us southward, close to the rim of the most southerly surveyed course.

"The Pacific welcomed the first modern Clipper bound for the Orient with a blazing sunset. Day passes into night with unmatched swiftness over the ocean, and before a final flying check was made by all officers we were swallowed by darkness. No stars were visible through the ceiling of clouds above. A solid floor of clouds two thousand feet below closed out the sea."

Experiencing this for the first time, Second Officer George King could not help himself and shamelessly radioed, "As the sun goes down, casting a flaming mantle over clouds beneath, scattered strips of cumulus high above the circular world sink into impenetrable blackness. . . . The radium-painted dials on the 197 flight and engine instruments glow eerily. . . . Through the portholes the blue flames off the outboard engine's exhaust flash out into pitch blackness."

Looking back retrospectively, Victor Wright viewed the event with some detachment: "With no passengers aboard, we could dress for comfort on the flight to Hawaii. As soon as we'd cleared the coast we got out of the uniforms we'd worn for the departure ceremonies and put on something comfortable, as they say, for the twenty-one-hour flight that lay ahead. I wore a pair of red pajamas and bedroom slippers, I remember, and the rest of the crew were just about as informal. We were a strange-looking bunch of trail-blazers.

"In those days," Wright continued, "we didn't have all the instruments and the cockpit indicators they now use, and the engineer had to roam around the clipper, spot-checking the various control systems. And whenever the navigator needed a hand, one of us would have to go back to the after-end of the cabin and check on our drift by sighting on the flares he had released. Then there were frequent fuel checks and conferences with the plane commander, as we were always trying to get as many miles as possible out of the engines for the fuel we used.

"All this kept me moving around from one end of the clipper to the other during that long night flight to Honolulu. I walked through the dawn, which caught us by the tail, and had breakfast from the sandwiches I carried in a paper bag. And I was still walking when the peaks of Hawaii rose out of a cloud bank in the west. And I was walking when we raised the Philippines. I often claim I'm the only man who ever walked across the Pacific."

The log takes up the story of the *China Clipper:* "In eight hours we are twelve hundred miles out over the Pacific and drilling through the black void of the night; we are in close contact with all points of the compass after eight hours of steady flying through layers of clouds above and below.

"We have been closely watched over by Pan American Airways ground stations at San Francisco and Los Angeles behind us and by the Honolulu and Midway stations ahead. Out of the limitless blackness ahead came the voice of the United States Coast Guard cutter *Itasca,* two hundred miles northeast. Immediately thereafter we spoke to the Norwegian motorship, *Roseville,* three hundred miles due north, and then to the U.S.S. *Wright,* nine hundred miles west."

At midnight (November 23): "We have just changed our fourth watch. Captain Sullivan, Engineering Officer Victor Wright, and Second Officer King are having dinner and then a forty-five-minute nap in the berths aft. Below, the radium-tipped dials glow dully. Behind the pilot on watch Radio Officer Jarboe is just acknowledging receipt by the U.S.S. *Wright* of our message of greeting. Navigation Officer Noonan is bent over the chart table like a form from another world. He is encased in a fur flying suit and leather helmet. He has just returned from the open aft hatch after taking a celestial sight through a vast hole in the cloud ceiling, affording the first view of the heavens in the last three hours.

"Across this section of the Pacific, even with head or cross winds, flying is remarkably smooth—a happy circumstance, since on this section of the twenty-four hundred miles the greatest amount of engineering is required, and regardless of the fact that the *China Clipper* is carrying a normal crew of seven—one extra engineering officer for actual training—every post requires relentless attention.

"Flight units of the size of the *China*

Clipper, twenty-five tons gross, function at the highest efficiency through the application of broad principles of marine operation routine. Throughout the night the navigation department has obtained seven celestial sights and received forty-one radio directive bearings.

"As night is thinning into the grayness of dawn all is quiet. Captain Sullivan is about to take over. From ten thousand feet above, the sea in the gray light is glassy, with long, unbroken swells. A flood of color suddenly spreads across that surface. Night has gone. Almost by the time you can raise your eyes from the sea below to the horizon behind, the sun is wholly in view.

"Navigation Officer Noonan makes a final check of our position. Before coming to his post the junior flight officer has nicely arranged our food, hot coffee and fruit, on the table in the lounge. For the first time on our many ocean flights all the officers off watch will sit down to breakfast together.

"Another watch change and the *China Clipper* is within three hundred miles of Honolulu. It is warmer now, and clouds are forming, so that the sea is again invisible. First Officer Sullivan has sighted a dark mass beyond the rim of the clouds. Mountains. Mount Molokai, our landfall, seen from an altitude of 10,300 feet, is still two hundred miles away. Many miles beyond we can see a great mantle of smoke, from the erupting crater."

"And then Captain Musick surprised us," Victor Wright remembered at this point in the flight. "We were told to shave (in cold water, at that) and get back into uniform. There was some grumbling, but we realized later that this was a master stroke. Getting cleaned up not only made us feel better—when the crew stepped off the Clipper all spic and span you'd have thought we'd just taken a swing around the harbor. It made the ocean crossing look routine."

After the change into the company uniform the log entry read: "In rapid succession then Hawaii's volcanic landmarks moved into range. Diamond Head loomed thirty miles ahead as all hands manned the posts while we slowly glided down from the heights to the patrolled channel on Pearl Harbor. Landing 10:19." This was in the morning of Saturday, November 23, 1935. The flight had taken twenty-one hours, four minutes.

"There was an official reception at Honolulu," Victor Wright remembers, "but it was small-scale. We'd been through Hawaii on four survey flights, and flying the Pacific was getting to be old hat to the people out there. But the welcoming committee and all our Navy friends seemed to be impressed with our carefully creased uniforms and our white caps and our bright and shining faces. There were some speeches and they handed out leis. All I wanted by that time was a place to sit down."

While the crew rested, Pan American ground (water?) crews removed the cargo for Honolulu (which included 46,561 letters) and serviced the ship for the next leg of the flight, to Midway.

The composite log takes up the tale again on Sunday, November 24: "Like a waterfront scene in the old days of sailing vessels when the clipper ships had to be loaded in a mad rush to sail with the tide, the marine runway of Pan American Airways Ocean Air Base No. 1, at Pearl Harbor, was a busy scene this morning. The *China Clipper* was being loaded to enable us to depart with the daylight on the next step of our eight-thousand-mile race with the sun across the Pacific with the first American air mail for the Philippines and the Orient.

"The early hour did not discourage pleasure craft carrying several hundred visitors, from assembling about the base to cheer our departure. They saw an interesting scene—lights bobbing on swells in the harbor, signal

First lap of its transpacific flight completed, the China Clipper *rests in the lagoon at Pearl Harbor, near Honolulu. (Smithsonian Institution, National Air and Space Museum)*

lights blinking from distant naval vessels, the lights aboard our airliner shining brilliantly. Dark forms of orderlies, rapidly wheeling a fleet of hand trucks carrying hundred-pound loads of our two-ton cargo for the big holds of the *China Clipper.*

"Following in rapid order, the trucks carried into the holds twenty-one crates of fresh vegetables of all descriptions for our island air bases to the west; nine crates of oranges and lemons; twelve crates of turkeys for the first Thanksgiving dinners in the history of those colonies on Midway and Wake; and cartons of cranberries, sweet potatoes, and mincemeat. Other crates, containing every conceivable item—paint brushes, typewriter ribbons, oil lamp wicks, among the eight hundred pounds of cargo labeled 'Guam.' Spare sewing machine needles, paper plates, napkins, baseballs, and tennis racquets among Wake's two thousand pounds. Lantern bulbs, refrigeration machinery parts, a complete barber's outfit, and nine hundred pounds more for Midway. All the results of accumulated radio requests for the past two months from those islands to Pan American's main base at Alameda, beginning 'On next Clipper send' —and then listing an incredible list of replacement articles and additional items they

believe they needed to add to the comfort of home on those tiny islands thousands of miles from each other and from civilization.

"After the mail was aboard, the fourteen passengers followed—two complete air base staffs replacing pioneers on Midway and Wake—and four Chinese cooks and a waiter for Wake Island. This was a great day for these Orientals, having the honor of being aboard on the first Pacific flight of the *China Clipper,* but they were to get off at Wake Island, still four thousand miles from China.

"The last cargo hatch was closed. Acting Airport Manager Parker Van Zandt reported all the cargo aboard and Second Officer George King reported the *China Clipper* ready, engines warmed, and all weather reports in and checked. The crew went aboard as daylight, held behind Pali and other great peaks, finally spilled over the green mountainsides. At 16:50 [Greenwich Mean Time; 6:20 A.M. Honolulu time] we cast off from the float.

"In the channel a breeze of only four knots ruffled the water, as daylight spread over the still-sleeping city. Captain Sullivan pointed the *China Clipper*'s nose into the north wind. The roaring of the engines

Servicing and loading the China Clipper *at Pan American Airways Base No. 1, Hawaii, in preparation for takeoff early in the morning for Midway, 1380 miles distant. (Smithsonian Institution, National Air and Space Museum)*

drowned the cheers of the crowd ashore, and at 17:05 [6:35 A.M.] we were off for Midway Island, thirteen hundred and eighty miles northwest.

"The first hour after the takeoff is always the busiest. During this period all officers stand watch. The mechanical details of the clipper are thoroughly checked, cargo finally adjusted for proper balance, and routine is set for the complete flight. . . . Ahead of us lay clear weather for seven hundred miles. At that point we would enter the cold front, which produces clouds and line squalls, but Midway Islands would be clear, beyond. . . .

"This stretch of twelve hundred miles [from Niihau Island, westernmost of the Hawaiian chain] to Midway, which presents few serious navigation problems, since we follow a long chain of islands and reefs, is like a great classroom to us. Navigation Officer Noonan conducted classes in celestial navigation problems among the flight officers on board.

"This was Sunday aboard the *China Clipper* as well as ashore. Some of our passengers were reading the Sunday Honolulu papers and others were playing bridge. Our four Chinese passengers seemed dazed, but made no comment."

The entire flight, which consumed 8½ hours of flying time, was uneventful. The cold front presented no problem except to reduce what had been nearly unlimited visibility to five miles. When the aircraft was still about fifty minutes away from Midway "the weather cleared suddenly and a cloudless sky appeared ahead. Despite the clear visibility, we were almost in Midway before we sighted the two islands breaking sharply above the sea."

The *China Clipper* settled down gently into the lagoon, after circling at five hundred feet in salute to the island personnel, one minute late: 2:01 P.M., Midway time. Even as the crew made for shore, ground crews were at work unloading, refueling,

The landing pier at Midway and two generally unsung heroes of the transpacific airline operation: members of the ground crew who remained in desolated spots to service the flying clippers. The men were rotated every six months. (Pan American)

and in general preparing the plane for an early morning takeoff.

This occurred at 6:12 A.M. (local time) on Monday, November 25: "Today's twelve-hundred-mile jump is the shortest but most difficult span in the entire aerial bridge and calls for one of the most exacting feats of navigation on record—striking 'on the nose' a tiny point smaller than a pinhead on the vast map of the Pacific Ocean.

"It is one thing to navigate a surface vessel, moving a mile every two minutes with a wealth of navigational aids at the command of the mariner. It is quite another to guide an airliner racing a mile every twenty-four seconds, enshrouded by clouds or above them, with endless horizons of open sea below, with the goal even from high altitude visible under best conditions scarcely twenty miles. . . .

"One of our only two checkmarks—the International Date Line—we crossed 203 miles out at 02:35 G.M.T., and the *China Clipper* flew into tomorrow from today.

"The only other check was a Matson liner charted on our map another 150 miles ahead. We mutually congratulated ourselves when First Officer Sullivan called out 'steamer ahoy' and all pressed against the portholes to peer thirty miles dead ahead. It took us only fourteen minutes to overhaul the S.S. *President Lincoln,* Captain Hansen, eleven days out of San Francisco and bound for Yokohama. We passed at 08:50 G.M.T. in Lat. 25:25 N., Long. E. 177.31. We exchanged radio greetings and dipped our wings in salute, getting an acknowledgment of three scarfs of white steam, although we did not hear the whistles.

"When we passed the halfway mark 621 miles out at 02:23 G.M.T. today, Second Officer King broke out the Chinese mess attendants aboard and had them serve us sumptuous lunch in grand style in the lounge room. It was mealtime for all aboard, including twenty-five canaries, each complete with a pound of birdseed. They are forcibly migrating to enliven the deadly silence of isolated Wake Island. . . .

"We covered the final four hundred miles in two hours and twenty minutes. Then Wake Island flashed by radio that we had been sighted fully two minutes before we aboard could distinguish the small dark spot, which is Pan American Airways midocean air base No. 3 on this skyway to the Orient. We covered the 1252 miles at an average speed of 148.7 miles per hour, landing five minutes ahead of schedule, at 02:40 G.M.T. [1:38 P.M. Tuesday local time], with 5242 miles of Pacific behind us and only two more legs remaining of this astounding eight-thousand-mile ocean airway."

The sight of Wake Island inspired this description in the log: "Five thousand miles from the mainland of America and a thousand miles from the nearest neighbors, the United States has a flourishing city, seen by fewer than a score of people. This unique way-station on the transpacific aerial trade route to the Orient is invisible until nearly atop the islet, then suddenly bristles a forest of orange-and-black radio masts, red roofs, white walls of a dozen buildings, walkways, gardens, windmills, a watchtower, and the Stars and Stripes floating atop a tall mast—a thrilling sight."

After greetings by Wake's manager, George Bicknell, a tour of the base, and a long-planned-for dinner, the crew retired for a night's sleep before the early morning departure at dawn, Wednesday, November 27:

"Although we were not awakened until five o'clock, the entire base staff was up and about at three, and in an hour had breakfasted, placed all cargo aboard the *China Clipper,* verified ship inspection, and had the engines warmed alongside the float, ready for departure.

"All night weather watches completed the final details on our flying map before six, and we boarded the clipper jumping the sun's appearance above the horizon by sixty seconds, our keel breaking the water of the

The dining room at Wake, after passenger service was established following the trail-blazing flight of the China Clipper. *A portion of the lounge may be seen through the double doors on the left. (Pan American)*

Wake lagoon at 19:04 G.M.T. [6:01 A.M.]. Like yesterday, dense clouds were pressing down to two thousand feet, putting the entire load of navigation on Officer Noonan's dead reckoning and those constantly alert radio compass stations fore and aft, which will not let us go a single minute.

"Below, a gray light skimmed across the glassy surface of a dead calm sea. Ahead on all sides was unbroken water. Aboard, the dull thunder of the engines beyond the cockpit. First Engineering Officer Chan Wright was behind his bulwark of instruments, levels, and buttons recording their errorless mechanical reports. . . . Radio Officer Jarboe recorded the arriving radio bearings that Officer Noonan was charting along our course, making a line like the markers on a highway, every twenty miles. . . .

"It was warm and pleasant twelve hundred feet above the calm sea, all windows wide open. The first three hours we made 470 miles, averaging 156 miles per hour on 60 percent of horsepower. . . . Climbing through a three-thousand-foot layer of clouds by instrument, we burst out on top in an empty world of dazzling sunshine, the cloud moisture on our wings flashing every color of the spectrum and the propellers describing great glistening arcs as we bore ahead in a world all to ourselves—except for nine radio stations [and] three radio compass stations, like the schoolteacher eyeing a suspicious pupil.

"We were in the realm of spanking trade-winds of the Eastern Hemisphere, which greatly varied our altitudes. We were flying a good course, but the altitude chart would resemble an erratic broker's graph, with a succession of peaks and valleys. The visibility was good below, the winds less."

Victor Wright revealed how they obtained additional radio bearings with the aid of the Japanese. "There was a Japanese radio station on Rota, an island about fifty miles north of Guam, and when we were about an hour out of Apra Harbor we'd send out a CQ or 'Do you hear me?' signal on the Japanese frequency. Then, while he was answering our call, we'd get a hearing on his station and combine that with a bearing from our station on Guam to get a good fix on our position. We couldn't use that one too often, though, because in 1935 the Japanese weren't interested in helping anyone establish an airline across the Pacific."

The last hour of the Guam leg was hurried along by an accommodating 30 mph tailwind, so that the China Clipper made 170 miles with engines reduced to one-half power. At 3:05 P.M. (Guam time) the big flying boat eased smoothly onto Apra Harbor.

"Everybody in Guam seemed to have turned out to give us a welcome," Victor Wright later recalled. "This was just as well, because after we'd landed we discovered that someone in Manila who had scheduled the arrival celebration had apparently been confused by the time changes caused by the International Date Line and had provided us with an extra day of flying time. This meant that if we continued our flight the next morning we would arrive in Manila a day before they were ready to greet us. So we laid over a day on Guam and tried to make ourselves as inconspicuous as possible. That wasn't too easy with people all around the world watching the news of the flight and wondering where you were. . . ."

On Friday (after the extra day of rest), November 29, "The China Clipper climbed quickly out of Apra Harbor at Guam today [at 6:12 A.M.] and raced westward across the Pacific toward the Philippines. Our goal, the end of eight thousand miles of ocean flying from San Francisco, was only 1608 miles away, closer now by 150 miles every hour.

"The roughest sea encountered on our

entire crossing was below us as we left Guam. We did not stay long at a low altitude to watch the whitecaps and the wind-tossed spray, but climbed quickly to six thousand feet, where a fifteen-mile east–northwest wind helped us along through a succession of clouds. Rising another thousand feet, we found a thirty-five-mile wind that enabled us to cover two hundred miles in an hour. . . .

"In 5½ hours, we had already passed the halfway mark.

"Then, reared sharply against the horizon from a distance of 150 miles, through the incredibly clear atmosphere from our altitude of eleven thousand feet, Mount Pandan and Catanduanes Island were sighted at 05:30 G.M.T.—a sight we had been looking forward to, unconsciously, for the past five days. Another sixty minutes would bring us in to Manila.

"As the rugged hills of the Philippines appeared on the port bow, the crew of the *China Clipper* came to a realization of the significance of this achievement in American aviation. Until then each officer had

Journey's end: The China Clipper *after landing at Manila Bay, Friday, November 29, 1935. Thousands of spectators line the shore to greet Captain Musick and his crew as small boats and large ships cluster near the plane. Overhead, a Navy reception flight passes over in salute. The* Clipper *has just flown the mail from San Francisco to Manila for the first time in history. (Pan American)*

been too occupied with the innumerable tasks at his exacting post to be concerned with more than a minute ahead. Those tasks were no lighter in the last hour, but the actual sight of the coastline, the hills, valleys, streams, and villages on the other side of the world we had left such a short time ago, forced a new conception on us. . . ." For so long preoccupied with the routine of flight, they had had little time to consider what it was they were accomplishing: They had crossed the Pacific by air.

There was little time for celebration aboard—Musick again ordered the men to clean up and to get into dress uniforms for the Manila reception. He then brought the *China Clipper* into Manila Harbor at 3:32 P.M., after eleven hours and thirty minutes of flying time. They had crossed from San Francisco to Manila, a total of 8210 miles, in fifty-nine hours, forty-eight minutes in the air.

The crew was welcomed ashore, and during the reception Captain Musick was forced up to the microphone. When asked of his impressions of the flight, he characteristically replied with two words, "Without incident."

Victor Wright, the flight engineer who had walked the Pacific, remembered that "They gave us a great reception at Manila. I particularly enjoyed the official banquet and the automobile tour around the city, because I could take them both sitting down. . . ."

The Pan American crew spent Saturday and Sunday relaxing, sight-seeing between messages of congratulation. Then in the early morning (2:35 A.M., Manila time) of Monday, December 2, 1935, all aboard the *China Clipper* once again, they lifted off the surface of Manila Harbor. A twenty-one-knot wind "beating steadily on our port bow" slowed them up, and for a long period the clipper remained at a minimal three hundred feet altitude. The glare of the sun so near the water was intense, and the wearing of dark glasses was a necessity.

"Flying eastward, the days are visibly shorter. We met dawn two hundred miles off the Philippines and, as we flew on, the sun moved entirely around us, coming in behind as though we had been suspended midway between the ceiling of clouds above and the sea beneath. Two hundred miles off Guam, the light began to fade."

Bucking the winds and racing with the sun, they arrived at Guam thirteen hours and fifty minutes after takeoff from Manila, landing after nightfall had already come (6:41 P.M., Guam time). "All landing instructions having been received aboard by radio, we followed them now as though on a chart. Ahead were six harbor lights outlining the channel. There were the white and green lights where the keel of the clipper was to strike the water, and there, a mile and a half farther, were the white and red lights where we would stop. Captain Sullivan, at the controls, nodded.

"Blinking our landing lights, we circled once to get the last-minute wind velocity and direction at the surface, picked up the signal of our standby launch in a parallel channel, and settled down. The clipper's keel struck the choppy water in a perfect line, our wake smothering the white and green lights. The white and red lights were nearly a mile distant when the *China Clipper* settled her nose into the bay, and we swung around to follow the launch to the flood-lighted float."

Guam was to be an overnight stop, with an early morning takeoff planned for the next day. While the plane rested in Apra Harbor, after having been serviced and refueled, a storm swept across Guam. A forty-mile-an-hour gale lashed against the bobbing *China Clipper,* as Musick and the rest of the crew kept a close eye on the developing weather map. This was no surprise, as Pan American weathermen had informed them that a typhoon was brewing in the vicinity and that its effect might

The China Clipper *docking at Manila; in the background: the Manila Hotel. (Pan American)*

The China Clipper *moored in Manila Bay after completing the San Francisco–Manila flight. First Officer Sullivan (left) and Captain Musick stand in hatches over cockpit. (Pan American)*

Gala reception at Manila. Musick and crew escorted by officials come ashore at Manila. (Pan American)

touch them along their Guam-to-Wake flight.

By morning, December 3, it was clear that the storm was moving northward rapidly and would not interfere with their course, except in the form of line squalls some two hundred miles out from Guam. In the protected harbor the *China Clipper* had ridden the storm safely, although, to be doubly certain, "mechanics swarmed over the airliner under brilliant floodlights augmented by hand flashlights, inspecting every rivet, strut, and every section of the great hull, wings, and engines."

In the dark of dawn they took off at 6:11 A.M., following in reverse the system of lights that had guided them into port the previous evening. Within minutes of takeoff the *China Clipper* had risen a thousand feet into the murky clouds, and Guam was instantly lost to sight. They flew into a headwind of thirty-five miles an hour, which made flying in the clouds bumpy. Bringing the plane down to six hundred feet helped to smooth out the path of the clipper. About two hundred miles out of Guam they began to encounter the line squalls (the center of the typhoon was then about 150 miles to the south of them).

"The wind shifted to north of east, directly over the bow. At our speed, rains lasted but a few minutes, creating a din on our metal hull and wings, pouring torrents down window portholes, while we flew by instruments. Then suddenly we came into clear weather again, and the entire plane became a mass of prismatic colors as sunlight struck the wet surfaces. Then back into the clouds we went again—a thousand feet above the surface—we were halfway between the clouds and the sea, with its crested whitecaps." Before they landed at Wake (at 8:57 P.M., local time) they would experience this intermittent pattern of squalls and clear weather eight times within an hour. Visibility during the rain was nil, and all flying was done by instru-

ments; their position was checked frequently by Noonan during this time—and watches were changed hourly, instead of the customary once every three hours. The fourteen hours it had taken them to get to Wake from Guam had been most strenuous.

Luckily, the following day, December 4, presented few flying-navigational problems. The clipper lifted off gracefully at 6:45 A.M. Wake time and flew into a "world . . . filled with brilliant sunshine, a smooth sea and only light clouds in the sky. Visibility was so unlimited we could peer across the entire sea." The one drawback was a steady twenty-five-mile-an-hour headwind, which cut down their speed to 110 miles an hour. On this leg of the flight also they recovered the day they had lost —November 25—when they had crossed the International Date Line. Although they had taken off that morning on Wednesday, December 4, they landed at Midway at 4:49 P.M. Tuesday, December 3.

It was thus possible (if only on paper) for the *China Clipper* to make a second early morning takeoff on Wednesday, the next morning, which it did at 6:11 A.M., Midway time. The flight was perfectly routine.

"Every thirty minutes the weather came aboard. Every sixty minutes the navigation officer on watch took sun sights, verifying our position computed by dead reckoning and by radio bearings. Every 120 minutes we dropped down near the surface to make a drift sight and compute the exact wind direction and intensity.

"Only when we were near the surface did we get any impression of speed. Then the heavy blue ocean slipped swiftly underneath. Today, this impression was heightened because we were passing islands and reefs, Hawaii's coral chain reaching forty miles beyond Midway.

"Three thousand feet above the clouds was unlimited visibility and dazzling sunshine. We were seemingly suspended motionless in the air. Occasionally, cumulus clouds piled up in fantastic forms above the general level, the only change visible."

In addition to the seven-man crew, the *China Clipper* by this time carried eighteen passengers, all Pan American employees returning to Honolulu after serving a stint of six months on Wake or Midway.

By noon they were nearly halfway to Honolulu. "We dropped down through the clouds again to show the passengers unique Perouse Pinnacle, the shape of a ship's sail, [which] rose abruptly out of a sea of white-tipped guano, then passed low over French Frigate Shoals, hemmed in by reefs over which foaming breakers formed lacy borders of lava shelves. Through the unusually clear atmosphere we sighted Necker Island, fifty-one miles off the port bow. . . ."

Nine hours and forty-five minutes after leaving Midway, the *China Clipper* settled with a flashing trail of foam into the waters of Pearl Harbor. It was five twenty-seven in the early evening in Honolulu.

Instead of taking off, as had been the practice, in the early morning of the next day, Thursday, December 5, the crew of the *China Clipper* waited until two minutes past three in the afternoon. For this last 2410-mile leg of the flight they timed the takeoff in order that they might arrive at their destination during daylight hours. Thanks to unexpected tailwinds the great flying boat arrived in California somewhat ahead of schedule, in seventeen hours, one minute of flying time (as compared to twenty-one hours, four minutes on the westbound flight), landing in San Francisco Bay at 10:36 A.M. It was the only port of the entire flight that happened to be clouded over on their approach, which was made by instrument.

When the *China Clipper* landed at Alameda it had officially come full circle;

it had flown into history, and what's more: back. "Even to us it seems incredible that we were across the entire Pacific and back again within two weeks of departure from this same port. The first air mail from the Philippines and Guam would be delivered in New York and Washington within a week of its departure from Manila. The Honolulu mail would reach its destination twenty-four hours after leaving the islands' post office. The cargo of flowers that we had brought was already en route east by air express, Railway Express Agency special, and would be in the East the next morning.

"The 108,000 letters that we had brought back were each a graphic testimonial of the new speed in transport communication over the old clipper ship routes across the Pacific, to speed American trade and commerce to the Orient."

The eastbound flight, against headwinds most of the time except for the welcome tailwind boost on the final leg home, consumed sixty-three hours, twenty-four minutes flying time from Manila to San Francisco (westbound had taken fifty-nine hours, forty-eight minutes). The total flight time for the entire trip of 16,420 miles was 123 hours, 12 minutes; the schedule had allowed for a total of 130 hours. In that brief moment in time, from Friday, November 22 through Friday, December 6, 1935, the world had shrunk a little, carried on the wide, graceful wings of the *China Clipper*.

Wide newspaper coverage placed the clipper in the celebrity class, and its photograph appeared from coast to coast and in the aviation magazines of the period. The *China Clipper* even appeared in a film that was named for it, the better portions being beautiful in-flight shots; the drama itself, starring Pat O'Brien and Humphrey Bogart, was not as memorable. The name, in fact, became generic and all three M-130s were called *China Clippers*.

Second Martin M-130 to go into transpacific service, the Philippine Clipper, *which set out for Manila three days after the* China Clipper *had completed its first roundtrip. Here the plane approaches the dock at Midway. (Pan American)*

The second to follow the *China Clipper* into service was the *Philippine Clipper*. On December 9, 1935, just three days after the return of the *China Clipper,* the *Philippine Clipper* (NC 14715) took off to traverse the same route, with Captain John H. Tilton in command and Captain Ralph H. Dahlstrom (who had delivered the plane from Baltimore) as first officer; first navigation officer was Judson Ingram. The first flight of the *Philippine Clipper* out to Manila was pretty much like that of the *China Clipper*—"without incident." On this flight, with a lighter mail load, three passengers were carried (all nonpaying)—Pan American's Louis Harmantas, a meteorologist destined for Manila, where he would establish weather bureaus, and the radio men from NBC, William Burke Miller and Harold See, who had been denied places on the *China Clipper*. They were the first non-Pan American employees to

make the transpacific flight. En route they broadcast from the clipper regularly, which contributed to the continuing excitement over the flying clippers.

The flight was pretty much routine, although to the laymen all sorts of routine operations were startling, such as coming upon Tilton and Dahlstrom in the cockpit. "Captain Ralph Dahlstrom, first officer, is flying the *Philippine Clipper* with his hands in his lap—and we are on a twenty-four-hundred-mile flight across water!" They were readily assured that with the Sperry automatic pilot operating all was well. They were impressed with the gooney birds on Midway and the surprisingly luxurious accommodations at the various way stations, in preparation for the day of the clipper's passenger flights. And there was the always puzzling problem with the International Date Line, especially if there was a broadcast schedule to maintain. "Imagine, for example, receiving a radiogram Friday morning telling us to originate a program for Thursday afternoon!"

It was on the return, eastbound, flight that certain incidents occurred. The original plan called for a two-day stay in Manila, which stretched to five because of a typhoon moving through their projected flight path, in the general vicinity of Guam. Their companion on the way out, Louis Harmantas, promptly grounded them (as meteorological officer in charge), which meant that the crew and their two passengers would not be home in time for Christmas, as they had hoped. To compensate for this a small three-foot Christmas tree was placed aboard the *Philippine Clipper,* along with wreaths, streamers, and holly.

The cautious Harmantas was good-naturedly nicknamed "Double Zero" (which was less than nothing) for having grounded them and thus spoiling Christmas. They were finally given the all-clear on December 23 and were ready for takeoff in the dark, at two-forty in the morning. While all precautions were taken to clear the area for takeoff, once on the step the clipper swerved to miss a sailboat that had supposedly moved out of the way, and then just as suddenly loomed up in the path of the plane. Then the engines were gunned again, and at two-forty-three the *Philippine Clipper* was off for Guam, Wake, and Honolulu. Tilton refused to push the ship, despite the not so very veiled hints that, with a little bit of luck, they might very well make it home in time for Christmas.

When they landed at Pearl Harbor, after celebrating Christmas Eve, the clipper nosed into the harbor with a large holly wreath hanging from the bowsprit.

Late in the afternoon, after a spell of poor weather in the morning of Christmas Day, the *Philippine Clipper* was again on its way. They were barely ten minutes out of Honolulu when it was noted that the No.

4 engine (right outboard) began missing fire. Tilton left the bridge "and for once —the only time in the entire trip—his smile and friendly expression were gone." Perhaps it meant nothing, but he was taking no chances. He ordered all of the fuel in the seawings ejected in preparation for a return to Pearl Harbor. For twenty minutes the clipper circled in view of Honolulu trailing a wide plume of vaporizing fuel— which led many to believe that the *Philippine Clipper* was afire.

After landing it was found that a blown spark plug had been the cause of the misfire; in forty-five minutes the plug was changed and the plane refueled. At dusk they were passing over Diamond Head, homeward bound again. Three hours later they were on the air, broadcasting personal greetings to family and friends and singing Christmas carols. After this touch of homesickness as many as could burrowed under the mail bags for warmth and went to sleep.

Miller was awakened when the "quiet purr of the motors was broken after 3:00 A.M. . . . by a blinding streak of sparks whisking past the windows on the left side. So close were they that the brilliance of the stars was dimmed. There was an unsteadiness in the clipper, and as we made

The Philippine Clipper *aloft, a good profile view of the Martin Ocean Transport—and a classic flight shot of the thirties. (Pan American)*

our way forward through the lounge, several ornaments on the tree crashed to the floor."

This time it was the No. 1 engine (left outboard). When power was cut, back-firing and sparking lessened. But the engine could not be cut, since No. 1 pumped fuel to the other engines. Once this was completed Tilton shut the engine down, the propeller stopped, and the flight proceeded more or less as planned. When the trouble had come they had been aloft for eleven hours out of Honolulu—1625 miles out, and 780 miles from San Francisco. There was nothing to do but to proceed for home on three engines. A forty-mile tailwind helped, and on December 26, 1935, the *Philippine Clipper*—not without incident—had completed its circuit of the San Francisco–Manila run.

The *Hawaii Clipper* (NC 14714) was the last of the Martins delivered to Pan American, arriving at Alameda on December 24, 1935. It went into service on May 2, 1936—arriving in Honolulu the following day, when it was christened. The *Hawaii Clipper* performed one of the most historic functions of the Martin flying boats—the inauguration of passenger service between California and the Philippines (one-way fare to Manila, by the way, was $799; round trip: $1438).

This flight began on October 21, 1936—just one day short of eleven months since the pioneer flight of the *China Clipper*—with a nearly even distribution between crew and passengers, of whom there were nine: Mrs. Clara Adams, Mrs. Zetta Averill, Colonel Charles Bartley, Alfred Bennett, R. F. Bradley, Wilbur May, Thomas Fortune Ryan III, and Mr. and Mrs. Cornelius V. Whitney (he was a member of Pan American's executive committee and board of directors). They were not lacking

The Hawaii Clipper, *third and last of the Martin flying boats to go into Pan American service. Passenger service to the Orient (Manila, at least) was inaugurated by the* Hawaii Clipper *in October 1936. Passengers in this photo are debarking at Honolulu during that flight. This aircraft was also the first of the Martin clippers to be lost during a flight, less than two years later. (Pan American)*

TABLE 12   U.S.A.-HAWAII-GUAM-PHILIPPINES

Daily	3:00	Lv. BOSTON, Mass., U.S.A. (AMA) ....E.S.T. Ar.	11:48	Daily
*	5:00	Lv. NEW YORK, N. Y., U.S.A. (UAL) .... Ar.	9:00	*
*	4:45	Lv. WASHING'N, D. C., U.S.A. (PAL) .... Ar.	10:45	*
*	9:30	Lv. CHICAGO, Ill., U.S.A. (UAL) ....C.S.T. Ar.	3:29	*
*	9:15	Ar. SAN FRANCISCO, U.S.A. (UAL) ...P.S.T. Lv.	1:15	*
Orient Express(z)		Pan American Airways Co. (PAAP)		Orient Express(z)
Wed.	3:00	Lv. SAN FRANCISCO (Alameda), U.S.A.P.S.T. Ar.	10:30	Sun.
Thur.	6:30	Lv. HONOLULU (Pearl Harbor), H.I...H.L.T. Lv.	12:00N	Mon.
Fri.	6:30	Lv. HONOLULU (Pearl Harbor), H.I...H.L.T. Ar.	5:30	Sun.
	3:00	Ar. MIDWAY ISLAND.................M.L.T.Lv.	6:00	
Sat.	6:00	Lv. MIDWAY ISLAND.................M.L.T.Ar.	5:00	Sat.
		(International Date Line)		
Sun.	3:00	Ar. WAKE ISLANDS.................165° Lv.	6:00	Sun.
Mon.	6:00	Lv. WAKE ISLANDS.....................Ar.	7:00	Sat.
	5:00	Ar. GUAM ISLAND.................150° Lv.	6:00	
Tue.	6:00	Lv. GUAM ISLAND.....................Ar.	8:30	Fri.
	5:00	Ar. MANILA (Cavite), P.I.........120° Lv.	4:00*	

*Departures from Manila subject to advancement to previous afternoon as occasion demands.
All times are approximate other than at San Francisco Westbound and at Honolulu Eastbound.

Light Face Type - A. M. — Bold Face - P. M.

U. S. Cy. PASSENGER TARIFF

Fares quoted below are One Way fares. Round Trip fares are twice one-way less 10%

TABLE 12	San Francisco Cal., U.S.A.	Honolulu H. I.	Midway Isl.	Wake Isls.	Guam Isl.	Manila P. I.
San Francisco, Cal., U.S.A.	....	$360	$445	$587	$704	$799
Honolulu, H. I.	$360	....	157	299	480	614
Midway Isl.	445	157	....	142	323	514
Wake Isls.	587	299	142	....	181	372
Guam Isl.	704	480	323	181	....	191
Manila, P. I.	799	614	514	372	191	....

TABLE 13   SERVICE IN CHINA

SHANGHAI—HANKOW—CHENGTU—KWEIYANG

Mon., Wed. Fri.	Tu., Thu. Sat., Sun.	China National Aviation Corp. (CNAC)	Mo., Wed. Fri., Sun.	Tues., Thur. Sat.
7:00 (t)	7:00 (t)	Lv. Shanghai.................Ar.	10:55 (t)	5:30 (t)
8:00	8:00	Ar. Nanking..................Lv.	9:40	4:15
8:20	8:20	Lv. Nanking..................Ar.	9:30	4:05
		Lv. Anking...................Ar.		
10:00	10:00	Lv. Kiukiang.................Ar.	8:00	2:35
10:55	10:55	Ar. Hankow..................Lv.	7:00	1:35
Tu., Thu. Sat., Sun.			Mo.,Wed. Fri., Sun.	
11:20	7:30(m)	Lv. Hankow..................Ar.	3:40 (m)	1:10
	9:10	Lv. Shasi...................Ar.	2:15	
12:35	10:10	Lv. Ichang..................Ar.	1:15	12:00
	12:30	Lv. Wanhsien................Lv.	10:55	
2:35	2:10	Ar. Chungking...............Lv.	9:00	9:55
	Daily(n)		Daily(n)	
3:00	2:30	Lv. Chungking...............Ar.	2:00	9:30
4:15	4:30	Ar. Chengtu.................Lv.	12:00	8:15
Tue., Sat. (n)				Tue., Sat.(n)
1:00	.....	Lv. Chungking...............Ar.	.....	5:00
2:45	.....	Ar. Kweiyang................Lv.	.....	3:15

SHANGHAI—HONGKONG—CANTON

Tue., Thu., Sat.	(s)	(CNAC)	(s)	Wed., Fri., Sun.
	6:30	Lv. Shanghai.................Ar.	3:45	
*	8:45	Lv. Wenchow.................Lv.	1:50	*
*	10:25	Lv. Foochow.................Lv.	12:10	*
*	11:55	Lv. Amoy....................Lv.	10:35	*
*	1:15	Lv. Swatow..................Lv.	9:20	*
*	2:45	Ar. Hongkong................Lv.	7:30	*
*	3:05	Lv. Hongkong................Ar.	7:10	*
*	3:45	Ar. Canton..................Lv.	6:30	*

SHANGHAI—PEIPING

Mo., Wed. Sat. (t)	(CNAC)	Mo., Wed. Sat. (t)
6:00	Lv. Shanghai.................Ar.	6:55
7:05	Ar. Nanking..................Lv.	5:40
7:20	Lv. Nanking..................Ar.	5:20
9:40	Ar. Tsingtao.................Lv.	2:35
Tue., Thur. Fri., Sun. (n)		Tue., Thur., Fri., Sun. (n)
6:30	Lv. Shanghai.................Ar.	2:45
9:30	Lv. Haichow.................Lv.	12:00
10:55	Ar. Tsingtao.................Lv.	10:25
11:05	Lv. Tsingtao................Ar.	2:25
2:05	Lv. Tientsin................Lv.	1:25
4:45	Ar. Peiping.................Lv.	12:45

Light Face Type - A. M. — Bold Face - P. M.

PASSENGER TARIFF IN U. S. CURRENCY
SHANGHAI—HANKOW—CHENGTU—KWEIYANG

	Shanghai	Nanking	Anking	K'kiang	Hankow	Shasi	Ichang	Whsien	Ch'king	Chengtu	Kweiyang
Shanghai	...	$14	$38	$54	$53	$90	$101	$150	$183	$216	$261
Nanking	$8	...	24	41	54	81	92	141	174	204	252
Anking	21	14	...	17	36	63	74	123	165	213	243
Kiukiang	30	23	9	...	20	47	57	107	149	197	227
Hankow	36	30	20	11	...	27	38	87	129	177	207
Shasi	51	45	35	26	15	...	14	65	108	156	186
Ichang	57	51	41	32	21	...	...	54	98	146	176
Wanhsien	84	78	68	59	48	36	30	...	47	95	125
Chungking	102	96	92	83	72	60	54	26	...	48	78
Chengtu	120	114	119	110	99	87	81	53	27	...	128
Kweiyang	147	141	137	128	117	105	99	71	45	72	...

SHANGHAI—PEIPING—HONGKONG—CANTON

	Shanghai	Nanking	Haichow	Tsingtao	Tientsin	Peiping			Shanghai	Wenchow	Foochow	Amoy	Swatow	Hongkong	Canton
Shanghai	...	$14	$29	$48	$72	$81		Shanghai	...	$35	$62	$81	$90	108	117
Nanking	$8	...	15	38	63	75		Wenchow	$20	...	30	54	69	95	102
Haichow	17	9	...	21	54	60		Foochow	35	17	...	24	42	72	81
Tsingtao	27	21	12	...	36	42		Amoy	45	30	14	...	18	48	59
Tientsin	39	36	30	21	...	14		Swatow	61	39	24	11	...	30	41
Peiping	45	42	33	24	9	...		Hongkong	60	53	41	27	17	...	14
								Canton	66	57	45	33	23	8	...

Light-face Type represents one-way fares. Heavy Type represents Round Trips. Round Trip Tickets Good for 30 Days.

Timetables and fare schedule of the clipper service between San Francisco and the Orient. (Pan American)

for attention nor accommodations across the Pacific, what with the clippers by then being comfortably fitted for as many as thirty-two passengers. The steward served well-cooked meals—a far cry from the apple and sandwich staple of the early days of commercial aviation. And the hotels at the island stopovers—Midway, Wake, and Guam—were a revelation of thirties' luxury.

When the *Hawaii Clipper* landed at Manila Harbor on October 27, 1936, another aviation milestone had been set. On November 2, 1936, the *Philippine Clipper* set down for the first time at Hong Kong, under command of Captain Tilton. The final leg of the Pacific track had been laid. However, the Martins would not regularly land in China; Captain Musick suggested that they should be retained on the San Francisco–Manila run; from Manila to Hong Kong it would be more economical—and a simpler maintenance problem—to use the Sikorsky S-42 as a shuttle between Manila and the Chinese mainland. This was, of course, the *Hong Kong Clipper*.

The Martin clippers logged thousands of hours in the air, and flights to and from the Orient by 1937 appeared to be a common occurrence. A year after passenger service had been inaugurated the clippers had flown 2,731,312 miles, carried 1986 passengers, and cargo amounting to 505,944 pounds.

But 1938 introduced a note of tragedy. Captain Musick's *Samoan Clipper* disappeared during a survey flight off Pago Pago. This accident, attributed to engine trouble, for a time discouraged Pan American's plans for the Honolulu to New Zealand air route. But the Martin clippers continued their regular runs to the Orient and back. Although they rendered excellent and efficient service, there were no others built —a fact that Martin found difficult to forgive, since he was stuck with the tools and jigs required for the M-130s. By this time

Life aboard a Martin clipper ca. 1935. The galley, with stewards preparing refreshments. (Pan American)

Dining aboard the Martin clipper, complete with linen tablecloth, silverware—and waiter. (Pan American)

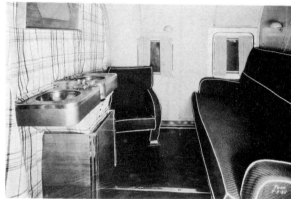

One of the private suites (of two) aboard the Martin M-130. (Pan American)

Double-decker berths of the Martin clipper. Night flights generally were made in the San Francisco–Honolulu leg; the flights were timed so that passengers could sleep at Midway, Wake, and Guam. (Pan American)

Decor of the Martin clippers was severely "moderne" in a characteristic thirties manner. This is a regular passenger compartment. In passageway behind are the curtains of berths. (Pan American)

Trippe had turned to another manufacturer he believed would build bigger and better clippers. For Martin, then, there had certainly been no profit in the giant flying clippers, beyond the gratification of knowing that his company had produced one of the most celebrated aircraft of its time.

The further misfortune was that none of the Martin clippers survived. The first to be lost had been the last to go into service. On July 28, 1938, the *Hawaii Clipper,* en route to Manila from Guam with six passengers and a crew of nine aboard, vanished without a word. The last position of the plane had been about three hundred miles from Manila; no word of any problems had come through—nor was any trace of the *Hawaii Clipper,* which had been under the command of Captain Leo Terletzky, ever found.

The remaining Martin boats continued in service until the coming of war in the Pacific. The *Philippine Clipper,* in fact, was attacked by Japanese aircraft in its dock at Wake Island on January 8, 1941. Although struck by several bullets, the clipper suffered no serious damage. After the bombing and strafing Japanese planes had left, Captain John R. Hamilton ordered engines started, loaded his crew plus all possible Pan American personnel aboard—a total of thirty-eight—and took off for Midway. On the way they passed over Japanese ships that had just shelled Midway, which was still burning when they landed in the dark. Quickly refueling, Hamilton got away also from Midway. However, landing at Pearl Harbor—nearly twenty-four hours after having left Wake Island—did not appear to have brought them to any sanctuary. Pearl Harbor was a burning shambles—and the realization came fully that the United States and Japan were at war.

The *China Clipper,* meanwhile, had missed the initial action because it was being serviced at San Francisco. Its shuttle, the S-42 *Hong Kong Clipper,* had not escaped the fate the Japanese had intended for the *Philippine Clipper;* it had been caught in the water at Manila when the Japanese struck and had been bombed into wreckage.

Early in 1942 both the Martin clippers were drafted into military service for use by the U. S. Navy. During the year both planes served as shuttles between San Francisco and Pearl Harbor (the *China Clipper* made no less than eighty-eight round trips that year).

The *Philippine Clipper* was making one of its routine flights from Pearl Harbor and on an approach to San Francisco in the early morning of January 21, 1943. The weather was not good, rainy with limited visibility. Besides the crew of nine, under Captain Robert M. Elzey, there were ten passengers aboard. Most of the latter was a high-priority group made up of Rear Admiral R. R. English, submarine commander in the Pacific, and his staff on the way to attend a high-level conference concerning submarine warfare matters. The tenth passenger was a fatally ill nurse, Edna Morrow, returning home.

Arriving almost four hours early in a pouring rain, the *Philippine Clipper* went into a holding pattern to wait out the storm and for better visibility. If there were no improvement, it was still possible to head south for San Diego—there was enough fuel. But also because of this extra fuel margin, Elzey could wait out the weather and still land at San Francisco as planned. The clipper berth was now situated at Treasure Island, rather than Alameda. The station tracked the clipper and kept Elzey informed of the changing weather situation.

For some reason, however, the plane was not holding over the Pacific, as Elzey believed. Instead, in the driving storm, he had drifted inland and was flying over land, in the vicinity of Ukiah, California. There being no satisfactory official explanation for this error, nor why it was not noted at Treasure Island, only speculation can account for what happened next. The guess, however, makes sense. Since it was common practice with the clippers when weathered-in while at sea to drop down for a look around at near water level to get bearings, it is very likely this is what Elzey did. Only he was not twenty-five miles off the coast, as he believed, but inland just west of Ukiah's hilly area. For just one moment Mrs. Charles Wallach, who had stepped out of their farmhouse when she heard the roar of aircraft engines, saw a large plane pass over headed north. A few minutes later the *Philippine Clipper* rammed into a hill and all but disintegrated in a roaring flame. All nineteen aboard the plane died.

Mrs. Wallach, although she did not know the plane had crashed, was worried about its altitude over so rough an area. When she attempted to phone, she found the storm had washed out the service. She even wrote a letter to the local district attorney, but to no avail. Meanwhile, for several days search planes were dispatched fruitlessly. No one could believe Mrs. Wallach, because it seemed incredible that the clipper could have been so far off course. Finally, after more than a week, it was decided that it was worth a look, and ten days after the crash a low-flying search plane spotted the wreckage five miles north of the Wallach ranch.

A great military cordon was drawn around the area, there being dark hints of sabotage, considering the presence of Admiral English and his staff aboard. This was buttressed when a search in the wreckage failed to turn up the admiral's briefcase, known to contain important military papers pertinent to the meeting he was to have attended (it was later found by a boy near the wreck some days after it had been decided the crash had not been attributable to enemy action but to a complex of human errors; the armed guard was relieved, and

souvenir hunters swarmed in to pick over the bones of the *Philippine Clipper*).

That left only the *China Clipper* still flying; by October of 1943 it was returned to Pan American by the Navy—the newer wartime aircraft, it was felt, could do the job more efficiently, for they had become faster and capable of carrying larger loads.

Berthed at Miami the *China Clipper,* with war paint removed, was again flying passengers and mail. Most of the long-distance military transport flying had been turned over to the larger Boeing flying boats or to such more powerful landplanes as the Douglas DC-4, the C-54 in military designation, as well as the Lockheed C-69 (Constellation).

The *China Clipper* plied aerial waters of the Caribbean and the South Atlantic to Léopoldville in the Belgian Congo, Africa (now Kinshasa, Republic of the Congo). This city had become an important air terminal in what was called the "Congo Route" during the perilous months in 1942 when the Japanese seemed invincible in the Far East and the Germans threatened North Africa. The Congo Route was established to assure an airway into the Middle East—and from there to the Pacific. This route took on less military significance when the Axis were crushed in North Africa. However, Léopoldville was still used by the Naval Air Transport Service, though not extensively, during the final months of the war.

On January 8, 1945, after having flown some three million miles in a decade, the *China Clipper* had set out from Miami on a flight, via South America, to Léopoldville. Captain Cyril Gayette was in command, and as the plane came in for a landing at Port of Spain, Trinidad, First Officer Leonard Cramer was at the controls. It was after nine in the evening and dark as the big plane began settling down on the water. Captain Cramer had had very little experience with landing on the water at night, and he prob-

Salvaging the China Clipper, *Port of Spain, Trinidad. (Pan American)*

ably was not able to discern between the darkness of the night and the blackness of the water.

This misjudgment caused him to fly the *China Clipper* directly into thirty feet of water. Hitting the surface at high speed the great plane broke up into several pieces and, although it did not burn, the fuel tanks ruptured, covering the water with a deadly scum. Those who did not die in the crash itself, died later of having swallowed ·the fuel as they attempted to get away from the crash. Of the thirty people aboard the *China Clipper,* twenty-three died (nine crewmen, of twelve; and fourteen passengers of eighteen). The impact had ripped away a portion of the hull, and the plane sank almost immediately. At first it was believed that the clipper had struck some object floating in the bay, but the investigation that followed found no such "unidentified object."

One of the three survivors in the crew, Flight Engineer J. W. Morse, was seated near a window observing the landing and noted the wingtip landing light "clearly illuminated the surface of the water, which was rippled." Morse, obviously, had no problem in making out the water's surface from where he sat; what Cramer saw will never be known, fcr he died in the crash.

Thus, tragically, did the saga of the Martin clippers come to an end. Although they had contributed immeasurably to the making of aviation less mysterious to the average man, the destruction of each of these beautiful aircraft contains in it a gnawing little seed of mystery.

* * *

This enigmatic quality has a sequel: Although he was denied further orders for the M-130s from Pan American, Martin produced a larger variation on the original theme, designated the M-156. Except for

The Soviet Clipper *headed for the water, 1937. (Martin Company)*

twin rudders, it bore a striking resemblance to its smaller antecedents. It was produced in 1937, tested and flown—and not found wanting. Since he could find no domestic purchaser, Martin sold the giant boat to Russia—thus acquiring the name, *Soviet Clipper*. As soon as the proper business arrangements had been worked out, the M-156 was dismantled, crated, and shipped to the Soviet Union.

It was never seen nor heard of again.

Awaiting testing, the M-156 nestles in the water alongside a miniature PBM which would grow into the giant Mariner. (*National Air Museum, Smithsonian Institution*)

The Soviet Clipper *aloft. A larger version of the classic clippers, the M-156 had a wingspan of 156 feet, was 91 feet long, and had a top speed of 190 miles an hour. (Span of the* China Clipper *was 130 feet). Twin tail was the major deviation from the original configuration. After plane was shipped to Russia its fate became a mystery. (Martin Company)*

8: Atlantic Conquest

If aerial mastery of the Pacific was redolent of romance and adventure, the conquest of the Atlantic represented a more tangible design: money. There was profit to be made out of the Orient, but there was something about the Atlantic community that spelled hard cash. There was a different, more reverent, attitude toward it among the nations ringing the Atlantic than could be found in the East. There, too, was a long tradition of trade between the Americas, Britain, France, and Germany. This trade was dependent upon swift communications as well as transportation of high-level personnel to distant centers of commerce and finance.

But the Atlantic was not easily con-quered; it was not merely a matter of distance but also one of recalcitrant weather and its related navigational problems. The North Atlantic was the most difficult, with its stormy skies, tricky winds, and general, in the word of a veteran, "cussedness." Logically, then, the better transatlantic route lay to the gentler south, a route that was slightly shorter (by less than a hundred miles) than the northern route, and blessed with less treacherous weather conditions. This was the route that connected Dakar, Senegal, the westernmost point of Africa, with Natal, Brazil, the easternmost point of South America.

The French were the first to explore this

route. As early as 1928 Compagnie Générale Aéropostale had initiated a kind of air mail route across the South Atlantic. The mail was carried from France to Dakar by air, then it was rushed across the Atlantic by fast destroyer and again, at Natal, was transformed into air mail again for delivery in South America. While this could hardly be classified as true air transportation, it was an attempt in the right direction.

Aéropostale made another, purer, effort in May of 1930, when on the eleventh, Jean Mermoz took off from Dakar in a Latécoère 28, a landplane converted for sea duty. Christened *Comte de la Vaulx,* the plane also carried Jean Dabry as co-pilot/navigator and Leopold Gimie as radio operator. Flying through the night, Mermoz brought the plane into Natal after nine-

Jean Mermoz, one of France's outstanding airmen and pioneer of the South Atlantic route connecting Africa and Brazil. Following several record-making flights Mermoz became an official of Air France, but continued with his flying. He was lost in December 1936 during a test flight of a four-engined plane in a flight over the South Atlantic. (Musée de l'Air)

teen hours, thirty-five minutes of flying. This was the first commercial crossing of the South Atlantic, the first delivery of transatlantic air mail, and set a new record for distance for hydroplanes. A month later, after a round of receptions and banquets, the crew once again climbed into the plane for the return flight. After literally more than fifty attempts, the *Comte de la Vaulx* finally rose off the surface of the Rio Potengi and headed back for Africa. However, when they were still about five hundred miles from Dakar (six hours of flying time) an engine oil leak forced them down at sea with a boiling engine. Luckily, their route was covered to some extent by two Aéropostale weather ships, the *Brentivy* (which had been posted six hundred miles off South America) and the *Phocée,* off Africa about the same distance. Mermoz set the plane down between two waves near the *Phocée* and he, his crew, and the mail aboard the *Comte de la Vaulx* were rescued. The plane, caught in the waves, lost a float and quickly sank into the sea.

The loss of the Latécoère 28 convinced Aéropostale that it was not quite ready for the South Atlantic run by air, although plans were made for the construction of larger seagoing aircraft for the future. However, financial misfortune overtook Aéropostale, and in 1931 it lapsed into bankruptcy; by the time it was merged into Air France, in 1933, it was possible for a landplane [the Couzinet 70, *Arc en Ciel* (Rainbow)] to make the passage nonstop. Fittingly, Mermoz—the "French Lindbergh" —made the first flight, in January 1933.

German ambitions perked up in the early thirties, also. By this time the Allies had relaxed their vigil on German aviation development (most of which was being carried on surreptitiously in foreign lands anyhow), and the aircraft industry began reviving more openly than had been obvious during the twenties. There being an extensive network of airlines inside Germany, as

Latécoère 28, of the type in which Jean Mermoz crossed the South Atlantic—west to east —for the first time in 1930; the plane, however, did not complete the return flight and came down 350 miles short of its destination, Dakar. (Musée de l'Air)

well as much mileage in South America, it followed that the two systems might be profitably linked. Even the once-dreaded airship, the scourge of London during the First World War, was revived.

By 1931 Deutsche Zeppelin Reederei began an air service between Friedrichshafen to Recife, Brazil (later extending the run to Rio de Janeiro) employing the majestic 787-foot-long *Graf Zeppelin* (LZ-127). This constituted the only direct air route between Europe and America at the time, albeit seasonal and leisurely. At a cost of

$461 (one way) it was possible to make a flight in quite grand style in from eighty to a hundred hours, depending on the headwinds, at a top speed of about seventy miles an hour. In 1931 the *Graf Zeppelin* made three round trips and by 1932 began a regular run, during the flying months of April through October, and continued until 1936. The destruction of the *Hindenburg* led to the grounding of the *Graf Zeppelin;* and the refusal of the United States to supply helium (in place of the highly combustible hydrogen) grounded the airships of Germany permanently.

Even as the *Graf Zeppelin* crossed the South Atlantic route Lufthansa was attempting to solve the problem of crossing as much of that water as possible by air. One ingenious solution was found in 1933 using catapult mother ships from which a Dornier Wal (Whale) could be flung with its load of mail and fuel. The mother ship, initially the *Westfalen* and later the *Schwabenland,* could transport the Wal part of the way from the African base at Bathurst, then catapult it on its way. The depot ships were equipped with recovery equipment to enable them to take the Wals aboard for

German ambitions in the Atlantic aerial conquest are graphically symbolized in this photograph of the Graf Zeppelin *passing over a Donier flying boat lifting off the water. Only the airship had the range that made a direct Atlantic crossing possible in 1931. (Lufthansa)*

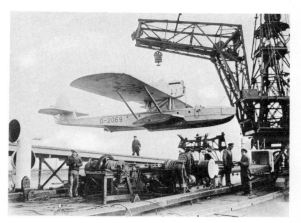

A Dornier Do-J, Wal, is hoisted aboard the Westfalen *for mail delivery by ship and air across the South Atlantic. Catapult is directly under plane. A good-sized aircraft, the Dornier Wal had a span of eighty-nine feet and fuselage length of sixty feet. (Lufthansa)*

refueling and servicing. These flying boats carried only mail—and not a great deal of that. But the service did speed up the delivery of those letters they did carry—a letter from Germany to Rio de Janeiro took only three days.

The Dornier flying boats were Germany's major bid for supremacy in overwater flight. The pioneer, Dr. Claudius Dornier, once an associate of Zeppelin and an advocate of metal construction in aircraft, formed his own company in 1922. He began almost immediately to produce commercial aircraft, among them the early (1921) flying boat, the *Delphin* (Dolphin), which was capable of carrying eight passengers. A characteristic of Dornier's design, aside from the metal construction, was the use of sponsons (later to be used for the first time in an American-designed plane on the *China Clipper*) instead of the more conventional wingtip floats. It was out of this design that the Wals developed, the first being introduced in 1922.

For some reason this design did not meet with the approval of the Allied Control Commission, which banned it, perhaps because a powerful (twin engines in tandem) flying boat appeared to have dire war potential. The Control Commission was noth-

ing if not inconsistent; although the German General Staff (also banned by the Versailles Treaty) was being resuscitated under their very collective nose and what would later emerge as the Luftwaffe was being born in Soviet Russia, they arbitrarily attempted to squash the Wal.

Whereupon Dornier moved his operations to Marina di Pisa in Italy and began producing the classic Do-J models of the type that was used by Lufthansa's catapult service and by several Atlantic aerial adventurers during the twenties and thirties. Not all of these attempts at Atlantic crossings were successful, but the bulk were, and the Wal proved itself as a design. Dornier was so pleased with it that the original design remained unchanged for some fifteen years. The only major difference was in size: The Dornier Wals grew and grew. But as they did they retained their original look: the boatlike fuselage, stubby seawings, the slabby wing, engines mounted atop the wing, tail structure complicated by a tangle of struts. Dornier's solution to the growth problem generally was to add more engines (and thus, considering their placement, to the drag).

Spurred on by the success of his flying boat design and the possibility that Lufthansa might consider expanding its transatlantic passenger service, Dornier proceeded in creating the most prodigious leviathan of all, the Do-X.

Although it was a grand conception, and it would be cruel to call it "Dornier's Folly," and inappropriate as well, the Do-X, simply, did not do. No matter—it served nobly in its time. It was to be a true ocean-liner that flew, massive in size as well as concept. A year was spent on the drawings alone, and construction began at the end of 1927 at Dornier's Swiss factory; by July 1929 the gigantic boat was rolled out of its hangar and put into the waters of the Boden See (Lake Constance), whose shores are formed by Germany, Switzerland, and

The Dornier Delphin of the early twenties. One of the first of Dornier's flying boats, it was the immediate ancestor of the Wals. It could carry eight passengers. The characteristic Dornier touch is already evident in the stubby sea wings and the rather thick, planky, wing. (U. S. Air Force)

Austria. When the Do-X was seen for the first time, many who saw it did not believe it would float, let alone fly.

The forward part of the fuselage resembled a cabin cruiser, and from tip of nose to tip of tail the plane measured 131 feet, four inches. The wingspread was no less than 157 feet, five inches; empty, the Do-X weighed well over sixty-one thousand pounds. Its most remarkable aspect was its size, for otherwise it revealed few innovations: There was the same, squared-off, hull-like fuselage fitted with the usual Dornier *stummel* (the stub-sponsons) and with a row of portholes along each side. The cockpit was situated on an upper deck above the passenger quarters, with accommodations for pilot and copilot, navigator, radio operator, and flight engineers to attend to the welfare of twelve engines.

These, originally 500-hp Siemens Jupiter air-cooled engines were arrayed back-to-back in six nacelles atop the wing; they appeared to have been nailed up there by carpenters rather than designed into the integral structure of the aircraft. It was possible, during the period of the Siemens engines, to perform in-flight maintenance. An engineer could crawl through the thick wing and emerge at each engine, inside a metal turret housing that rose up from the wing to the engine. But then it was found that the Siemens did not provide sufficient power, and they were exchanged for Curtiss Conquerers of greater horsepower.

These were placed on the original mountings, although the turrets were removed, which left the engines all aclutter on the wing. This engine change did not really solve the problem, despite the additional power, for the rear six engines had a tendency to overheat, which caused loss of power whatever the engine make.

Not that the plane was a failure. When it took off, after some three hours of water-taxiing, on July 12, 1929, it took to the air so readily that it was obviously a flyable aircraft. For the test, of course, the Do-X

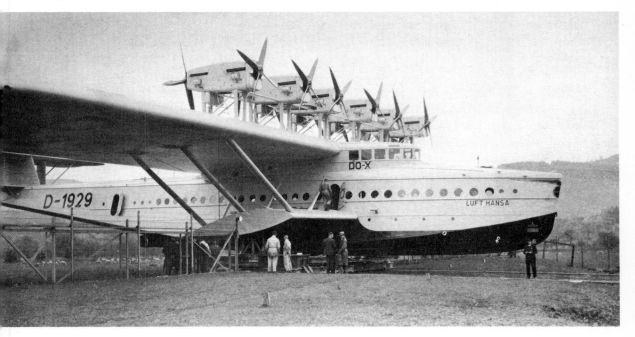

The Do-X, still landbound, fitted with a dozen Curtiss engines—the installation of which did not in the slightest decrease resistance and drag. Larger propellers might have improved the performance, but no one seems to have thought of that when the engines were changed. (U. S. Air Force)

was not burdened with payload—which was its chief reason for being. It was hoped that it might carry a hundred passengers over the Atlantic in splendid comfort, which included everything from a smoking room to showers.

Meanwhile, testing proceeded as the various problems were considered. Operating the big plane was no joyride, as the control system, though complex, was simplified to the point of asceticism. The pilot, for example, had no actual control over his various engines; this fell into the province of the flight engineer, who had his control panels some distance away from the cockpit. In between was the navigator's compartment, which he shared with the ship's captain, and the radio room. This arrangement called for a good deal of dashing hither and yon, and yelling. Despite all these inconveniences, which at the time may not have been considered inconveniences, the Do-X continued to prove itself. In one test, made on October 31, 1929, it was decided to show what the plane could do in a weight-lifting attempt, so that in addition to the crew of ten, 150 passengers were taken aboard for a flight around the Bodensee.

The Do-X took off without any trouble, circled, and landed—and then it was found that besides the authorized 160 persons the plane had also lifted nine stowaways, who had hidden in its capacious interior.

In the waters of the Boden See, the Do-X is poised for a run. Note complexity of tail-bracing and controls. (U. S. Air Force)

Dornier, pleased with the results of the tests, hoped to show what the plane could do under more or less flight conditions. There were some disappointments: With its gross weight up to 123,000 pounds (Dornier had originally planned on 118,000 pounds), speed was reduced to around a hundred miles an hour (from a hoped-for 115) and range was down to around two thousand miles—provided no heavy payload was carried. The engine change actually made little difference in the performance. Nor was advantage taken of the fact that the Curtiss engines could have turned larger propellers; they were simply fitted with the originals from the Siemens. Despite the obvious shortcomings, Dornier decided that the Do-X should make a tour to the New World, stopping along the way to publicize the flying leviathan.

It was officially announced that the Do-X would set out for the Americas in the summer of 1930, but ominously this was delayed for one reason or another (one being the change of engines). Finally, on November 5, 1930, the plane lifted off the surface of the Bodensee and headed for Lisbon, its first stop. Under command of an ex-First World War naval pilot, Friedrich Christiansen, the Do-X was piloted by Horst Merz and Cramer von Clausbruch; sixteen other men comprised the crew. There were no passengers, although a good cargo of mail was carried.

As an exercise in public relations, or even in the making of a historic flight, the progress of the Do-X was no triumph. Dornier contended that "Our main object was to supply practical proof, proof that the upper limits set on increasing the size of aircraft are far greater than theorists suppose." This statement was made, of course, after the big plane had made its tour and had proved itself to be underpowered. It still did not really prove the point for aerial giantism (although there appeared to be a rash of international competition over "the world's largest airplane" around this time).

The Do-X was scheduled to visit several countries on the way to America, among them the Netherlands and England (where it was flown by the Prince of Wales for about ten minutes); shortly after this misfortune began setting it. On its way to Portugal for the beginning of its South Atlantic crossing, the Do-X encountered a heavy fog and was forced down at sea. Captain Christiansen covered sixty miles of open sea on the surface and taxied the big boat into a convenient French harbor.

But they pressed on, accompanied by vicissitudes of assorted degrees of peril. One of the worst occurred at Lisbon, where a fuel tank fire caused considerable damage to the wing, necessitating a month's layover for repairs. That accomplished, the Do-X headed for the Canary Islands, specifically Las Palmas, where during a takeoff attempt

The plane that looked more like a ship. Rubber tires along edge of stummel *protected it during docking operations. (U. S. Air Force)*

the hull suffered damages that led to a three-month layover for more repairs. The next stop was Cape Verde, where little seems to have happened except that five members of the crew were left behind, as was all that was considered not absolutely essential, to enable the Do-X to carry enough fuel for the next step of the journey, the actual flight over the Atlantic. The big boat took off from Cape Verde on June 4, 1931 (it had started out on November 5,

The plane that actually flew like a boat, the Do-X beginning to lift off the Bodensee. A beautiful, if not very practical flying boat, it had arrived before the engines it required. (Lufthansa)

1930) and found, despite the lesser load, that it could not attain altitude and flew most of the way to Natal barely thirty feet above the water.

The next day the crew and their impressive plane were treated to a great welcome by the people of Brazil, and the news of the safe arrival was heralded throughout the world. The Do-X never failed to attract attention wherever it appeared and, unless embarrassing questions were asked about performance—or fuel consumption, which was voracious—it was an overpowering tourist attraction. When it became known to Captain Christiansen that the plane was to make a series of guest appearances along the coast of South America, he began muttering uncomplimentary views on "joyriding." Consequently he was relieved of his command, which was then taken over by Fritz Hamer.

It was Hamer who brought the Do-X, finally, into New York on August 27, 1931 —more than nine months since it had left Germany. Since it had not been engaged in any record attempt, the fact that the plane arrived at all, in all its immensity, was reason enough for the crew to be treated to one of New York's classic ticker-tape parades and a bemedaling by Mayor James Walker.

The plane then went into drydock for the winter—as Dornier hoped he might interest American capital in the monster; Lufthansa had gone rather cold on the idea of a giant airliner during the plane's trial (and tribulations) flight over. On May 19, 1932, the Do-X took off from Manhasset Bay, and via Newfoundland and the Azores headed homeward without unreasonable incident. However, just six miles short of Portugal, and low on fuel, the plane was landed in the water and made the rest of the way, shipshape, to Horta. Back in its homeland, after an absence of about a year and a half, the Do-X was greeted enthusiastically; the crew was accorded proper recognition. But the plane itself was little more than a large curio; except for two others, there was no great fleet of Do-Xs filling the air. Instead the Do-X went into retirement in the German Air Museum in Berlin—where it was totally destroyed in a bombing raid during the Second World War.

Although he had found no takers in Germany or the Americas, Dornier did succeed in selling two Do-Xs to Italy for use as commercial airliners. Although when delivered the planes proved capable of getting over the Alps (thus discrediting *Jane's All the World's Aircraft* damning claim that its service ceiling was a mere 1640 feet), they

The Do-X, airborne at long last. (U. S. Information Agency/National Archives)

New York, August 5, 1931, the Do-X finally arrives at its destination. (Smithsonian Institution, National Air and Space Museum)

still could not lift the weight claimed for them, nor achieve anywhere near the range. Ultimately the planes were turned over to the *Regia Aeronautica* (the Royal Italian Air Force), which quickly lost interest also. The two big planes were dismantled, finally, and that ended the line. Even Dornier abandoned the big plane concept and produced a better performer in the less pretentious Do-S, which was built almost simultaneously with the Do-Xs. Not afflicted by underpowering as were the bigger craft, the Do-S proved to be a worthy craft although denied the press coverage that had celebrated the Do-X.

Germany in the early thirties was regaining its "rightful place in the sun," politically as well as aeronautically. Italy, too, was anxious to make its mark in the annals of flight. Dictator Benito Mussolini was decidedly air-minded, and numbered among his favorites a politician-airman, Italo Balbo, one of whose contributions to the resurgence of a new Italy was the organization of a group known as the Blackshirts. Thus did he help put Mussolini into power and, although *Il Duce* kept a wary eye on a possible rival (he usually managed to "promote" them out of harm's way), he rewarded Balbo with various important positions in the new government of Italy. In

The Dornier Do-S, less spectacular in bulk and general appearance than the Do-X, was superior in performance and practicality. (U. S. Air Force)

1929 Mussolini even bestowed the office of Under Secretary of State for Aeronautics, one he had planned to fill himself, upon Balbo.

Italian aviation was not particularly impressive in its achievements during the early Lindbergh era, although like every nation Italy produced its share of intrepid airmen. There was the airshipman Umberto Nobile, who had an affinity for polar flights in airships—and whose popularity did not please Balbo. And there was the Marchese Francesco de Pinedo who, in 1925, flew from Rome to Tokyo and, two years later, crossed the South Atlantic and toured the United States in his aircraft, a Savoia-Marchetti twin-hulled flying boat. This plane, named the *Santa Maria,* was inadvertently destroyed by fire in Arizona when spilled fuel caught fire.

The destruction of the *Santa Maria* all but led to an international incident, and promises were made to punish any guilty person. It turned out to be a young boat tender who had dropped a lighted match into the enfueled water in a wrestling match over a cigarette in a rowboat, which just happened to be near the plane. A second plane, *Santa Maria II,* was dispatched to the United States under armed Italian guard, and de Pinedo continued with his tour of the country and then set off for home. He did not quite make it—in any sense. The plane ran out of fuel short of his goal and was towed into port by schooner. De Pinedo's not so glorious arrival, while greeted wildly by Italians and by a pleased *Il Duce,* had a good deal of the edge taken off because Charles Lindbergh had succeeded just days before in flying the Atlantic alone in a monoplane.

Although a favorite of Mussolini, de Pinedo did not remain so for very long, and it was Balbo who climbed high in Italian political circles. He agreed with Mussolini that something should be done "for the glory of Fascist Italy" with aircraft. He also

Savoia-Marchetti 55X flying boat which, though not a foolproof aircraft, was popular with Italian airmen during the thirties. Originally designed as a torpedo-bomber, the twin-hull boat was a good choice for long overwater flights. For such flights the guns had been removed from the plane and the positions faired over in front and rear of hulls. Pilots sat side by side in cabin under tandem engines. Span was an inch less than eighty feet. (U. S. Air Force)

thought big: If de Pinedo could make the crossing in the Savoia-Marchetti, why not make the same flight with a great flying armada? A large formation of aircraft would make quite an impression and would certainly be noted. So the first formation flight of the South Atlantic got under way from Orbetello, the seaplane base north of Rome, on December 17, 1930 and landed at Rio de Janiero on January 6, 1931. The crossing was not without incident; of the fourteen Savoias that began, two crashed, resulting in the deaths of five men; one of the replacement aircraft sank in mid-Atlantic after colliding with a cruiser that attempted to take it in tow—and a second replacement suffered some damage, although it was repaired and eventually joined Balbo's armada. Ten planes eventually landed at Rio,

a feat of airmanship and formation flying that were outstanding.

But Balbo had even greater plans. The tenth anniversary of the Fascist revolution would occur in 1933; it was Balbo's suggestion to Mussolini that the event be marked by another mass flight—this time to North America, but instead of a dozen aircraft, twenty-four would make the crossing. This kind of thinking pleased *Il Duce,* and arrangements were set afoot and training of aircrews began at Orbetello.

Once again the craft selected for the flight was the Savoia-Marchetti 55X, which had been designed some years before as a torpedo-bomber flying boat. Although it had been in service for years (in fact, it had once been rejected by the Italian Air Force, a rejection ultimately overruled by

Balbo), the plane was not without its flaws. During the planning stages of the projected North Atlantic flight nearly a hundred different propellers were tested before the engines were fitted with them; over a dozen radiator types were tried. And once the twenty-six aircraft were selected for the flight, all were returned to the factory for structural reinforcement, the installation of more modern instruments, and larger fuel tanks. Finally, by May, the planes were ready. Also, Balbo's carefully laid-out plans were set in motion, with ships stretched out along the route, with radio communications set up, and with full safety precautions (down to the last collapsible boat) in order. Practice flights had prepared the crews well in advance of the mission. The entire enterprise was beautifully planned, organized, and, in fact—except for some mishaps— well carried out.

Each of the Savoias carried a standard crew of four, although some carried five— in all, the final selection of twenty-four planes (plus one in reserve) were manned by 115 men.

While Balbo awaited good flying conditions he and his crews were treated to news-

Italo Balbo, Italy's aviation hero of 1931. (National Archives)

paper chiding about the delay. May stretched into June and June into July, and then on July 1, 1933, the armada took off from Orbetello. Balbo led the formation, which was divided up into eight flights of three planes each in "Vs." The first stop was Amsterdam, a flight of 875 miles over the Alps—a flight that took seven hours and fifteen minutes. To Balbo's dismay it was at Amsterdam that disaster struck for the first time. One of the planes coming in for a landing capsized in the Zuider Zee, burying the hulls deep in the mud. Two men were injured, but one died in the mud before anything could be done. It was not a good beginning—and the prestige of Italian aviation was at stake.

The flight had been long publicized, and it was known that the destination of the flying boats was Chicago, then the setting of a world's fair. It would not have been wise to cancel out at the first accident, so the reserve Savoia was placed in service and the Balbo armada continued on its way. Except for the exigencies contributed by the weather that lay in their path, the rest of the flight, in fact, proceeded as well as could be expected. From Amsterdam, the two dozen double-hulled boats crossed the North Sea, cloudy, rainy, and then clear, on a Sunday and landed in Londonderry, Northern Ireland. Weather again interfered and they were held up for three days before chanching the first long overwater hop to Reykjavik, Iceland, a distance of about 950 miles.

All went well until, at about the halfway mark, the formation encountered heavy fog and was forced to descend close to the water and to depend a great deal on their instruments. Despite the potential for calamity, all twenty-four Savoias safely landed at Reykjavik in a heavy rain.

After some delay because of the weather, and the fact that Balbo, for some reason, could not get his plane off the water, the armada eventually continued on to Cartwright, Labrador; from there, after a refueling, they proceeded on to Shediac Bay, New Brunswick, and then to Montreal. In this, their first great population center in North America, the Italian airmen were greeted by throngs of people lining the banks of the St. Lawrence River, and the river itself swarmed with numerous small boats, many of them carrying overzealous newsmen. Balbo and his formation landed first and taxied up to the mooring buoys. The press boats then moved into midstream to complicate the landings of the planes that followed, many of which were forced to swerve to avoid collisions in the water. Balbo, who had left his plane and had boarded a launch, was disturbed by the mad scene unfolding before him. He began shouting, using language that revealed his anger, for

someone to clear the landing area of the small boats. Aboard the launch was a Canadian Broadcasting official with a mobile radio and a microphone that he promptly stuck into Balbo's face. Since he did not understand the language, the radio man may have thought Balbo was merely excited by the frenzy of the greeting from Montreal. Those who understood Italian were treated to a colorful flow of vituperation via the airwaves.

Fortunately, thanks to the skill of the pilots, all the Savoias managed to land safely. The crews rested overnight and pushed on for Chicago the next morning. This final leg of the flight was again complicated by weather, and Balbo was forced to change their course now and then to avoid storms over the lake area. At one point three of the planes had separated from the forma-

Balbo's armada arrives at its destination, the Chicago World's Fair ("A Century of Progress"), July 15, 1933. Though he soon passed out of aviation history to devote himself to the military life, the flight's leader was remembered during the Second World War: RAF fliers called large formations of aircraft "Balbos." (U. S. Air Force)

tion, but all were joined up again over Detroit. The flying boats were also met by a big formation of little planes of the First Pursuit Wing from Selfridge Field. The U. S. Army pilots, escorting the Italians to Chicago, entertained them along the way with aerobatics, which delighted the visitors.

Then the twenty-four Savoias settled down onto Lake Michigan on July 15, 1933 —two weeks from the day on which they had taken off. They had covered a total of 11,495 miles in forty-eight hours, forty-seven minutes at an average speed of 124.6 miles an hour. When he landed Balbo carried as a passenger the Italian ambassador to the United States, Augusto Rossi, who had joined the flight at Montreal. Chicago greeted the armada warmly, and after a formal greeting from Governor Henry Horner, Balbo accepted all the good tidings and replied that he was proud to have carried out his leader's command and that the feat of his men was an indication of the greatness of the new Italy. Italo Balbo Day was declared in Chicago, and a street was renamed in his honor to open the festivities celebrating the safe arrival of the twenty-four planes.

On July 19 the Italians took off again, heading for New York (where they were met by aggressive camera planes); then went to Washington to lunch with President Franklin Roosevelt, to whom Balbo presented a commemorative medal. Upon his return to New York, Balbo was treated to a ticker-tape parade and by July 25, festivities over (and somewhat eclipsed by the round-the-world solo flight of Wiley Post, completed on the twenty-second), the armada began its homeward flight.

It was pretty much like the outbound trip, plagued by small problems and the weather, with some of the original place names running in reverse. However, the weather over the northern route turned so bad that, despite earlier arrangements, Balbo decided to pursue a more southerly course through the Azores. From there it would be possible to get to Lisbon, Portugal, and then home. By August 8, despite engine troubles and some bad weather, all of the aircraft were safe in their harbors in the Azores. The following morning, Balbo's luck took a bad turn. During a takeoff one of the Savoias flipped over and splashed into the harbor of Ponta Delgada. Balbo was then circling above observing the takeoffs and was informed by radio that the accident had not been serious; one crewman, Lieutenant Enrico Squaglia, was in shock and was sent to the hospital, but the three other men were only bruised.

When he landed in Lisbon with the twenty-three remaining planes Balbo could look forward to celebrations—except that he received word of the death of Lieutenant Squaglia. All festivities were canceled, and Balbo sought privacy in his hotel room. He was bolstered somewhat by a telegram from Mussolini, but it did not improve the situation, for in what should have been a moment of triumph, Balbo was saddened and disconsolate. Early in the morning of August 12, the twenty-three planes set out for Rome—a long flight of fourteen hundred miles, but within the range of the Savoias. Even this final lap was afflicted with problems—a headwind that reduced their speed to a hundred miles an hour (Balbo had wished for 140) and overheating engines, which caused some of the planes to lag behind and spoiled the formation. It would not do to arrive before the *Duce* in poor formation. But arrive they did in the early evening (the engines cooled off and the formations were perfect) accompanied by fifty seaplanes of the *Regia Aeronautica* to be greeted first of all by *Il Duce* and the cheers of thousands of people. This helped to heal the wounds of loss—two men and two of the Savoia-Marchettis—and Balbo had, with considerable success, proved that Italian-made aircraft, manned by Italian crews, could cross the Atlantic.

A grateful Mussolini promoted all the crew members and made Balbo Italy's first air marshal, and later made him governor general of Libya, North Africa. And it was there that Balbo's aviation-military-political career ended on an ironic note—a plane in which he was flying was shot down over Tobruk, when it failed to give an identification signal, by Italian antiaircraft guns.

While Balbo and his armada had proved that, with planning and organization (and a more or less qualified aircraft), it was possible to fly the Atlantic, there was no eagerness on the part of the Italian commercial aviation firms to make a regular thing of it. That still remained in the hands of the French and the Germans (with Juan Trippe of Pan American watching anxiously). The *Graf Zeppelin* continued in service, as did the Dornier Wals with their mother ships. By February 1934 (the year after Balbo's mass flights) Lufthansa had begun regular air mail delivery over the Atlantic; in 1936 Air France joined the German firm in regularly crossing the Atlantic over the southern route. The two lines even worked out a system of cooperation in order to avoid the waste of competition; this, at least, lasted until the coming of the Second World War.

An improvement in the German mail service—for mail continued to be the major item, not passengers—came with the introduction of the Blohm und Voss Ha-139 floatplane, which was catapulted off the deck of the *Schwabenland* in 1938. The Ha-139 was faster than the Wal, although limited range still required dependence upon the depot ships in the Atlantic. The name of Dornier came to the fore again the next year with the introduction of the Do-26, a sleek, four-engined flying boat, a far cry in design from the cluttered old Do-X. By this time Dornier had even abandoned his seawings, and an interesting innovation in the design were retractable floats located in the center of each wing panel. Just how well the plane might have served was not demonstrated because of the coming of war. Planned for the North Atlantic route, the Do-26 had a top speed of nearly two hundred miles an hour and a range of five thousand miles. In ten years Dornier had come a long way, although few would forget the romantic Do-X.

Surprisingly inconspicuous, at least so far, from the competition for the commercial air conquest of the Atlantic were the seafaring British. Willing to leave the South Atlantic

Blohm und Voss Ha-139 float plane in place on its catapult aboard the Schwabenland *in the late thirties. This plane, the* Nordwind, *carried only mail. The plane was powered by four Junkers Diesel engines and operated in both the North and South Atlantic. (Lufthansa)*

The Nordwind *coming in at New York on one of its scheduled flights between Horta, Azores, and New York. The plane was built at the Blohm und Voss shipyards at Hamburg, thus the "Ha" in its type designation. (U. S. Air Force)*

The Dornier Do-26 Seeadler, *prototype of this aircraft series that flew for the first time in May of 1938. The plane, one of Dornier's most attractive, was designed for the North Atlantic mail service, although later models were modified for wartime transport. Four Jumo 205E engines powered the Do-26, with the rear engines being raised ten degrees (as in this photo) to keep propellers clear during takeoff. In this plane Dornier, for the first time, produced a seaplane without his usual* flossenstummeln *(seawings), and used instead retractable wing floats. (Lufthansa)*

to the French and Germans, British interest lay to the north. The initial truth was that the British had no planes capable of crossing the Atlantic with a healthy payload. Early British commercial airline development concentrated on linking the Empire, as Imperial Airways built lines to Africa, the Middle East, Asia, and Australia. Most of these routes were flown by landplanes and biplanes at that, such as the Armstrong-Whitworth Argosy, the Handley Page Hannibal, and the de Havilland Hercules, among others.

Not that the British were not interested in rise-off-water aircraft; even before Henri Fabre managed to get his craft into the air in France, an Englishman, J. E. Humphreys (actually an air-minded dental surgeon) produced a kind of unsuccessful flying boat

in 1909. After the success of Curtiss, both British and French activity in rise-off-water craft quickened, and the coming of the First World War brought a series of true, hulled, flying boats—most of them bearing a distinct family resemblance to the Curtiss flying boat of 1912. These took on an increasingly British "look" under the hand of John Cyril Porte in the Porte/Felixstowe series of flying boats, which culminated in 1918 in the Fury, a giant (123-foot span) seagoing triplane.

Soon other British names joined the earlier pioneers, among them Sopwith, Supermarine, Vickers, and Saunders. It was also in 1918, the year of the Porte/Felixstowe Fury, that one of the classic names in British seaplane development—Short Brothers —nearly emerged—"nearly" because in that year Short began construction of their first

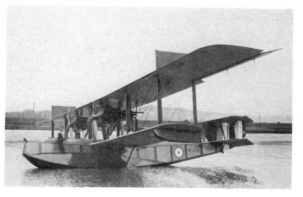

The first in a long line of great British-designed flying boats from Short Brothers, the Cromarty. Originally intended as a warplane, the Cromarty was begun in January 1918 and not completed before the war ended. The economic crisis that followed the war held up production until 1921. Although not granted a government order, this plane was the predecessor of the Short boats that followed. (Short Brothers & Harland)

Supermarine Sea Eagle about 1924. Passenger cabin is in bow of hull forward of the wheels, which folded up under wing; pilot sat in open cockpit just under radiator. Teardrop-shaped forms on top of wing are fuel tanks. Engine is a Rolls-Royce Eagle—top speed about ninety miles an hour. (BOAC Photo)

flying boat (following previous successes with floatplanes). This was the Cromarty which was designed to be a long-range patrol bomber, complete with two gun positions and provision for a bombload. The war ended before the plane was completed, and during the economic pinch that followed, work was delayed so that the Cromarty did not come to light until 1921 as the first Short Brothers flying boat.

In this same period, also, the Supermarine Company was struggling to survive the postwar slump and produced several flying boats hopefully for the civilian and commercial market, with varied, but mostly good, success. These were given such names as Sea King, Sea Lion, Seal, and Seagull and reached a high point in the Sea Eagle of 1923. Designed by R. J. Mitchell, who designed the famed Schneider trophy winners for Supermarine and the Spitfire that followed them, the Sea Eagle was used as a six-passenger cross-Channel transport. These popular little amphibians were initially used by Supermarine's own British Marine Air Navigation Company to fly passengers from Woolston to the Channel Islands. In 1924 the company merged with several other

small airlines to form Imperial Airways Ltd., which later emerged as the giant British Overseas Airways Corporation. Three of the Sea Eagles were built: One was lost while competing in the King's Cup Air Race in 1924; another was sunk when rammed by a ship in Guernsey Harbor in 1927. The single survivor was withdrawn from service in 1929.

One of the most successful of the Supermarine designs of the twenties was the Southampton, which was produced to replace the Porte/Felixstowe F-5 of First World War vintage. The Southampton bore a close resemblance to its predecessor, the Swan of 1924, a passenger transport. Originally constructed with an all-wood hull, the Mark II Southampton had an all-metal (duralumin) fuselage. The craft was manned by a crew of five—the two pilots (one of whom doubled as navigator) in two cockpits just aft of the front gunner/bombardier's position in the nose. A rear gunner sat in the aft cockpit, and a midgunner/radio operator was situated amidships, directly aft of the wing's trailing edge. Southamptons were widely used by the RAF in the latter twenties, especially in long-distance training flights to the far corners of the British Empire. The standard Southampton had a

wingspan of seventy-five feet, with a fuselage length of fifty-one feet. Their average
speed was just a little over eighty miles an
hour; standard endurance was nine hours,
although, with maximum fuel, flights of
eleven hours' duration were possible. Southamptons remained in RAF service until the
mid-thirties.

Although the Short Cromarty had not
been accepted for government contract, it
did lead to further work along the same
lines, resulting in such experimental aircraft
as the Short S-1 Cockle, the first all-metal
flying boat (except for ailerons, rudder, and
elevators). Short used this craft to test the
feasibility of metal construction and applied

*The Short Cockle, the first of the all-metal
flying boats and certainly one of the smallest.
The wingspan measured thirty-six feet. Originally built for a private flier (who seems never
to have claimed it), the Cockle was used by
Short for testing the concept of metal hulls
and the effect of seawater on them. (Short
Brothers & Harland)*

*One of the finest of all British flying boats, the Supermarine Southampton, which
served well with the RAF from 1925 to 1935. (Charles E. Brown, FRPS)*

The first Short Singapore, the fruit of the experiments with the little Cockle. The Singapore was the first large all-metal flying boat. (Short Brothers & Harland)

what they learned to future designs. The result was, in 1926, the S-5 Singapore I, the first of the large all-metal boats. The work of Short design team Arthur Gouge and C. P. Lipscombe, the Singapore was to enjoy a distinguished flying career both in military and civil dress.

Late in 1927 the Singapore was loaned by the RAF to Alan Cobham for an extensive survey flight of Africa. With a crew of five (which included his wife and a photographer), Cobham set out on his aerial survey. However at Malta, even before Africa had been reached, the plane was damaged seriously in a bad storm. Nearly two months were consumed in repairing the wing, elevators, and wingtip floats (which had been washed away). Then in January 1928 Cobham and his party continued with their twenty-three-thousand-mile air safari, returning to England in June. The flight of the Singapore proved that an all-metal flying boat was capable of covering great distances, could sustain the shock of landings, and lift good payloads. After its return to the RAF the Singapore was slightly modified, with the engines changed—from the Rolls-Royce Condor to the Buzzard—which

brought its top speed up to 132 miles an hour.

By 1928 the name of Short Brothers meant something in the field of the flying boat. So it was that when Imperial Airways planned its trunk lines to Africa and India, much of them over water, Short Brothers were approached to provide the aircraft for the job. This was the Short S-8 Calcutta, which drew upon the experience afforded by the Singapore in the production of metal-hulled flying boats. A trio of engines (originally Bristol Jupiters, later more powerful Armstrong Siddeley Tigers) powered the craft, which could remain airborne, and even take off, with only the two outer engines operating.

A crew of four—pilot, copilot, radio operator, and steward—attended to the aerial needs of fifteen passengers; the Calcutta cruised at around eighty miles an hour and had a maximum capability of 118 mph. It proved to be a most successful design and six were eventually built, serving well into the thirties (two, however, were lost in accidents, although through no fault in the design).

The reputation of the Short boats was not

confined to Britain; in 1930 the Japanese government ordered a long-range reconnaissance aircraft, the resulting design resembling the Calcutta, with three interwing engines and the usual nearly total metal construction. Larger than the Calcutta, the S-15 had a wingspan of 101 feet, 10 inches and was 74 feet, 7 inches long. It was a warlike ship, with positions for three machine guns and external bomb racks. After testing, the plane was dismantled and shipped to Japan, where it was reassembled by the Kawanishi Aircraft Company, under license by Short; they were also the Japanese agents for the Rolls-Royce engines that powered the plane. Subsequently additional copies of the flying boat were built for the Japanese Navy. Short, however, retained the general design ideas and used them in the later S-14 Sarafand (although powered by six engines, in tandem, in three nacelles).

By the beginning of the thirties Imperial Airways was ready to replace the trusty Calcuttas on the Mediterranean stretch of the London-to-India run. This resulted in the larger, four-engined S-17, the Kent, the first of which was christened Scipio and which flew for the first time on February 24, 1931. Powered by four Bristol Jupiter

The Short Kent, one of the first of the big luxury flying boats used by Imperial Airways on its Mediterranean run. Plane in photo is the prototype of the series, Scipio, *which was flown for the first time in February 1931. (Short Brothers & Harland)*

engines, with a wing spanning 113 feet and a fuselage of seventy-eight feet in length, the Scipio had room for sixteen passengers besides the usual crew of four. An interesting feature was that of the seat upholstery, which was pneumatically inflated and could double, if necessary, as a life preserver. There were three of the Kent types built and, like the previous Short boats, proved very worthy craft, indeed. Only one, however, survived long enough to be scrapped. One was burned by a disgruntled Italian with, in the phrase of G. R. Duval, "a grievance now lost to history." The prototype, *Scipio,* suffered a landing accident at Crete, killing two passengers, the sole fatalities suffered in these craft. The Kents were comfortable and reliable aircraft, and when their day as seacraft was over, proved their flexibility by continuing to serve as landplanes, the Short L-17.

The same year, 1934, that the Kent became a landplane Short Brothers produced their last biplane flying boat, the Singapore III. It was a military design and was powered by four engines set in tandem nacelles—a kind of step backward after the engine arrangement of the Kents. But the Singapore III was a modification of the 1930 Singapore II (the first of their flying boats to employ the twin tandem engine). The

The Short S-15, built for the Japanese Navy as a long-range reconnaissance flying boat. Examples of this type were produced, under license, by the Kawanishi company in Japan. (Short Brothers & Harland)

The last of a worthy line, the Short Singapore III—the last biplane flying boat built by Short Brothers. Introduced into squadron service with the RAF in 1935, the Singapore III remained in active operation into the early months of the Second World War. Short Brothers & Harland)

Singapores did not figure in the battle for the Atlantic commercial revenue except to contribute further to the skills of Short Brothers and their response to the challenge of crossing wide stretches of water.

In 1935 Imperial Airways' planners began to consider another challenge: passenger service throughout the Empire and across the Atlantic. Some of this could be attributed to a decision the previous year of the British government to ship all mails to the far corners of the Empire by air; another reason was the ambitions of Juan Terry Trippe and the expanding Pan American empire, not to mention the Germans, with their Zeppelins and catapult planes. Trippe was blocked from advancing in the Atlantic by the simple expedient of denying Pan American landing rights. But it was galling to know that Trippe already had the aircraft, the Sikorsky S-42, capable of transatlantic flight—and Britain did not.

When Imperial Airways issued a request for a such a plane, a decidedly advanced type, only Short was able to promise delivery. A design was worked up by Short's Arthur Gouge fulfilling Imperial's ambitious specifications. It would have to be a large flying boat to carry the expected large payload (including room for twenty-four passengers); no plane of such dimensions had ever been built in Britain. Imperial was pleased with the design, but Short hesitated. It seemed a good idea to construct a prototype and test it before launching on an ambitious building program. Imperial countered with the answer that there was too little time and ordered twenty-eight of the new boats off the drafting table.

And so was conceived the Short S-23 "C" Class Empire Flying Boat. A high-winged monoplane, powered by four 920-hp Bristol Pegasus engines, with a deep hull, the Empire was ready for its first flight on July 4, 1936, the prototype being named *Canopus* (after an ancient Egyptian city). Short's chief test pilot, John Lankester Parker, took up the handsome boat, after it had been slipped into the Medway River, at Rochester. Thanks to the design of the hull bottom, the heavy boat (eighteen tons) lifted off the Medway after a run of only seventeen seconds. The flight itself was a demonstration of the solidness of the design —the only hitch coming during the landing, when a small problem in the electrical system prevented the use of the special Gouge-designed flaps. Parker brought the plane down without using flaps, and no one among the laymen—company shareholders and newsmen—was aware of the difference. By October the *Canopus* had gone into service in the Mediterranean—and a new era in British aviation began.

Soon the S-23s began rolling out of the Rochester plant at a rate of nearly two a month; when the initial order of twenty-eight was well under way an additional eleven were ordered. Almost the instant they were completed, had been tested, and flown, they were delivered to Imperial Airways for the Mediterranean run. Others went to Qantas for use in the Pacific. Soon the S-23s were winging over Egypt, Africa, Malaya, India, and Australia—thus the name Empire flying boat.

The runs of these boats were not in the

The first of a great line of flying boats: rollout of the S-23 Canopus, *prototype of the Empire flying boats. On the slipway, the* Canopus *is undergoing last-minute engine adjustments—note open engine access panels on port wing. (Short Brothers & Harland)*

category of long-range, not such as would be required to make an Atlantic crossing. The S-23s could manage a comfortable seven hundred miles or so at a cruising speed of 165 mph. They were capable of a top speed of two hundred miles an hour, which was about as good as some fighters could do in their day. But it was range and payload that counted if the British were to rule the waves. They were willing even to share this rule with Trippe. Sometime in the spring of 1937 an agreement was drawn up between British and American (that is, Imperial Airways and Pan American) airlines for a shared transatlantic service. There was a small catch in the agreement, which stated that no American company could begin any service unless the British could provide a reciprocal service at the same time.

The hitch in the catch was that Pan American, with its Sikorsky S-42, was ready in the summer of 1937 when the *Pan American Clipper III* (formerly the *Alaskan Clipper*), commanded by Captain Harold Gray, made the first Atlantic survey flight. Leav-

ing from Port Washington, New York, the *Clipper III* flew via Botwood, Newfoundland, to Southampton, England in great style: Dinner was served at ten thousand feet consisting of shrimp cocktail, soup, filet mignon with mushroom sauce, a salad, ice cream, cake, and demitasse.

At the same time, per Clause H of the agreement, an Empire boat, *Caledonia,* under the command of Captain A. S. Wilcockson, set out on the crossing in the opposite direction—the hard way. Westbound crossings of the Atlantic invariably had to contend with headwinds. The *Clipper III* made the flight from Botwood to Britain in twelve hours, thirty-four minutes; *Caledonia,* flying a slightly longer route and bucking the headwind, took fifteen hours, three minutes to reach Botwood. The Empire eventually bettered its mark in other trial crossings (the last being made on September 13, 1937), but the fact was that, although the Atlantic had been crossed, the Empire boat carried no payload. It proved that it could be done, with plenty of fuel in special tanks, but

Canopus *on the Medway River awaiting testing by John Lankester Parker. An L-17, landplane version of the* Kent, *flies over. (Short Brothers & Harland)*

Empire *boat* Cameronian *takes off. Wingspan was 114 feet, fuselage length eighty-eight feet. (Short Brothers & Harland)*

The famous promenade deck of an Empire *flying boat, a touch of spaciousness unique at the time in aircraft. (BOAC Photo)*

without passengers and without cargo. The *Clipper III,* however, was capable of carrying a payload. This closed the reciprocal Atlantic route for the time being.

Trippe took some consolation in getting a foothold in the British Atlantic when, in June before the long-range Atlantic trials, Pan American and Imperial shared regular runs between New York and Bermuda, Pan American with the Bermuda Clipper (S-42B, NC 16735) and Imperial with the Empire boat *Cavalier,* which unfortunately was lost at sea in January of 1939. With no reserve aircraft available, Pan American carried on alone with the Sikorskys. For Trippe the landing rights at Bermuda meant a foot in the door, for it placed the Azores and Lisbon within range of Pan American's boats. However, although he was permitted to fly between New York and Bermuda, the British would not permit him to land en route from Europe.

Meanwhile the British continued with the Empire boats. The S-23 was followed by the S-30, with no alteration in general specifications. The major difference between the S-23 and the S-30 was in the installation of smaller, less powerful engines. Despite this, the S-30 performed as well as the more powerfully engined S-23. The S-33 followed (it also had the same dimensions), but with a return to the original Bristol Pegasus engines; two only of these were built, and a third was never completed, thanks to the eruption of the Second World War.

The last of the Empire boats, or rather an outgrowth of them, was the larger "G" class flying boat, of which three were built in 1939–40. With a wingspan twenty feet wider than the "C" class boats, the newer craft were notable for their increase in size over the earlier ones as well as a slightly different rear step. These planes (the S-26) were specifically designed for transatlantic crossings and had a range of more than three thousand miles, which would have made it possible for them to cross the Atlantic nonstop with a full mail load. The S-26 came upon the scene just in time for the war; it never went into commercial service and almost immediately went into wartime paint and the RAF for duty as long-range reconnaissance aircraft. Of the three built only one, the *Golden Hind,* survived the war. The *Golden Fleece* suffered failure in two engines and fell into the sea of Cape Finisterre (off the coast of Spain); its survivors were rescued by their quarry, a German submarine. The *Golden Horn* caught fire in the air during a test after repairs and crashed into the River Tagus (at Lisbon), resulting in the death of thirteen passengers. The *Golden Hind,* following its military service, was returned to British Overseas Airways Corporation (which had been formed from Imperial and British Airways in 1939). Finally, in 1954, the last of the S-26s was scrapped. Of the S-25, more later.

To solve the problem of range, and its cognate, the heavy fuel load in place of payload, an ingenious method was devised in 1937 using an Empire boat as a flying mother ship. Some of the S-30s (the second series of Empires) were also fitted for in-flight refueling, this being accomplished by Alan Cobham's Flight Refuelling Ltd., and were used for lifting the mail between Southampton and New York.

The idea originated in the mind of Imperial's Major R. H. Mayo, who believed that it would be possible to place one aircraft atop another, to use the power and lift of both to take off—with the upper plane loaded with plenty of fuel and payload—and fly together toward the destination. Once the *Composite* (as it came to be called) was well on its way, the smaller upper aircraft would be released to continue on its way (carrying a load that would have made an unassisted takeoff impossible); the mother plane would then return to port.

The only plane large enough to serve as the "mother" was Short's Empire flying boat. An S-23 was used as the base for the

An S-30, variant of the S-23; the only difference was the installation of less powerful engines. The Aotearoa *enjoyed a long productive life with Tasman Empire Airways, Ltd. and flew between Auckland, New Zealand and Sydney, Australia from April 1940 until October 1947. (U. S. Air Force Photo)*

Last of the Empire boats, the S-26 "G" Class flying boat. Though still bearing a distinctive family resemblance to the S-23, the S-26 was larger (wingspan was twenty feet greater) and was characterized by a knife-edged rear step. They were intended for the transatlantic traffic, but the coming of war altered that. (Short Brothers & Harland)

design (and given the designation S-21), the result being a slightly swollen "C" class flying boat. The original span of 114 feet was retained, but the chord was increased, which in turn added 250 square feet of wing area. To the top of this wing was fitted a special superstructure that would carry the smaller aircraft, (which, in fact, was no light plane, but one with a span of seventy-three feet); the engine nacelles were moved outward from the centerline to assure clearance of

A new idea in flight: the piggyback Short-Mayo Composite, an attempt to solve the problem of range in seagoing aircraft. The idea was for the bottom, and larger plane, to use up its fuel in getting the fully loaded upper plane into the air. The upper plane then could be released with an ample load of fuel (plus payload) to proceed to its destination. (Short Brothers & Harland)

the propellers by the floats of the upper craft. Control surfaces were also enlarged (as compared to the standard Empire) because during the takeoff the controls of the upper plane were locked, and control of the Composite during takeoff and in flight was in the hands of the pilot of the S-21 component, which was given the name *Maia* (Latin for "the great one"). The fuselage was broader than that of the Empires.

The upper craft, the S-20 *Mercury* (the winged messenger of Roman mythology) was a high-winged monoplane with twin floats. It was manned by a crew of two—pilot and radio operator. Like the *Maia,* the *Mercury* was powered by four engines. When the two units were combined they produced an eight-engined seagoing biplane. The engines of the upper plane, incidentally, were started from inside the flying boat via

compressed air. Indicater lights inside the *Maia* informed the pilot if the proper parts of the *Mercury* were snapped into the right places on the wing pylon.

Both aircraft were tested individually by Lankester Parker and found flyable with excellent performances late in 1937. When they were joined, however, trouble developed in the all-important telephone with which the duo-pilots communicated. Harold Piper, another Short test pilot, was to fly the *Mercury* for the combination flight and Parker the *Maia.* Once the communications problem was straightened out the Composite was ready for a test flight on January 4, 1938. The curious contraption actually flew. A month later, on February 6, it was felt that the time had arrived for the real test, complete with separation. Again the pilots were Parker and Piper who,

170   SEAWINGS

as before, had no trouble getting their eight-engine double-decker craft off the water.

To keep out of the limelight as much as possible Parker flew them out over the Thames Estuary for the test. With everything in obvious order and readiness the *Mercury* was released from the *Maia*. The larger flying boat dropped away and gently dived until it picked up the lift that it had lost when *Mercury* had been released. The floatplane ascended swiftly, its floats clearing nicely away from the pylon structure and the engines. It was obvious that Mayo's conception worked.

In July it was decided to give the *Composite* its real acid test—an Atlantic crossing. On the twenty-first, with veteran Empire Captain A. S. Wilcockson in the *Maia* and Captain D. C. T. Bennett (pilot) and A. J. Coster (radio operator) in the *Mercury,* the *Composite* took off from Foynes, Ireland, in a remarkably short run of eighteen minutes despite an enormous load of mail and newspapers in the *Mercury*. Well out to sea, the craft separated and the *Mercury* winged its way to Montreal after a flight of twenty hours, twenty minutes over a distance of 2930 miles nonstop.

This was followed in October with a long-distance attempt, planned to go from Dundee, Scotland to Cape Town, South Africa. After being released from the *Maia, Mercury* (without payload), although it did not reach Cape Town, did cover no less than 6045 miles before it ran out of fuel near Orange River, South Africa. Bennett again was the pilot and succeeded in establishing a distance record for a seaplane that stands to this day. On the *Composite*'s thirteenth flight, which occurred on November 29, 1938, a nonstop mail service was inaugurated between Southampton and Alexandria in a flight time of nine hours; the crew again consisted of Bennett and Coster. This service was continued regularly until the war.

It was obvious that with the Short-Mayo

Positioning the Mercury *atop* Maia, *a delicate operation; an elaborate assemblage of struts joined the aircraft, as can be seen.* (*BOAC Photo*)

The Short-Mayo Composite *over a smoky Rochester, England, headed seaward on its first official Atlantic crossing, July 21, 1938. This newsreel shot was taken from the promenade deck of an Empire boat.* (*BOAC Photo*)

Composite the British had come up with an answer to long-distance flights with heavy payload. But it was not yet the answer to the question of scheduled passenger service. Although Imperial had come close with the *Composite* and, especially, with the "G" class flying boat, their future was interrupted by the war.

Even so, even before the *Mercury* had crossed the Atlantic and before the great *Golden Hind* had made its first flight, Juan Trippe had already acquired the ultimate weapon for the conquest of the Atlantic— freight and passengers—in the magnificent Boeing clipper, if only the British would let him fly the Atlantic.

9: B314

The Boeing Company's experience with hydroplanes went back a long time, to its very first plane—a collaboration in design between William E. Boeing, an aviation enthusiast with timber holdings (and the money that went with them) in the state of Washington, and Conrad Westervelt, an ex-Navy engineer with an aeronautical bent. The plane they produced, given their own initials—B&W—as a designation, was a simple floatplane put together by local carpenters and cabinetmakers and with its spruce frame covered with linen sewn by neighborhood seamstresses. The plane flew gratifyingly, and the two built in 1916 were bought by the government of New Zealand.

By 1917 the Boeing Airplane Company was solidly launched in business (Westervelt had by then been recalled to the Navy).

The next plane, also, was a floatplane, based to some extent upon the B&W, but with refinements (most of them contributed by a young graduate of the Massachusetts Institute of Technology, T. Wong) and was designated the Model C. More than fifty were ordered by the U. S. Navy as trainers and two landplane variants by the Army.

The flying boat concept was introduced to Boeing during the First World War when Boeing was contracted to produce the Curtiss HS-2L for the Navy. The order was not completely filled when the Armistice

Boeing and Westervelt B&W, first aircraft to bear the Boeing name. Fuselage length: twenty-seven feet, six inches; wingspan: fifty-two feet. (Boeing Company)

came, and Boeing again turned to producing its own aircraft.

During the postwar slump the B-1 (actually the sixth Boeing design) was conceived by Claire Egtvedt, Boeing's chief engineer, and his assistant, Louis Marsh. It was a floatplane designed to carry a pilot, two passengers, and mail or cargo. Though obviously inspired by the Curtiss boat, the B-1 was an original design. It was much smaller (fifty feet span against seventy-four feet), somewhat cleaner in design, and not intended to be used as a military plane. It was a good design also, but came at the wrong time. Anyone who was buying aircraft then could get them cheaper by buying them from the government's surplus pile of aircraft of practically every description. By 1919 Boeing considered getting out of the airplane business.

But the company kept alive by working on planes designed by others, such as the U. S. Army, or remodeling existent warplanes such as the DH-4 to extend their life as military procurements dropped

sharply immediately after the war. Finally, in 1923, Boeing again contributed an original design, Boeing Model 15, a pursuit plane based to some extent on the Thomas-Morse MB-3 (which Boeing had built for the Army under a postwar contract during the "keeping alive" period). The Model 15, the Army's PW-9 and the Navy's FB, brought in healthy orders throughout the middle twenties, which sustained Boeing until it again turned to commercial designs.

During this period Boeing produced another flying boat for the Navy, the PB-1 (Patrol Boeing-1; Boeing's Model 50). It was an ambitious design for 1925, with a capability of covering the waters between California and Hawaii nonstop—a distance of twenty-four hundred miles—with a ton of bombs, plus various guns. The result was a boat with a span (top wing) of eighty-seven feet, six inches and a fuselage of nearly sixty feet in length. Metal was used widely in the construction, although the top of the hull was of wood and the wing and tail covering was fabric. Powered

The B-1, designed as a three-place commercial transport carrying two passengers with pilot and mail. Hull was of laminated wood veneer, with spruce and plywood wing construction. The B-1 had a top speed of ninety miles an hour and a range of four hundred miles. (Boeing Company)

Lower wing of Boeing PB-1 being covered in the Boeing factory in Seattle. Ribs were metal. Upper and lower spans were equal, measuring eighty-seven feet, six inches. (Boeing Company)

Hull construction of the Boeing PB-1—planing bottom (right) was metal while top of hull (left) was wood. (Boeing Company)

by two tandem 800-hp water-cooled Packard engines, the PB-1 was capable of a top speed of about 125 mph. The engines, however, did not prove satisfactory and eventually were replaced by the air-cooled Pratt & Whitney Hornets. With the engine change the original PB-1 became, in the Navy's books, the XPB-2. Only one had been built (the Navy by then had branched out into designing its own patrol boats, and then assigning their manufacture to private firms).

Except for a brief return to the B-1 (as Boeing Model 204) in 1929, the single PB-1 ended Boeing's concern with flying boats. In the meantime the company concentrated on the production of a series of classic commercial planes (Model 40, Model 80, the Monomail and the Model 247) and such military aircraft as the F4B/P-12 series for the Navy and Army, the P-26, and the bomber sequence, beginning with the B-9 and culminating in the B-17 Flying Fortress and B-29.

Design features of note in both the commercial and military aircraft, particularly the most successful, were all-metal construction and the single wing.

When Boeing received a letter from Pan American, dated February 28, 1936, asking if the company was up to the conception and construction of "a long-range four-engine marine aircraft" (a plane that Trippe hoped would outperform the Sikorsky S-42), the initial step by Boeing's chief engineer, Robert Minshall, was to reject the idea. Not that Minshall thought it was, in an engineering sense, beyond Boeing, but because money was tight, the facilities for such a large craft would stretch the factory's limits, and it would require a lot of hands. In addition, Pan American was in a hurry to see the blueprints, and it seemed improbable that even that deadline could be met.

Curiously, it was a scoffer who really forced the issue. Wellwood Beall, an engineer turned salesman, happened to be in Shanghai selling Boeing pursuits to the Chinese, when word had come through that Musick had begun his Pacific survey flight in the *Pan American Clipper*. When the Sikorsky landed at Midway, there was excitement and speculation in the Cathay Hotel, and even rumors that soon the American mainland and China would be joined by air.

Beale, a practical man, dismissed this idea with, "That's a lot of poppycock"— or words to that effect. This satisfied most of those who heard the pronouncement, except his young wife (of just a few weeks), Jean, who chided him—"an airplane man"—for saying it would take fifteen years before such a thing, on a regular schedule, would be possible. "Don't you think," she teased, "you might have to eat those words?"

This bothered Beall, who had returned to Seattle to become Boeing's service engineer, and it bothered him that Minshall had been forced to turn down Pan American's contract. He took the nagging idea home with him and began sketching at his dining room table under the occasional eye of Jean Beall. As his point of departure Beall took the wing of the XB-15, the giant (though underpowered) "Old Grandad," the predecessor of the Flying Fortress. Then he proceeded waterward on the hull, which he visualized as of double-decker construction, one deck for the control cabin and crew and the other for passengers—no less than seventy-four of the latter and six of the former. To lift the craft, crew, and payload the boat would require more powerful engines than were available when the XB-15 had been conceived; these existed in the Wright Twin Cyclone fourteen-cylinder engines, which could achieve 1600 hp each. According to his calculations, Beall concluded that the

Launching the PB-1; tandem Packard engines powered the craft. (Boeing Company)

plane's range would be about thirty-five hundred miles.

Beall showed his idea to Minshall who, impressed with it, developed it after requesting an extension on the deadline date for blueprints and projected performance figures. On June 21, 1936, after the usual hard-headed discussions, as could be expected from Trippe and his merry men, a contract was signed for six of what was designated Model 314 for three million dollars, with an option for an additional six.

Work soon got under way at the Boeing plant near Seattle; the 152-foot wing and 106-foot fuselage precluded assembling in the plant. The units were built separately, then assembled outdoors on a ramp. It would be, when completed, the most luxurious, the largest aircraft of its time—with one qualification: The span of the Do-X exceeded the 314's by five feet, five inches. But the Do-X was not a truly successful,

Model 314 takes shape in the Boeing factory, nestled in the launching cradle. (Boeing Company)

A wing panel being joined to center section. Circular opening just behind nacelle was large enough to permit an engineer through in order to work on engines (if need be) during flight. (Boeing Company)

176   SEAWINGS

operational, aircraft. Two features of the Dornier reappeared in the Boeing—the seawings, and in-flight engine accessibility. A passageway inside the wing and behind the engines was large enough for a man to crawl through to make minor repairs on the engines in flight.

Although the wing configuration was based upon the bomber wings Boeing was using at the time, the hull of the 314—as observed by Jean Beall when she peered over her husband's shoulder to see his sketches—owed more to the whale—the Cetacea, not the Dornier. Inside that cetacean form Beall and Boeing's design team had provided for the most modern airliner imaginable. The flight deck was unusually spacious—twenty-one feet long and more than nine wide—with comfortable working space assigned to the crew. The pilot and copilot's section could be curtained off during night flying while the navigator, engineer, and radio operator could work with lights. From the flight deck (rear) the engines could be reached through hatchways; a spiral staircase, just forward of the radio operator's station, led down to the main passenger deck. Crew's quarters, baggage, and mail compartments were directly behind the flight deck and were reached through an ironing-board-shaped door.

Passenger accommodations were even more grand, with plenty of room for as many as seventy passengers (by day; thirty-four could be carried, snug in their berths, at night). The size of the crew varied, depending upon the type of flight, from six to ten—the greater number being made up of stewards to attend to the needs of the great number of passengers. And, like its

Model 314 nearly complete; engines and port aileron have not yet been installed; nor has second letter of license number—which will be a "C" for "Commercial"; until tested and passed, the 314 will officially be regarded as an "X" for "Experimental." Rest of number identifies this model as being the future Honolulu. *(Boeing Company)*

The left-hand—pilot's—seat of the Boeing 314.
(Boeing Company)

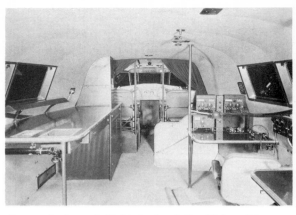

Forward view of flight deck of the 314—with navigator's table on left, then the cockpit with pilot on left and copilot on right. Angular hatchway (open), in front of radio operator's station, led down to main passenger deck. (Boeing Company)

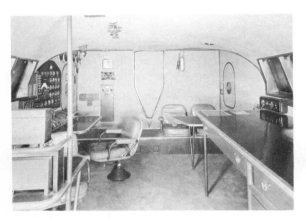

Flight deck of the B314, looking aft. In left foreground, the radio operator's station; directly behind that is the flight engineer's station. Small hatches with small circular windows are engine access openings. Ironing-board-shaped door led aft to crew's quarters and baggage and mail compartments. Table on right was navigator's work space. (Boeing Company)

Closeup of radio operator's and flight engineer's stations. (Boeing Company)

predecessors, the S-42, and the *China Clipper,* the 314 was aesthetically pleasing to look upon. Its very appearance, its mien, was that of an airplane that was destined to perform beautifully.

Initially, however, this did not appear to be so. At the end of May 1938 the first completed 314 was ready for launching. On the thirty-first it was lowered into the water. On June 1, the aircraft was towed into Puget Sound off Duwamish Head. Test pilot Eddie Allen ran up the engines to prepare for a taxi test; for a time the hills around Seattle reverberated with the powerful sound of the Wright Cyclones. Then it stopped; all the plugs had to be changed.

The next day, a Thursday, with the plugs changed, Allen taxied the big plane easily across the waters of the Sound. On Friday, June 3, 1938, he took it into open waters in the afternoon; in its wake the little picket boats, one of them carrying Beall, followed like goading minnows. Allen turned and headed back for port. Suddenly a wind caught the 314 and tipped it to starboard. The right wingtip sliced into the water and the left rose at a crazy angle into the air. For a frightful moment it appeared to Beall, and to Pan American's André Priester riding with him, that the

314 would go under; in fact, the right outboard engine was dangerously close to being swamped.

Allen gunned the right engines, which raised the wing, but then it appeared as if the left wing would slip under the water. He then quickly cut the engines and, although the left wing was still low, the rolling stopped. To level the ship, Allen sent life-jacketed men out through the navigator's hatch onto the left wingtip; they threw out the sea anchor and waited to be towed back to the plant. The only explanation for the near swamping was that because of the light load carried for the test, and the fact that the fuel had been in the wing tanks and none in the seawings, the plane's center of gravity had been too high for true stability in the water.

The next day, even with ballast, the same thing occurred—this time, it appeared, because the copilot, unaccustomed to handling so large and complex a plane, had inadvertently raced the engines on the wrong side in a turn. About at this point, however, it was thought that perhaps the seawings might be lowered a bit.

Tuesday, June 7, was selected for the first flight; even this was delayed until the wind died down. Then, at six-seventeen in the evening, Eddie Allen again poured on full power, turned into the wind, and lifted,

Key men in the Boeing 314 conception and development: in the nose, with lifejacket, Wellwood Beall, and peering out of the hatch, test pilot Eddie Allen. (Boeing Company)

skimmed, and rose into the sky. Gracefully the plane arched higher and disappeared into the dusk. The takeoff was applauded and cheered, for the past several days had proved rather monotonous and frustrating; at last the B314 was airborne.

After thirty-eight minutes, Allen set the plane down on Lake Washington—but there was another problem. "We had power to spare," he said, "but when I got off the water I couldn't turn." In order to turn for the flight back Allen had been forced to do it with the engines rather than with the rudder. Obviously the rudder was too small for the big plane. The first attempt at a solution was to eliminate the center rudder and add two rudders to the tips of the horizontal tail. That did not seem to solve the problem; eventually the center tail was restored, and with the triple rudder the 314 performed beautifully. These changes, plus the change in the positioning of the seawings (the angle of the leading edge to the water was lessened) added to the man-hours and to the cost of the B314 to Boeing.

All six of the initial-order Boeing clippers

Eleanor Roosevelt, wife of the President, shares water gathered from the seven seas, with the Yankee Clipper, *which she christened at the Tidal Basin, Washington, D.C., on March 3, 1939. The* Yankee *was the first of the Boeing clippers to cross the Atlantic roundtrip. (Pan American)*

were delivered to Pan American between January and June 1939. These were, in order of production, the *Honolulu Clipper* (NC 18601), the *California Clipper* (18602), the *Yankee Clipper* (18603), the *Atlantic Clipper* (18604), the *Dixie Clipper* (18605), and the *American Clipper* (18606).

The second group of six was already under way at the Boeing plant; these were designated B314As and differed from the earlier series in that they were fitted with larger fuel tanks and more powerful Wright Cyclones (1600 hp each as against the earlier 1500). By this time war had come—as well as an understanding between the British and Trippe, who held no grudges. Three of the Boeings, with Pan American's blessings, were sold to British Overseas Airways Corporation: *Berwick* (NC-18607; G-AGCA in British registration), *Bangor* (18608; G-AGCB), and *Bristol* (18610; G-AGBZ). These were not clippers in the strict sense, since Pan American had already made that into a trade name. The aircraft were the same, however.

The remaining three went into service with Pan American as the *Pacific Clipper* (18609), the *Anzac Clipper* (18611), and the *Capetown Clipper* (18612). All six of the latter B314s were delivered between April and August 1941. Around this same time the initial six were converted into 314As; the conversion made it possible to carry three additional passengers.

With the delivery of the first Boeing clipper Trippe had the aircraft capable of spanning the Atlantic—even without a refueling stop at Bermuda. Thus Pan American planes could fly directly to the Azores, and beyond. Better, they could fly nonstop to France. In February 1939 (a month after the delivery of the first 314), Trippe had worked out an agreement with France, giving him landing rights at Marseilles— a short three hours from Paris. The French, when they were able, it was agreed, could use Pan American facilities in the United States.

This move meant that Trippe had, just as he had at Singapore, flanked the British. It seemed pointless of them to continue resisting him and, by early 1939, Imperial Airways voiced no objections to Pan American's incursion into their royal air. The *Yankee Clipper,* by this time—May 20, 1939—had made its first Atlantic crossing from Port Washington, New York, to Lisbon, Portugal, in twenty-six hours, fifty-four minutes. By the twenty-second the Boeing was at Marseilles delivering the mail. This marked the first delivery of regularly scheduled mail by a heavier-than-air craft from the United States to Europe. When the *Yankee Clipper,* under its captain, Arthur E. LaPorte, returned to Port Washington on May 27, it had completed the first scheduled round trip across the Atlantic. In June—by which time the British had come around by not invoking the reciprocity clause of their old agreement

—the *Yankee Clipper* made the crossing with passengers (albeit nonpaying passengers, as the first crossing was made with newsmen and Pan American officials aboard). This was followed on June 24, 1939 with the first mail flight to Britain with the *Yankee Clipper* again, commanded by Captain Harold E. Gray. Then, on June 28, Captain R. O. D. Sullivan, who had been Musick's first officer on the *China Clipper,* took off from Port Washington and headed out over the Atlantic to make the first scheduled passenger flight; the big boat carried twenty-two passengers.

Soon all six of the new clippers were in Pan American service—the *Honolulu* and *California* in the Pacific and the *Yankee, Atlantic, Dixie,* and *American* in the Atlantic. The three 314As that went to BOAC entered Atlantic service also, linking Poole, England with Baltimore; later another route—a wartime expediency—was run between Lisbon and Portugal. The *Pacific, Anzac,* and *Capetown* clippers went to Pan

The Honolulu Clipper, *after tests fitted with twin rudders after the original single rudder had proved in tests to be inadequate. (Boeing Company)*

American's Pacific Division. Like the Martins before them, the advent of the Boeing clippers was an event of great interest to the man in the street. They were much written about, photographed and, most importantly, performed dependably and were soon making the ocean flights as a matter of course. But their advent, unfortunately, coincided with the coming of the Second World War.

The beautiful aircraft had barely begun scheduled operations when the political tragedies of war forced route changes, disrupted schedules, shunted the big boats off to war and, in time, brought about those conditions that made the flying clippers obsolescent.

It was as if, like their human masters, the flying boats were caught up in untoward and unexpected events. As has been related, the Martin *Philippine Clipper* was caught at Wake Island, and shot up there though not seriously, when the Japanese ignited the war in the Pacific. Likewise two of the Pacific Boeings, the *Anzac* and *Pacific Clippers,* were overtaken by events. The *Anzac* was en route to Singapore from Hawaii when word came of the Japanese attack. Captain H. Lanier Turner turned around, avoided Honolulu by landing at Hilo, Hawaii—the most southeastern island of the group and about as far away from Pearl Harbor, then smoldering, as he could get. Once the passengers were safely ashore, Turner took off and headed for San Francisco—and a flying career in the U. S. Army.

The *Pacific Clipper,* captained by Robert Ford, had just completed its San Francisco to Auckland, New Zealand, run when the war came. Rather than risk the loss of the crew and its plane flying through what might easily have become enemy territory, the War Department ordered Ford to take the long way home. Instead of returning to California over the Pacific, the *Pacific*

Clipper proceeded westward to Australia, India, Arabia, central Africa, and South America and then up to New York where, after flying some 34,500 miles, it landed on January 6, 1942. By the time of the landing the *Pacific* had already been inducted into the U. S. Navy. Except for the breadth of the United States the plane had flown around the world.

This was, in fact, accomplished by the *Anzac Clipper* with Captain William M. Masland in command. The 314, designated then by the Army as a C-98, was to have picked up President Roosevelt at Casablanca to fly him, Churchill, and Stalin to Australia for a conference there with China's Chiang Kai-shek. At the last minute the Australian conference was canceled —"because the Japanese got word of it," according to Captain Masland—but he continued with the original flight plan, taking along with him General Albert S. Wedemeyer and his staff for delivery in Australia. Masland then continued on until he had circled the earth before landing at New York. The *Anzac Clipper* had logged a total of 36,728 miles and was in fact the first airliner intended for commercial use to accomplish this (excepting the *Graf Zeppelin,* of course). In this way the clippers blazed new routes that brought about their own end.

The *Honolulu Clipper,* with the Navy's permission, remained in Pan American operation in the Pacific. The *Yankee, Pacific, Dixie,* and *Atlantic Clippers,* like the *Honolulu Clipper,* had been sold to the Navy, but only the *Pacific Clipper* was actually used by them. The stipulation was that the others would be diverted to military use should the need ever arise. Meanwhile, they were employed in carrying passengers, many of them military, and important war materials to far-flung corners of the world.

The Army took over the *American, Captetown, Anzac,* and *California Clippers,*

Model 314, now fitted with its final triple rudder, flies in company with another famous Boeing aircraft, the B-17C. (Boeing Company)

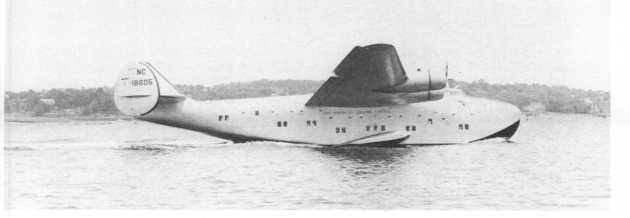

The Dixie Clipper, *the Boeing flying boat that inaugurated Pan American's first transatlantic passenger service in June 1939. (Pan American)*

California Clipper *awaiting its launching for service in Pan American's Pacific Division. (Boeing Company)*

The Boeing clippers in port awaiting wartime disposition: at left, the bow of the Anzac *(which flew 'round the world when the war struck); on the right, the* American, *which was used by the U. S. Army during the war. The rear clipper's identity was not recorded. (Boeing Company)*

which were active in similar wartime activities. They were manned by Pan American crews and, while engaged in warlike missions, were not technically combat aircraft. They were not armed, nor could they carry bombs: only men and supplies. Their crews were not inducted into the Army or the Navy, but the planes were.

The 314s carried many important passengers: Franklin D. Roosevelt was transported to the Casablanca Conference in January 1943, in the *Dixie Clipper,* an event marked also by the celebration of his sixty-first birthday en route. The plane

was under the command of Captain Howard M. Cone. Harry Hopkins, a special assistant to the President—although uneasy about the whole idea of flying—noted the effect of the flight upon his chief. "I sat with him," Hopkins wrote in his diary, "strapped in, as the plane rose from the water—and he acted like a sixteen-year-old, for he has done no flying since he was President. The trip was smooth, the President happy and interested."

The clippers were captained and piloted by some of the finest airmen ever to fly, but it was undoubtedly BOAC's *Berwick*

President Roosevelt (with hat, center) and party boarding the Dixie *for the flight to Casablanca. (Navy Department, National Archives)*

Boeing clipper in war paint: this is the Capetown, *first of the 314s to see war service and the last completed Boeing flying boat. This plane was renamed the* Bermuda Sky Queen *after the war. (Boeing Company)*

that could have boasted of the most distinguished pilot of all. This occurred actually in the earlier weeks of the war—a year before Casablanca. The "Arcadia" meeting had been held at Washington, during which Roosevelt and Britain's Winston Churchill had discussed certain strategies, namely that despite the fact that the Japanese were a threat in the Pacific, the better action would be to concentrate on "Hitler first." Following the meetings Churchill was scheduled to be flown from Norfolk, Virginia to Bermuda, where he would board a ship, the *Duke of York,* with its destroyer escort for the return trip to England in the U-boat-infested waters of the Atlantic.

"I traveled in an enormous Boeing flying-boat," he later wrote, "which made a most favorable impression on me. . . . I took the controls for a bit, to feel this ponderous machine of thirty tons or more in the air. I got more and more attached to the flying-boat."

So attached did he become that Churchill spoke with Captain J. C. Kelly Rogers to learn if the flying boat was capable of crossing the Atlantic. Rogers' eyes lit up, and he assured the Prime Minister that it was indeed possible. Churchill found some-

thing grand in the idea, but when he discussed it with his aides, Chief of Air Staff, Air Chief Marshal Sir Charles Portal and First Sea Lord, Admiral of the Fleet Sir Dudley Pound, they disapproved. They argued of the risk, and Churchill countered with, "What about the U-boats you have been pointing out to me?" No less than twenty German submarines were already charted in their homeward path by sea.

After discussions with Rogers the two men were assured of the plane's capabilities, but there was still hesitancy. Then Churchill promised that they, too, would make the flight. This made the difference, and so far as the Chief of Air Staff and First Sea Lord were concerned, everything was fine. Only Churchill's personal aide, Commander C. R. "Tommy" Thompson, R.N., was disappointed when it was learned that with a full contingent of Very Important Persons and cartons of papers with war plans and a heavy load of fuel, there was no room for him. Thompson went so far as try to change jobs with one of the stewards, offering to do his chores of washing up, but Captain Rogers was firm and Thompson was left at the dock when Churchill and party boarded a launch at Bermuda to continue on to England by air.

The Berwick *under construction, one of three that Pan American released for use by BOAC. This plane was the one that Winston Churchill piloted. (Boeing Company)*

Winston Churchill at the controls of the Berwick, *with Captain Kelly Rogers looking on. (BOAC Photo)*

Although heavily loaded, the plane took off from the harbor, clearing a reef and the hills surrounding it with ease. The night before, Churchill confessed, "I felt rather frightened. I thought of the ocean spaces, and that we should never be within a thousand miles of land until we approached the British Isles."

But once the *Berwick* had become airborne, Churchill relaxed and thoroughly enjoyed the flight—"I had always regarded an Atlantic flight with awe." He enjoyed the luxury of the craft and its smooth flight characteristics; he had been assigned the peacetime bridal suite in the stern of the plane with its wide berth and windows on either side. He was impressed with the size, too, for it was a walk of thirty or forty feet to the dining room, "where nothing was lacking in food or drink."

Ever curious, Churchill explored the great plane and clambered up to the flight deck where Rogers explained the workings of the various instruments in the cockpit as well as the function of the rubber de-icer boots on the wings and tail surfaces to splinter away the ice that may have formed. Completely at ease—"we were in sure hands" —Churchill retired to the bridal suite "and slept soundly for several hours."

Upon rising the next morning, just before dawn, he made his way to the bridge and found all was not absolutely right. The Atlantic had clouded over during the night; also, they appeared to be off course. The flight through the misty night had made star sighting impossible. They were supposedly on an approach to the British Isles from the southwest, but they could not discern any glimpse of the Scilly Islands through the occasional break in the clouds. It was obvious that they had strayed during the blind flying in the night. After a conference between Portal and Rogers it was decided they would make a turn and head directly north (unknown to Churchill, at the time, another six minutes of flying would have brought them over Brest, France, the nest of German submarines and a hotbed of anti-aircraft guns).

Even so, they were not out of trouble, though now on the correct bearing. Now coming in directly from the south, they had become an Unidentified Aircraft. Picked up by a radar station in Kent as a possible lone bomber headed in from Brest, the *Berwick* became the quarry of a half dozen Fighter Command Hurricanes.

According to Churchill they "were ordered to shoot us down. However, they failed in their mission." Before the Hurricanes intercepted the *Berwick* Captain Rogers brought the big boat down nicely at Plymouth Harbor, saying, "I never felt so relieved in my life. . . ." Although Churchill, as always, enjoyed the proximity of hazard, it was unlikely that the Hurricane pilots would have shot them down, unless their aircraft recognition was terribly off. No German plane remotely resembled the Boeing 314. But had they continued on toward Brest the tale might have had a sad ending. The "Formal Naval Person" characteristically delighted in the entire exploit—and he may very well have been the only head of government to pilot one of the last of the clippers.

The clippers served well in the war, although their chores were generally supplanted by the newer landplanes. Although both surviving Martin clippers were lost during the war, only one of the Boeings suffered such a fate.

This was the *Yankee Clipper,* which had accumulated so many "firsts" to its credit in the first historic days of the 314's advent. When war came, the *Yankee,* although officially a Navy plane, continued making its flights over the Atlantic to Lisbon and Southampton. It was on one of these flights, on February 22, 1943, that the *Yankee,* having crossed the Atlantic, was coming in to land on the Tagus River, near Lisbon, Portugal. It was early evening, and as the plane turned to port in the landing approach the left wingtip brushed the water. In a moment the plane splashed violently into the river, broke up, and within ten minutes sank under the freezing surface of the Tagus. Of the thirty-nine passengers aboard, twenty-four were killed. Among the fifteen survivors, most of whom had spilled out of the torn aircraft, was singer Jane Froman, who was traveling with a USO troupe that was on tour entertaining troops. In her company, another vocalist, Tamara (who had achieved a kind of fame by introducing "Smoke Gets in Your Eyes" in the Jerome Kern musical, *Roberta*) did not survive the crash. Miss Froman, who had suffered severe injuries, was kept afloat by another

Bristol, *the Boeing flying boat in British wartime dress in service for BOAC. (Boeing Company)*

The historic Yankee Clipper *during its period of "first" accumulations before the Second World War. (Pan American)*

A portion of the wing of the Yankee *being salvaged from the Tagus River, February 1943. (Boeing Company)*

A "hazard to navigation," the Honolulu *derelict in the Pacific shortly before being sunk by Navy gunfire. (Boeing Company)*

of the fifteen survivors, Fourth Officer John C. Burns, whom she subsequently married. When it crashed the *Yankee Clipper* had logged over a million miles and 240 safe crossings of the Atlantic. It was the only one of the B314s to be lost in a flying accident, one that could obviously be attributed to "pilot error."

Eventually all of the Army C-98s were turned over to the Navy; the Air Force, which had actually built up a world-wide airway system, turned to the more economical, wider-ranging, faster, greater payload carriers such as the Douglas C-54 (the civilian DC-4) and the Lockheed C-69 (the Constellation), both landplanes. The handwriting, as far as the flying boat was concerned, was written in the wind.

Pan American even did not repurchase the clippers when the Navy was ready to release them, for Pan American, too, had already begun to convert to landplanes. Thus were the *American, Atlantic,* and *Dixie* placed in drydock at the Naval Air Station at San Diego and put up for sale by the War Assets Administration. By this time, early in 1946, Pan American had flown its last clipper flight—this was on April 8, 1946, when the *American Clipper* came into San Francisco from Honolulu; it eventually joined the other three retirees at San Diego—as did, in short time, the *California* and *Anzac.* The three British

B314s eventually ended up in similar retirement at Baltimore.

Only the *Honolulu Clipper,* the first of the Boeing clipper line, escaped that fate— but that proved to be no triumph. Just before Pan American closed out its clipper service to the Pacific, the *Honolulu,* en route from Honolulu to San Francisco, developed engine trouble. On November 3, 1945, the plane made a smooth landing in the Pacific. Soon the Navy sped the carrier *Manila Bay* to the rescue, and all twenty-three passengers and crew were safely taken aboard. The undamaged clipper was then taken in tow by the seaplane tender *San Pablo.* For five days the unusual procession headed landward and then the *Honolulu Clipper* rode down the crest of a wave and smashed into the side of the *San Pablo.* With bow crushed and starboard wingtip sheared away, it was obvious that the plane would never fly again without extensive repairs.

Declared a "hazard to navigation," the *Honolulu Clipper* became the target of U. S. Navy guns. No less than thirteen hundred rounds of 20 mm gunfire were consumed in sending the great plane to the bottom of the Pacific.

After Pan American and BOAC retired the surviving clippers, some were actually put into flying shape again by new airlines that popped up after the war. One of them was the short-lived Universal Airlines, which began its nonscheduled clipper operations by taking the wind-damaged *Pacific Clipper* apart for replacement parts for use on the other ships. This too was the immediate fate of the *Atlantic Clipper* when yet another new, nonscheduled airline, followed Universal; this was American-International Airways.

The former *Capetown* was reconditioned and back flying again as the *Bermuda Sky Queen*. On October 2, 1947, it was flown to England and chartered by Air Liason Limited of London, to bring sixty-two British delegates to the United States for a United Nations meeting. On the return flight, bucking the curse of the west-to-east route, strong headwinds, the *Capetown/ Bermuda Sky Queen* was forced to land in the choppy Atlantic because of fuel shortage. In the rough waters it took the U. S. Coast Guard a full twenty-four hours before the passengers and crew could be taken off the floundering plane.

A recapitulation of the *Honolulu Clipper*'s accident ensued. When the Coast Guard ship, the *Bibb,* approached to attach a tow line, a wave tossed the flying boat into the *Bibb,* stoving in the nose of the *Sky Queen.* The *Bibb*'s captain, Charles Martin then ordered what had become a derelict to be sunk by gunfire. Blazing, the plane sank into the sea.

Soon after, American-International Airways sank also; the seven remaining B314s were bought by yet another hopeful, World Airways. These were the four ex-Pan American *American, Anzac, California,* and *Dixie Clippers* and the *Bangor, Berwick,* and *Bristol.* These survivors numbered among them the flying boats that had flown with history—Roosevelt's *Dixie* and Churchill's *Berwick.* After using up the *Dixie*—so much for history—and the *California* for parts, World employed the boats to carry cargo and for charter flights along the eastern seacoast of the United States and to the

Bermuda Sky Queen *after colliding with the* Bibb. *(National Archives)*

Bermuda Sky Queen *aflame in the Atlantic after being fired upon by the Coast Guard ship* Bibb. *(National Archives)*

End of the last flight by a Boeing clipper, and the last of any Pan American flying boat: the American *in San Francisco Harbor after coming in from Honolulu, April 8, 1946. Disconsolate ground crewman "Shorty" Greenough is silently expressive in the foreground. (Pan American)*

Caribbean. They were not inexpensive craft to operate, and World had to contend with more economically sufficient rivals; by 1949 World was in financial trouble and sold out to new management. Once again the clippers were beached, awaiting a new call to service. But none came, and by 1951 all of the B314s had been scrapped except the *Bristol,* which was moored at Baltimore. Finally it was sold to a minister who called himself "Master X," who intended to use the plane to fly to Russia to talk peace with Stalin. But this was not to be. Baltimore Harbor was hit by a sudden storm, "late in 1951 or early in 1952," according to John F. R. Scott, Jr., who was stationed at Friendship International Airport near Baltimore, and the *Bristol* was blown loose of its moorings, struck something, and sank. It was later raised out of the mud and, like so many of the other 314s, scrapped. It was the very last of the line.

End of an era: A new DC-4 takes off from New York's LaGuardia Airport, passing over clipper anchored in Bowery Bay, bringing an end to the days of the flying clippers (although Pan American continued naming their landplanes clippers). (Pan American Airways)

10: Warwings

The idea that a flying boat could be operated as an effective military aircraft dates back to before the First World War. The U. S. Navy had encouraged Glenn Curtiss in his rise-off-water experiments (although reluctantly because of the inborn resistance of traditionalists to flying machines) and was rewarded with the first truly successful seaplane in 1911. Within a year Curtiss produced a fine flying boat. By 1913 the U. S. Signal Corps had purchased the Burgess Model I "Coast Defense Hydro" (sometimes called the Burgess-Wright). It had been preceded by the Model H, already mentioned. But Burgess and Wright came to a parting, and soon after, the former made an arrange-

ment with an English soldier-designer, John William Dunne. Determined to produce an extremely stable aircraft, Dunne came up with a very striking design—a tailless biplane with a marked sweepback of the wings. The plane proved to be what Dunne had hoped for and then Burgess, his agreement with Wright over, arrived to arrange for a Burgess variant of the plane. This became the Burgess-Dunne. One of the features was a float, the trademark, practically, of Burgess aircraft. Although Dunne worried about the efficiency of this modification, the floatplane proved as air- and seaworthy as the landplane. Burgess succeeded in selling the design to the U. S.

Navy, the U. S. Signal Corps, and to the Canadian government. What was hoped would prove to be a more refined version of the Burgess-Dunne was produced for the Navy some time in 1915, but did not prove out. More sleek than the earlier models and with less of a wingspan, the plane exhibited certain unfortunate flight characteristics and was not used. Later models, less streamlined and with a longer, boxy, float, looked more gawky; but they performed better.

When war came to Europe the Curtiss proved an influential design, particularly through the Porte/Felixstowes, although several British and French designs already existed. When the United States was drawn into the war, the Navy turned to Curtiss for its flying seacraft. The design evolved through the years of war, and one of the most successful was the HS-2L of 1918, of which more than a thousand were produced. Most of these were built by Curtiss, but others were turned out of the factories of L. W. F. Engineering, Standard, Gallaudet —where are they now?—as well as Boeing and Loughead (later simplified to Lockheed). The experience introduced Boeing and Lockheed to the flying boat, which each pursued independently, Boeing with its B-1 and Lockheed (more correctly still Loughead in 1918) with its F-1.

Allen and Malcolm Loughead designed the F-1 with the help of an architectural draftsman, John K. Northrop, and built it in a garage near the Santa Barbara waterfront. First flown on March 28, 1918, the F-1 was intended as a naval patrol boat, but of course came too late in the war. It was powered by two Hall-Scott engines (of the Hall-Scott Motor Car Company) and was hailed as the largest seaplane (the upper wing was seventy-four feet) "ever constructed on the Pacific Coast," a curious distinction. This was brought out in an advertisement in which Hall-Scott acknowledged an achievement of the F-1: "On April 12 [1918], the Loughead Seaplane F-1 established a new American duration record. This seaplane, the largest ever constructed on the Pacific Coast, made the trip with a pilot and three passengers, from Santa Barbara to San Diego, a distance of 211 miles, in 181 minutes. The F-1 is designed for aerial patrol and is motored by two Six-Cylinder *Hall-Scott* A-5 150 *h.p.* Airplane Engines."

The primary function of the flying boats was, as noted in the advertisement, aerial patrol. Reconnaissance over coastal waters was the initial job of the land-based boats, with the spotting of approaching enemy ships of especial importance; with the introduction by the Germans of unrestricted submarine warfare, the flying boats were confronted with a new kind of menace. Spotting the U-boats and destroying them transformed the large, rather clumsy aircraft into offensive weapons, and soon they were weighed down with machine guns, torpedoes, and bombs.

Although all the warring powers employed aircraft during the 1914–18 war, it was not, in fact, a war in which aircraft contributed much more than a touch of romance. Fighting in the air could be deadly, but the First World War was a ground war,

A few steps in the post-Curtiss evolution of the military seaplane. Opposite page: 1, the Burgess Model I Coast Defense Hydro employed by the U. S. Signal Corps in the Philippines in 1914; 2, the Navy's Burgess-Dunne, which turned out to be a reject, though not the end of the line for this design; 3, a Loughhead (later Lockheed)-built HS-2L, a Curtiss-designed flying boat of 1918—the "L" indicated that it was powered by a Liberty engine; 4, a Dornier flying boat ca. 1914–15. 5, a curious Caproni Triplane on floats and with a twin fuselage; 6, a one-place Macchi M-7, a speedy design; an M-8 won the 1921 Schneider Trophy and, 7, a Lockheed F-1 of 1918, which was completed too late for use in the war—it was later converted for use in charter service. (U. S. Air Force/Lockheed)

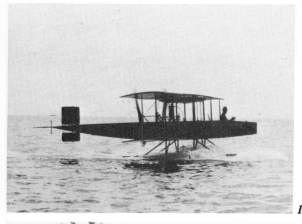

1

2

3

4

5

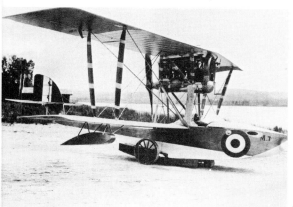

6

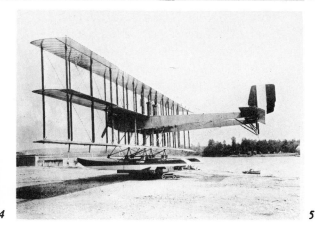

7

commanded by traditional ground commanders who had little use for the noisy, flimsy flying machines. Most aerial action was devoted to duels between individual fighter planes—and later between large formations—or bombing. The flying boats, confined to the sea, confronted the submarine or an occasional Zeppelin. They proved themselves to be reasonably effective, although had they been attacked by the faster, more nimble fighters they would not have fared too well. They were not incapable of self-protection, for many of the boats bristled with gun positions—from four to seven. Late in the war—June 1918—a formation of three Felixstowes and a Curtiss H-12 ran into an enemy formation of more than a dozen Brandenburg seaplanes. Since the latter were burdened by floats, it made the performances of the contenders somewhat equal—for none of the aircraft was very speedy. In the fighting that followed the Curtiss was shot down; a Felixstowe was forced down, but after repairs took off to return to its base. However, six of the German planes were lost.

It was during the war that Germany's Dornier first began considering the flying boat, adding such refinements as metal construction, multimotors, and a dash of giantism. These would be developed after the war in the Wals, the Do-X, and later Dornier designs that flourished between the wars. France's concentration was on the development of fighters, but other powers, such as Italy, explored the idea of the flying boat, ranging from small to large—from the tiny Macchi boat to the gigantic Caproni Triplane. The former led to an entire line of great Italian seaplanes—boats and floatplanes—among them the winners of the Schneider races, when these were re-established again after the war.

The between-the-wars period was generally given over to floundering. Germany was crippled (temporarily) insofar as the production of any kind of aircraft was concerned. As for the three major powers, the victors, France, Britain, and the United States, all had been caught by the Armistice with a surplus of warplanes and a surfeit of war. At least Germany, France, and Britain began to re-enter early onto the aviation lists by the formation of commercial airlines. The United States, as is known, lagged behind.

This was even more evident in military aviation, despite the admonitions of the vociferous Brigadier General William Mitchell. As one of the few American military men who had served in France and who exhibited a grasp of the implications of air power, Mitchell was an advocate of a separate air force. But this did not sit well with his own Army nor with the more conservative Navy. In time Mitchell's most dangerous contender was the U. S. Navy—which, eventually, got him. He was court-martialed for making uncomplimentary remarks in public about the Navy.

Consequently U.S. naval aviation peacetime development was conservative. There was little public money, for one thing—and less public support, for another. No one, during the twenties, wished to hear anything about weapons of war. The "war to end wars" had been fought. In the Army, however, Mitchell's fight and subsequent quasi-martyrdom had stirred up the younger theoreticians, who began thinking in terms of the heavy bomber—and more surreptitiously, a separate air arm. The Navy thinkers were happy as they were. They played with their boats and maintained a small aerial unit tucked in among the battleships, destroyers, and cruisers. It was admitted that aircraft, indeed, did have a fleet function ("the eyes of the Fleet"), but must not be permitted to get out of hand or, to mix metaphors, to let the tail wag the dog.

While the Navy indulged a kind of aerial tokenism, not all Navy men were antiaircraft, to coin a phrase; but the top brass was,

Loening amphibian of the U.S. peacetime Navy (also of the Army); this plane was a classic of the time, although hardly a thing of joy and a beauty forever. (Navy Department, National Archives)

Navy Vought O2U Corsair floatplanes on their catapults sometime in the latter twenties. These planes were supposed to scout for lurking enemy ships, after which their home ships would move in to attack in a surface-to-surface engagement. (Historical Collection, Title Insurance and Trust Company, San Diego)

generally (they seemed also to favor airships, no doubt because they so much resembled flying battleships). However, the Navy's air branch did not go entirely under, and there was a small and steady trickle of amphibians, carrier-based fighters, seaplanes, and flying boats. These ushered in the colorful, but parsimonious, era of the gawky but wonderful Loening amphibian, the conception of a young designer, Grover Loening. The Loening was used by both the U. S. Navy for various tasks and by the U. S. Army (for a good-will tour of Central and South America in the latter twenties). It was the era, too, of such carrier-based craft as the early Vought Corsair and the little Boeing FBs.

A swarm of Boeing F4B fighters on the flight deck of the Langley, *the first U.S. carrier (converted from collier* Jupiter). *(Boeing Company)*

But the Navy's airmen were not above attracting attention to themselves in order to encourage public interest and congressional funding. The Navy, like the Army Air Corps, participated in history-making flights and entered various speed and endurance competitions—all to advance aviation as well as the Navy's image. The flight of the NC-4 had done much along these lines, although the Army followed that with its round-the-world flight. The next year, 1925, the Navy

was ready with its PN-9, a product of the Naval Aircraft Factory at Philadelphia.

Although the Navy had no intention of duplicating the Army's world flight, the wide Pacific seemed a greater challenge than the Atlantic. So when an Australian scientist, Dr. David Stead, made the suggestion that a flight from, say, Honolulu to Australia would prove the point for any future Pacific air travel by civil airlines, the chief of the Navy's Bureau of Aeronautics, Rear Admiral W. A. Moffett, liked the idea and contributed his own variations. The flight should begin, he believed, at San Francisco, employing the Douglas SDW floatplane for the job. Although it did not have the range, it did have twin floats, and a system of refueling was devised all along the proposed route. But when the PN-9 was ready, this plan was dropped in favor of two PNs and a Boeing flying boat making a flight from San Francisco to Honolulu, nonstop. One PN and the Boeing were eliminated early in the flight, which began on August 31, 1925. The craft, under Commander John Rodgers (who held the No. 2 position in the list of naval aviators) proceeded on its way across the Pacific.

Twenty-five hours later, about 450 miles from Honolulu, the plane ran out of fuel. Rodgers had time to set it down safely in the water, but for some reason the plane's radio went out and, despite the presence of many ships in the general area, there was no means of communication between the plane and ships.

Rodgers had no other recourse except, as had been the fate of the NC-3, to head for safety over the waves. The PN-9 was one of the first of the flying boats with a metal hull, and it proved seaworthy during the ordeal that followed for Rodgers and his crew of four. For nine days they bounced over the Pacific, using a sail fashioned of fabric torn from the wings, without so much as a word of their fate being known to the

The Naval Aircraft Factory PN-9, none the worse for wear, after flying some eighteen hundred miles by air and sailing 450 miles on the surface of the Pacific. This photo was taken over Oahu after the flight and nine days at sea—plus a little repair work to the wings. Length of fuselage was forty-nine feet, and wingspan, nearly seventy-three feet. (Smithsonian Institution, National Air and Space Museum)

world. They were, in fact, presumed lost, a point of which the angry Mitchell would make much.

It was the submarine *R-4* that spotted the downed plane off the island of Kauia, and soon men and aircraft were safe in port. Although their flight had failed, the distance covered by the PN-9 before it came down (1841 miles) was a record for a seaplane. And, although the wings had suffered, the metal hull had stood the test, and within days the refurbished PN-9 was flying again over Hawaii.

This was the time also of the first of the large Navy flying boats, the Consolidated XPY-1, which when it was not ordered by the Navy (having chosen the lower-bidding Martin's version), became the *Commodore* of Trippe's Caribbean epoch. Martin con-

tinued producing flying boats until Consolidated returned in 1932 with the P2Y-1, which was similar in configuration to the XPY-1 but with the addition of a stubby lower wing, converting it into a sesquiplane. Although incapable of high speeds, the boats were capable of flying great distances. Their wings spanned a hundred feet and their sleek fuselages measured nearly sixty-two feet. Top speed of the craft was about 125 miles an hour, and the range approached two thousand miles.

The new variant of the flying boat not only proved itself soon after it was introduced by Consolidated—it was also instrumental in helping to keep the company solvent during the Depression. The first production models of the P2Y-1 were delivered to Patrol Squadron 10 (VP-10), stationed at Norfolk, Virginia, in 1933. Under its commander, Lieutenant Commander Knefler McGinnis, the squadron began flying six-plane patrols in formation. As a curtain raiser the squadron made a nonstop flight from Norfolk to Coco Solo, Panama, a distance of 2059 miles. They made the flight in twenty-five hours, nineteen minutes, bettering Balbo's distance flight from Rome to Rio in the Savoia Marchettis two years before.

Early after the turn of the following year the six P2Ys winged north westward in three long hops, arriving in San Francisco in readiness for a Pacific crossing. This was a stretch of twenty-four hundred miles of open sea, which had never been flown by a formation before—although it had been done successfully in a single plane by two Army pilots, Lieutenants Lester Maitland and Albert Hegenberger in 1927.

"The squadron took off from San Francisco Bay the afternoon of January 10 [1934]," a historian later wrote in *Convariety,* the house organ for General Dynamics (which eventually absorbed Consolidated). "The boats were heavy with 1750 gallons of fuel each, and there was almost no breeze."

Commander McGinnis held a less matter-of-fact view: "They chose the worst month of the year. There were only two or three days in January favorable for a flight of that kind." Since they did not have the engine power then, it was impossible to fly above the poor weather they encountered at cruising altitude. Instead, McGinnis brought the planes under the clouds; at times, even at night, the little formation flew within only a few hundred feet of the Pacific.

Once off the water they "headed west through the Golden Gate (where workmen building the new suspension bridge stopped to watch) at 2:22 P.M. McGinnis and his copilot, Commander Marc A. Mitscher, led the boats through a long night of almost blind flying in thick overcast.

Consolidated P2Y-1, which had evolved from the old Commodore; it was one of the first successful large flying boats of the early thirties. (Historical Collection, Title Insurance and Trust Company, San Diego)

"Visibility improved after dawn, and at noon the formation swept past Diamond Head, crossed over Honolulu at 1000 feet, and flew on to Pearl Harbor. . . . The lead boat alighted off Ford Island at 12:29 P.M. and the last at 12:37. Elapsed time was twenty-four hours, fifty-six minutes for a distance of 2408 miles." There was excitement in Honolulu, in Washington (President Roosevelt sent his congratulations, calling the flight "the greatest undertaking of its kind in the history of aviation"), and in Rome (where Balbo had been eclipsed a second time as far as distance was concerned—although his formation had been much larger and had flown a greater accumulated mileage the previous year); from Rome, too, came the prediction that the flight of the P2Ys was a demonstration of the future potential of aircraft in war.

An ominous note was heard also from Tokyo, where a Japanese naval officer observed that each new step forward in aviation gave man additional power. "It remains to be seen," he concluded, "whether these powers will be used beneficially or destructively."

For the time being, constructively—for within a year Pan American would initiate its Pacific survey flights in preparation for mail and passenger service to the Orient.

The P2Y-1, having proved itself (two

dozen were ordered by the Navy), led to refinements and even better performance. The major changes were connected with the engines. Instead of dangling under the wing, as on the P2Y-1s, they were raised and faired into the leading edge of the wing. In addition, the engine was cowled in the more efficient NACA cowling, which had been developed by Frederick E. Weick of the National Advisory Committee for Aeronautics. These comparatively small modifications increased speed, range—and orders, for the Navy ordered twenty-three of the P2Y-3s. Foreign sales of the P2Ys helped sustain Consolidated: six were purchased by Argentina and one each by Colombia and Japan. The same design eventually appeared in Japan as the Navy Type 99 (H5Y1) medium flying boat (American code name "Cherry"), although in its Japanese variant (perhaps because of being underpowered) it proved unsuccessful. Only six were built and none actually saw war service.

Meanwhile, off the other ocean, Britain too was devoting some thought to the development of larger, aggressive flying boats. At around the same time as Consolidated's P2Y-3 had emerged, the Blackburn *Perth* had made its debut. Based on the *Iris* of 1926, the *Perth* of 1933 was regarded as a most formidable seaplane. Powered by three Rolls-Royce Buzzards, it had a wingspan of ninety-seven feet (as did the later models—or Marks—of the *Iris*), a fuselage seventy feet long, and could remain aloft for six hours (i.e., it had a range of fifteen hundred miles), and had a top speed of 132 miles an hour. Of all-metal construction, the *Perth* was fabric-covered except for the hull, which was plated with Alclad.

The *Perth* was the largest flying boat then in service with the RAF. Its armament was particularly impressive. Besides carrying a bombload of a ton, it also carried three Lewis machine guns and, jutting from its nose, a 37-mm gun capable of firing one hundred 1½-pound shells a minute. In its time the *Perth* was regarded as an "aerial battleship," and it was, but its time proved brief. By 1937 it was seeing its final days of service with No. 204 Squadron. Short

The P2Y-3 with engines faired into the wing, an improvement over the P2Y-1, whose engines dangled under the wing, causing drag. (Navy Department National Archives)

The Blackburn Perth *makes a bombing run over the Humber, on England's east coast, during its trials in October 1933. (U. S. Air Force)*

Singapores replaced the *Perth,* as did a newer Short design—the Sunderland—which is getting slightly ahead of the story. The scene shifts again to the United States.

Having displaced Martin in the Navy's affections (temporarily and in the flying boat category) Consolidated continued to modify their flying boat, hoping for continued Navy procurements. A great step was taken in the summer of 1935 when the firm packed its belongings (in seventy-one freight cars), as many of its employees who agreed to move, and left Buffalo, New York and headed westward for San Diego, California. It had been a move that had been contemplated for some time and was one primarily dictated by the weather. With its influx of seaplane orders Consolidated hoped to have access to flying conditions and to harbor facilities without the problems of snow, sleet, and the need to chop the ice in order to launch a seaplane.

The business end of the Perth, *showing the .37-mm gun installation in the nose; boat was powered by three Rolls-Royce Buzzards and could cruise for about six hours. Top speed was about 130 miles an hour. (U. S. Air Force)*

Of the seventy-one cars, twenty-one were devoted to carrying household goods of the moving employees. Not all, however, went west: Lawrence D. Bell, then vice president and general manager of Consolidated, chose to remain behind to form his own company, and several Consolidated employees stayed on with him. To many who followed the company, the West was a fairly total mystery. Howard Golem, traffic manager, drove a friend's car to San Diego and recalls, "When I started to drive from Buffalo, everyone advised me that I was going into wild country. They told me to carry extra water and fuel and once west of the Mississippi I wasn't to stop except in populated areas, because of bandits!"

Golem made it, despite the hazards of the American West circa 1935, and the new plant was opened on October 20, 1935. Founder and President Reuben Fleet in his opening-day address noted that "For 12½ years we have striven for this day. It marks the culmination of a dream for a factory of our own in a city of our own choice." He found good words to say about San Diego, its people, its community, and even its air. "For flying it seems to have a 'body' found nowhere else."

He spoke of the need for more powerful aircraft engines that would make it possible "to build gigantic flying boats that will carry a hundred passengers to Honolulu or across the Atlantic in twelve hours." He pointed out that on that opening day Consolidated's employees numbered 874, but that within a year he predicted the total would reach three thousand. This was no idle guess, for Fleet was aware of a Navy contract that had arrived the previous June, in the middle of the confusion of moving the company, for sixty of the latest in the flying boat series, the XP3Y-1.

This was chief engineer I. M. Laddon's newest brainchild. The prototype had been ordered in October of 1933; the new plane was available for flight tests by March 1935.

A PBY taxies into the water for a test run—a new step in the evolution of Consolidated's flying boat design. (General Dynamics, Convair Division)

The latest variation on the P2Y introduced some innovations. The sesquiplanes had been eliminated, and with them a good deal of the struts; the twin-and-a-half rudder had been replaced with a generous swooping tail. As reported in the company paper, "The flying boat was a broadwinged monoplane, having the cleanest lines of any seaplane yet designed. A single pair of lift struts connected fuselage to wing on each side, and the tail assembly showed no external braces. Until now, fixed wing floats had increased the parasitic drag of all seaplanes. Laddon designed a retracting float that folded into place as an outer tip of the wing. Thus, the float actually increased lift by a small amount.

"Exhaust gases were utilized for the first time in a thermal de-icing system. Engine heat, previously wasted, was deflected through a system of internal ducts to warm the leading edges of wing and empennage. Further, the airplane employed the first integral wing tanks. Instead of building separate gasoline cells, Laddon sealed off internal sections of the wings as reservoirs. The weight saving was calculated as a half pound per gallon of fuel capacity—a substantial addition to payload."

The first production model of this aircraft —the first of the sixty ordered by the Navy —was launched on October 5, 1936, in Coronado Bay, near the spot where Glenn Curtiss had lifted his hydroplane off the water a quarter of a century earlier. The new Consolidated boat was, of course, the first of the PBYs, the Catalinas, as they were named by the British. The Navy by this time had somewhat simplified its nomenclature, and the initials stood for Patrol-Bombing Consolidated (under the Navy's system the letter Y was assigned to Consolidated and later, when they merged, to Consolidated-Vultee).

". . . a generous swooping tail . . ." Man is dwarfed because he is standing in background on port wingtip. (Smithsonian Institution, National Air and Space Museum)

The U. S. Navy began ordering the high-performance (for their time) flying boats in batches of fifty and sixty in 1935–36, then down to thirty-three for the PBY-4 (on which the first blister side gun turrets appeared) and up to two hundred for the PBY-5 in 1939 (the first war year) to which were added, in 1941, an additional 586. More than seven hundred of the 5As (the amphibious version with a tricycle landing gear) and 225 PBY-5Bs went to Britain. The line came to an end with the PBY-6A (with an altered tail) in 1944–45 when 235 were built. All told, counting the contributions of other manufacturers, more than three thousand Catalinas (the name eventually adopted by the U. S. Navy in October 1941) were produced in the decade 1935–45. They were, in fact, the most numerous of any flying boat ever built.

The PBY-5A, first of the amphibious versions of the Catalina. (General Dynamics, Convair Division)

Not all served in warlike operations. The early Navy models were employed in making mass flights from San Diego to Pearl Harbor or the Canal Zone. One was built, in 1937, for use by Dr. Richard Archbold of New York's Museum of Natural History for an expedition to Dutch New Guinea.

This PBY, named *Guba* (a Motu word meaning "sudden storm"), became the first flying boat to cross the country when on June 24, 1937, it took off from San Diego and landed in New York seventeen hours, 3½ minutes later. But Dr. Archbold was not destined to make the flight to New Guinea just then. A Russian aviator, Sigismund Levanesky, had been lost while on an attempt to fly over the North Pole. The Soviet government bought the *Guba* from Archbold for use by polar expert Sir Hubert Wilkins in an attempt to find Levanesky and his crew. From Aklavik, Canadian Northwest Territories, a hundred miles north of the Arctic Circle, Wilkins flew the *Guba* some nineteen thousand miles for a month before giving up the hopeless search. The PBY was then returned to Russia (from where the following year an order for three export model PBYs arrived).

Archbold ordered a second *Guba* and set out from San Diego on June 2, 1938. His pilot was Russell Rogers; the copilot was Steve Barinka (who doubled as flight engineer); navigator was Lewis Yancey, radio operator was Ray Booth, and the full-time flight engineer was Gerald Brown.

PBY on the step; this is a model 5A. Large side blister was introduced on the PBY-4. (General Dynamics, Convair Division)

The Catalina in flight with wingtip floats retracted. (Boeing Company)

A double-exposed photograph demonstrating retraction of the main gear of the PBY-5A. (General Dynamics, Convair Division)

The *Guba* logged thousands of air miles in its long life; Rogers hopped the Pacific in three legs: Pearl Harbor, Wake Island, and Hollandia, New Guinea, where the expedition arrived on June 11. "During the next eleven months," a Convair historian has written, "Guba made 168 flights and carried more than 280 tons of supplies to expedition field camps in the interior. Many of the landings were made on Lake Habbema, two hundred miles inland and eleven thousand feet above sea level.

"While the New Guinea work was nearing an end, the Australian and British governments enlisted Archbold's participation in a survey of an air route across the Indian Ocean, which had never been flown.

"After installation of new engines shipped from San Diego, *Guba* left Hollandia May 12, 1939, and flew to Sydney via Port

Moresby and Townsville. From Sydney the boat flew nonstop across Australia to Port Hedlund, the jumping-off point. The survey was carried out with stops at Cocos Island, Direction Island, Diego Garcia, and Mahe. News of the boat's arrival June 21 at Mombasa, on the Kenya coast, stirred interest throughout East Africa.

"Heading homeward, *Guba* bridged Africa in two hops, letting down on Lake Victoria and on the Congo River at Coquilhatville. On June 29–30 it made an overwater flight of 3190 miles from Daker to St. Thomas in the West Indies (time: nineteen hours, thirty-three minutes). The next afternoon *Guba* landed at New York, and Archbold and his crew were whisked off to the Aviation Building at the World's Fair for an official welcome. *Guba* returned to San Diego Bay July 6, completing the first

The Guba, *first of the PBYs to be used in the Pacific. This was the Museum of Natural History's exploration aircraft flown to New Guinea and used there by the expedition headed by Dr. Richard Archbold in 1938 and was the first seaplane to fly around the world. (General Dynamics, Convair Division)*

round-the-world flight ever made by a seaplane, and the first made by any aircraft at the globe's largest diameter."

Shortly after, the *Guba* was bought by the British Purchasing Committee and went into service for BOAC in Africa; later it was used as a utility plane by Saunders-Roe and was finally turned over to the Ministry of Aircraft Production and used in northern Wales in testing flying boat moorings. After being damaged and sunk in a gale, the *Guba* was raised, all usable equipment was removed, and what remained was taken out to sea and sunk for the last time. As for its history-making globe-girdling voyage, Steve Barinka, who had served as copilot and later worked for Convair, recalled it as "a thrilling experience, but without major incident."

It had, however, been a preview of the kind of worldwide operations in which the PBY would figure during the war years. Even as the new variants were coming off the Consolidated production line, a larger craft was forming in the imagination of

Chief Engineer Laddon. Initially he had envisioned an enlarged Catalina, only powered with four engines instead of two; otherwise it would have the same swooping vertical fin and rudder and the wingtip floats. The hull was somewhat deeper at the bow, but the new plane, the XPB2Y-1, bore a decided family resemblance to the Catalina.

The prototype was ready for test in December 1937. As with the Boeing 314, it was found that the boat lacked satisfactory directional stability. More tail area was added to the plane until finally the problem was solved with a broad twin tail. Eventually the PB2Y, the Coronado (thanks to the name-conscious British), was born. The Navy did not exhibit the same interest in the Coronado as it did in the Catalina; operating a large four-engined boat was costly and complex (and the PB2Y cost three times more than the PBY). About two hundred Coronados were ordered and were used by both the United States and the British as patrol bombers and transports.

The British had, just a month before the

The XPB2Y-1, evolved out of the Catalina into the prototype of the Coronado. This early variant was fitted with auxiliary vertical rudders to overcome lateral instability, which had proved a problem in early testing of the prototype. Eventually tail surfaces evolved into the twin tails (as on the B-24) and deeper hull. (General Dynamics, Convair Division)

PB2Y Coronado in a relatively late form, the PB2Y-3R, converted into a transport. Military equipment was removed and low-altitude engines installed. In this form the Coronado could carry forty-four passengers along with the crew of five. (General Dynamics, Convair Division)

prototype Coronado had emerged, brought forth their own four-engined patrol boat—the Short S-25 Sunderland, the military version of the Empire flying boats. The first Sunderland flew in October 1937, and the first production models began appearing in April of the next year. The wingspan of the military plane was slightly less than that of the Empires: 112 feet, 9½ inches as compared to the 114 feet of the S-23. Hull configurations differed also, with the Sunderland's being somewhat more efficiently shaped for better planing and the reduction of drag. The vertical fin and rudder were also slightly different, being taller in the Sunderland. The nose of the military plane was blunter and housed a gun turret; there was also a turret in the tail.

The Sunderland, like Short's previous flying boats, was of all-metal construction, was powered by four Bristol *Pegasus* engines, and could reach a top speed of about two hundred miles an hour; cruising speed was in the 170–80 mph range. It could remain aloft for a little over thirteen hours. During its long lifetime, the Sunderland underwent various modifications and reached the end of its line with the improved Mark V, in which the Bristol engines were exchanged for

Consolidated's Model 31, an attempt at a civil transport that did not work out—at least not in its original purpose. However, as may be seen, the tail and wing surfaces eventually appeared on other Consolidated aircraft, most notably the B-24 Liberator. (General Dynamics, Convair Division)

Pratt & Whitney Twin Wasps. With the coming of peace the Sunderlands continued in service for years, and many were converted to civil aircraft such as the *Hythe* (1942), the *Seaford* (1945), the *Sandringham* (1945), and the *Solent* (1946)—the first being a conversion from the Mark III, the second from the Mark IV; the *Sandringham* resulted from a modification of one of the *Hythes* and the *Solent* from the *Seaford*. The *Solent* was, in fact, to be the last of the large British civil flying boats, which ceased operations officially on September 30, 1958.

As the Sunderland progressed through its various Marks in Britain—and went into service with the RAF Coastal Command by the spring of 1938—the development of large military flying boats continued in the United States also. Consolidated, having contributed the Catalina and Coronado, once again gave way to the incursions of Martin. In 1938 Consolidated had attempted to enter the civil transport business with its Model 31, a flying boat designed to carry fifty-two passengers over long distances in hopes of getting a contract from Pan American. But the Model 31 lost out to the Boeing 314—although not that it was a total loss. When the Air Force approached Consolidated to design a new bomber that could become the partner of the Boeing B-17 in

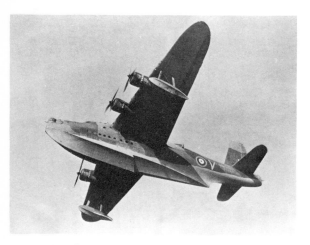

The Short Sunderland, the classic British military flying boat. Introduced in 1937, Sunderlands were used throughout the war and even later. (U. S. Air Force)

long-range bombing, the slender Davis wing, tail, and beaching gear concept (that is, a tricycle landing gear) were borrowed right off the Model 31. The result was a swift design and production job on the XB-24, the prototype of the famed Liberator.

Martin engineers and designers, meanwhile, were busy building a large model airplane. It was a quarter-scale flying model (capable of carrying one man) of a new two-engined flying boat. It was possible to study water and air characteristics of the design without the expense of first making a full-sized prototype. This testing was done during the early months of 1937, and on June 30 an order was placed by the Navy for the XPBM-1 (followed in December for twenty PBM-1s). The prototype flew for the first time on February 18, 1939.

The two Wright engines were set into the gull wings, outboard tip floats retracted into the wings, and twin rudders rested on the stern. The plane's armament was an indication of the imminence of war: a .30-caliber gun was mounted in a nose turret, and was balanced with a .50-caliber in a tail turret;

another .50 was mounted in a top turret, and another two were in the waist. The plane could carry a bombload of a half ton over a range of more than three thousand miles. Top speed was a bit over two hundred miles an hour so that the Mariner, as the boat came to be called, was a formidable craft.

With the actual coming of war the plane underwent changes: The most obvious physical ones were the installation of nonretracting floats and a dihedraled tail; armament was increased, self-sealing tanks were added, more powerful engines were installed and, eventually, when the menace of the German submarine had become acute, radar housing was added immediately behind the cockpit. Like so many other American-designed flying boats (as well as land-planes) the Mariner was used also by Britain in patrolling its waters and hunting submarines.

Simultaneously with the development of the Mariner, Martin worked on yet another, but more ambitious, flying boat project. Begun in September 1938, the new design was

The one-quarter scale model prototype of what became the Martin PBM Mariner. Various tests were run in the one-man model to develop the final production aircraft. (Martin Company)

The full-scale Mariner after some modifications, notably the dihedraled tail and, in the flight photos, the addition of a radome over the cockpit for sub-hunting. (Martin Company)

projected as a super patrol boat or transport and was completed by the summer of 1941.

"Construction statistics emphasized the size of the future Pacific Queen," Lieutenant Commander Andrew Serrell wrote in *United States Naval Institute Proceedings.* "Into the air frame was crammed 7½ miles of wiring, over three million rivets, 60,000 pounds of aluminum, almost thirteen tons of steel, 750 pounds of rubber, 650 cubic yards of fabric, 2000 pounds of copper, tin, and zinc, 300 gallons of paint—and twenty-four separate telephone outlets for internal communications.

"Out of a contract which represented an initial outlay of almost eight million dollars emerged a seaplane giant the likes of which the aviation world would not see again until her successor came along almost two decades later. From the deep recesses of the Baltimore factory's largest hangar burst into view and into print an airplane which had the cubic capacity of a fifteen-room house within the confines of her 117-foot double-decked hull, whose wingtip dimensions measured only 100 feet shorter than a regulation football field, and whose gross weight of 144,000 pounds embodied the ability of air-lifting over twenty-five tons of payload. With the unveiling of the Mars the day of the water-based transport aircraft had truly arrived."

Given the initial designation, XPB2M-1, the Mars was to have been officially flown for the first time in November of 1941. Before this could occur a fire broke out in the plane and the takeoff was delayed until the summer of the next year. By then the United States was at war. The big plane—its wing spanned two hundred feet—with a remarkable range of seven thousand miles and designed to carry bombloads of from seven to ten tons, had been produced a little too early to serve as a battle plane. A good deal had been learned during 1939–41 and the Mars, it was decided, would have required too much costly and time-consuming modification to make it a really potent warplane. So it was converted, in 1943, into a transport and designated JRM-1, the JR indicating that the Navy employed it as a utility transport. In the Naval Air Transport Service the Mars proved an impressive weight-lifter in the Pacific, particularly in Air Transport Squadron 2 (VR-2). On one flight the Mars carried 308 passengers and the crew (eleven men) in a flight from Alameda to San Diego. During the war it transported some three million pounds of freight—ranging from blood plasma to replacement parts—in the Pacific.

When war came to Europe in the late summer of 1939 all the contenders, except Poland, had tested flying boats for sea reconnaissance. France possessed several for patrolling the Atlantic and Mediterranean. The state of France's air power was not encouraging, however; its air force was, in fact, no match for the Luftwaffe.

France, of all the warring nations, could draw upon the largest array of flying boats —most of them, however, obsolete or obsolescent. The bulk of French designs dated back to the latter twenties and early thirties. The oldest operational boat was the CAMS-37, the initials standing for Chantiers Aéro-Maritimes de la Seine. These all-wood boats, which flourished in the French Navy

An idea of the size of the Mars (*two hundred foot span*) *may be gleaned from this photo of the aircraft in war paint and with more than a hundred men lined up under the wing.* (*National Air Museum, Smithsonian Institution*)

The later Mars with the single rudder: the JRM transport, around 1945. (*Navy Department, National Archives*)

The Mars on a takeoff run; it was the largest flying boat of its time, but had come a little late to be used as a combat reconnaissance plane. During the war it was an outstanding cargo transport capable of lifting heavy payloads. (*Martin Company*)

The oldest French flying boat, CAMS-37, still in use when the Second World War began. Its obsolescence is underscored by the fact that it was of wood construction; this craft, designed by Maurice Hurel, flew for the first time in 1926. (*Musée de l'Air*)

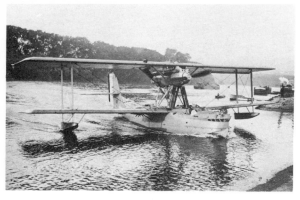

The military development of the Cargo commercial flying boat, the CAMS-55. Like the CAMS-37, these boats were also made of wood. First flown in 1929, the CAMS-55 production ended in 1935, although the plane itself remained in French Navy service throughout France's participation in the war. (Musée de l'Air)

The Loire 501, a multipurpose amphibian of the early thirties. It served as a trainer and a communications plane, and even carried mail. Wingspan was fifty-two feet, six inches; fuselage length was thirty-six feet, four inches. (Musée de l'Air)

The Potez 452, designed for operations from shipboard. First flown in 1932, the plane was equipped with a single outthrust Hispano-Suiza engine and folding wings. Span was forty-two feet, seven inches; length, thirty-three feet, six inches. (Musée de l'Air)

between the wars, were practically out of service by the time war came. In their operational days they had been either shore-based or operated from ships. By 1939 they were either used as communications craft or as trainers, although some continued being used for patrolling the French coastal waters until the summer of 1940; likewise the CAMS-55, which came a little later (1929), a variant of a successful commercial boat (the model 53). The 55 was a more powerful aircraft than the 37 (the 55 was equipped with two engines, one pulling and one pushing) and, despite its almost instant obsolescence, two managed to survive the fall of France and were used by the Free French for reconnaissance.

The thirties brought an upsurge of French production of flying boats, generally of a multipurpose design. They could be used, it was hoped, either commercially or militarily. Such were the Loire 501 (a small three- or four-place liaison craft), an early variant of which first flew in 1931. Another small plane, the Potez 452, was designed for operations from a ship, complete with folding wings for storage. The planes were raised from or lowered into the water by crane. Of the sixteen 452s built, only one appears to have survived the war, the major reason being no doubt the inability to acquire spare parts—and the fact that, following the capitulation of France to Germany, the dated planes were scrapped or destroyed.

Almost simultaneously Ateliers et Chantiers de la Loire produced two flying boats, the first being the Loire 70, a comparatively large (span ninety-eight feet, five inches) aircraft powered by three engines, two pulling and one, mounted in the center of the wing, pushing. Its prototype flew for the first time in June 1934. Its factory mate, the smaller Loire 130 (wingspan fifty-two feet, five inches), flew for the first time in November of the same year. The latter was one of the most extensively employed of any French-produced flying boats. Like so many others used by the French Navy, the Loire 130, technically described as a *"hydravion de surveillance catapultable,"* was stored aboard various ships for reconnaissance duties with the fleet. It was also shore-based for coastal patrols.

The Loire 70, used generally to supplant the aging CAMS-55s, did not proliferate and only eight were built, six of them being used by Escadrille E7 for patrolling the Mediterranean when the war began. One 70 had been "written off" by then after a hard landing. By June of 1940 only four still remained operational—and then the *Regia Aeronautica* swooped down upon the base at Karouba, destroyed one totally, and damaged two others beyond all hope of repair. When France was eliminated from the war, Escadrille E7 had but one Loire 70 still flying when the squadron was disbanded according to the treaty impressed upon France by Hitler.

Another early, perhaps venerable would be the apter word, French flying boat was the Breguet 521, popularly called the *Bizerte*. Based on the British Short Calcutta of 1928, the French variant flew initially in 1933 and the prototype went into operational testing (with the Escadrille 1E2) in April of 1935. Of all-metal construction (a Short hallmark), the *Bizerte* was one of the last biplane flying boats to be used in the Second World War. *Bizertes* were flown by Escadrilles de Surveillance in patrolling the Atlantic and Mediterranean; after France's defeat some remained in the service of the Vichy Government's Navy and others were confiscated for use by the Luftwaffe as air-sea rescue craft. At least one *Bizerte* was still operational in the summer of 1944 in the Mediterranean, but was eventually retired because of a lack of parts.

One of the largest of the French flying

The Loire 70, an all-metal three-engined reconnaissance flying boat of 1934, two tractors and one pusher. Its top speed was about 145 miles an hour. (Musée de l'Air)

The single-engined (Hispano-Suiza) Loire 130, shipboard-stored reconnaissance plane. (Musée de l'Air)

The old Breguet 521 Bizerte, trimotored biplane flying boat inspired by the Short Calcutta. Designed as a long-range reconnaissance boat, the Bizerte had a span of 115 feet, three inches and a fuselage length of sixty-seven feet, two inches. (Musée de l'Air)

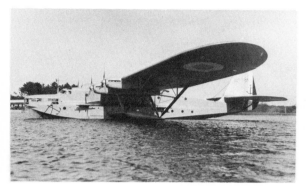

Some later French flying boats of the Second World War: the Latécoère 302; Potez-CAMS-141; Latécoère 523; the Sud-Est LeO H-470; the Sud-Est LeO H-246—all prewar designs; and the wartime, and too late, products: Breguet 730 and the Latécoère 611. (Musée de l'Air)

boats operational when the war began was the 144-foot wingspan, four-engined Latécoère 302, a long-range reconnaissance craft evolved from the slightly earlier commercial boat, the Latécoère 300, a veteran of the Dakar-to-Natal Atlantic route. Other multiengined boats that followed the 302, (which flew for the first time in 1936) were the Potez-CAMS-141, the Latécoère 523 (with no less than six engines), and the Sud-Est LeO (for Loiré-et-Oliver) H-470. All of these planes appeared in 1938, just on the eve of the war. The Sud-Est LeO H-246, also a multiengined craft, was produced in time to see some action with the French Navy—as well as with Air France as a commercial airliner. However, most fell into German hands during the occupation of France.

During the war, there was some degree of business as usual, and France did manufacture a trickle of new boats—the Breguet 730 and 790 and the Latécoère 611—all of which appeared in 1940. By this time France was finished as a warring nation. And despite the large number of interesting types of flying boats at France's disposal, they amounted to little in the outcome of the war, mainly because of obsolescence. When the newer, faster, more efficient boats appeared, it was too late.

Britain was second in the number of types on hand when the war came again to Europe. These ranged in longevity from the Supermarine *Walrus* (1933) to such stalwarts as the Saunders-Roe A-27 London, the Short Singapore III and the Supermarine Stranraer, all of which had arrived upon the scene by the mid-thirties. The major debut occurred, however, in 1937, when the first of the Sunderlands lifted off the surface of the Medway under the hand of test pilot John Lankester Parker, with Harold Piper aboard as copilot. The burden of wartime reconnaissance, submarine hunting (and sinking), and bombing would

The doughty Supermarine Walrus, a prewar design that served well with the Royal Navy during the war until 1944, when it began to be replaced by the newer Sea Otter. Tough and reliable, the Walrus was a popular plane. (National Maritime Museum)

Supermarine Sea Otter, successor to the old Walrus. (Imperial War Museum)

Saunders-Roe (Saro) London, one of the older British designs to be used in the war. Dating from the mid-thirties, the London carried a crew of six, had a range (maximum) of 1740 miles, and a top speed of 155 miles an hour. Wingspan measured eighty feet; fuselage, fifty-six feet, six inches. (Imperial War Museum)

descend upon the very capable wings of the Sunderland.

During the war Britain could depend upon the flying boats already operational— but eventually the concentration would be placed upon land-based fighters and bombers. Still, some new designs appeared during the war, one very interesting in its conception and the other a failure.

Supermarine Stranraer, one of the older types in active service when war came. It developed out of the old Southampton V in 1935 and was supplanted by the Catalina in 1943. (Imperial War Museum)

The Blackburn B-20 was especially fascinating because its design featured a retractable hull. Actually this was more of a large float that, when down, kept the fuselage of the aircraft at the correct takeoff attitude, with the propellers clear of water spray. Once off the water the pontoon raised and faired into the hull, resulting in a perfectly normal appearing flying boat. Tests, in early 1940, proved that the idea worked. But before testing was completed the B-20 crashed. All aboard the plane were killed, and the project was abandoned.

Also abandoned was the Saunders-Roe S-36 Lerwick, designed to fulfill the same specifications for a medium-range reconnaissance boat as the Blackburn B-20. Something inherent in the design of the Lerwick led to problems—the major one being instability in both water and air. Throughout the testing various little faults were remedied, propellers were raised, tailplanes were moved around and modified and, finally, the Lerwick proved practically fatal

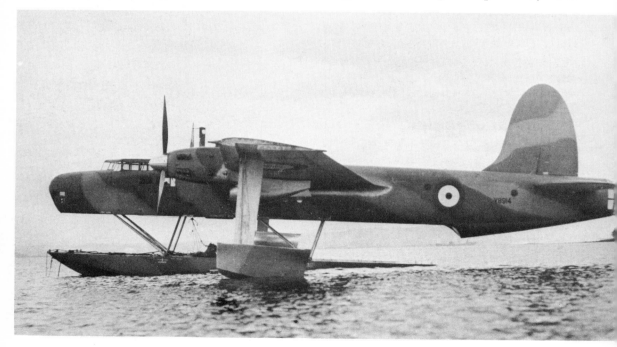

Blackburn B-20, the flying boat with a retractable hull. With wing floats up, the span measured eighty-two feet, two inches; the fuselage was sixty-nine feet, seven inches long. Destruction of prototype ended research along this development. (Imperial War Museum)

Saunders-Roe S-36 Lerwick, the flying boat that lacked real airworthiness and that was abandoned during the war. Span was eighty feet, ten inches; length, sixty-three feet, seven inches. (Imperial War Museum)

in a stall. Despite this, twenty-one Lerwicks were actually built in numerous variants—the hope being that the correct balance in the design just might appear. But a series of accidents (generally after a stall) led to the withdrawal of the Lerwick from operations. A crew member described his experience in the S-36: ". . . one minute flying, the next swimming . . ." It was one of the rare British failures with a flying boat.

Like France, Germany tended to depend upon older, proven boats such as the Dorniers Do-18, Do-24, and Do-26, and the Blohm und Voss 138 (the latter designed specifically for long-range reconnaissance). The Do-24 had been initially produced for the Royal Netherlands Naval Air Service. Several of the boats produced before the war began were sent to the East Indies (those under construction in Dutch plants were seized for the Luftwaffe) to be flown by the Dutch and later the Australians. The plane achieved the distinction of being used by several of the warring powers: Holland, Australia, Germany, France, and even one neutral, Sweden, which impounded one of the Do-24s that had made a forced landing at Hällevik. The

The Dornier lineup when Germany went to war: the Do-18, Do-24, and Do-26. (Imperial War Museum)

Luftwaffe found it a most useful aircraft during the Norwegian fighting, when it was employed as a transport.

The Do-26, of which Lufthansa's *Seeadler* and *Seefalke* were well known in the late thirties, was almost immediately taken over by the Luftwaffe when war began. They were used as transports during Hitler's Norway campaign in the spring of 1940 and could carry at maximum a dozen fully equipped troops—troops equipped to fight in snowy, mountainous terrain. Like all flying boats, they were quite easily victimized by the faster, more maneuverable fighters, such as the Hurricanes and Spitfires, and very few survived the Norwegian campaign.

As for the Blohm und Voss 138, its twin-boomed design (in a sense a throwback to the old Sikorsky S-38) was unique among the wartime flying boats. It was designed at the Blohm und Voss shipyards at Hamburg as a long-range reconnaissance aircraft and flew for the first time in 1937; it passed through several modifications—the hull and vertical rudders undergoing several changes over the years. The Bv 138 proved to be a versatile flying boat and was used for several functions besides reconnaissance —including troop transportation (Norway again), bombardment, and mine sweeping when equipped with a large dural hoop— this last being a Bv 138B-O converted into the Bv 138MS.

The Blohm und Voss 138, this one being fitted with a mine detector (which also, electrically, detonated the mines). (Heinz J. Nowarra)

This handful of types sufficed for Germany's aerial effort, since the Luftwaffe's major emphasis had been placed upon fighters, dive bombers, and medium bombers. In time, a great deal of overwater reconnaissance was taken over by the land-based Focke-Wulf 200 *Condor*. During the war two large German flying boats were produced by Blohm und Voss, the Bv 222 Wiking (1940) and the Bv 238 (1944),

One of the final wartime German flying boats, the Blohm und Voss Bv 222 Wiking, an exceptionally large aircraft, impressive in performance but late in arriving. (Imperial War Museum)

both powered by six engines. The Wiking had been originally intended for use over the Atlantic by Lufthansa; with a wing spanning 150 feet, 11 inches it could have carried two dozen passengers by day and sixteen comfortably by night. The first Bv 222 did not fly until the war had begun so that it no longer could fulfill its peacetime function and was taken into the Luftwaffe as both a transport and a reconnaissance flying boat. It was used during the African campaign to bring supplies to Rommel's beleaguered Afrika Korps, as well as to other points in the Mediterranean. As a troop transport the Wiking could carry more than ninety troops to battle; and it could return with seventy casualties. It was, of course, vulnerable to fighter attack and rarely ventured out without fighter escort of its own. But the RAF generally dealt harshly with it over the Mediterranean and, as the war turned sour for the Germans, the Wiking, as many other Luftwaffe aircraft, was destroyed by its crews or by Allied fighter attacks where they rested on the water.

The fate of the Bv 238, which emerged in 1944, was even more dismal. Coming late in the war, it was an ambitious multi-purpose design: patrol, bombardment, and transport. The wing spanned nearly two hundred feet and would have required the services of a ten-man crew. But the aircraft had arrived too late in the history of the Third Reich for, by the spring of 1944, when the trials of the Bv 238 were taking place on Lake Schaal, Allied fighters ranged pretty much at will over Germany. One day, then, as the Bv 238V1 rested on the waters of the lake, American P-51s swooped in over the water and left the big boat a flaming wreck. Work on future aircraft was eventually abandoned, for Germany's war-

making and the making of aircraft was all but over.

When Russia went to war its outstanding flying boat was the little single-engined Beriev MBR-2. Designer G. M. Beriev produced it as a four- to five-man short-range reconnaissance plane: thus the MBR (which stood for Morskii Blizhnii Razved-chik, Navy Short-Range Reconnaissance). The MBR first flew in 1931, went into operation in 1933, and was produced until 1942. The war in Russia was a massive ground war; the Russians, in fact, tended to skimp on aircraft production, relying a great deal upon Lend Lease for modern aircraft—at least until late in the war. Beriev followed the MBR-2 with a larger, improved MDR (Long-Range) flying boat for operations over the Baltic, Black Sea, and the Pacific. The MBR, however, was

Beriev MBR-2, Russia's outstanding wartime flying boat. It was also operated as a land-plane and with skis. The wingspan was forty-three feet, eleven inches, and the fuselage measured thirty feet, two inches. (U. S. Air Force)

built in great numbers (an estimated fifteen hundred) and was the backbone of Russia's seaplane strength. But Russia's war effort was aimed at wiping out the German Army and piercing the Reich to its very heart, Berlin, with infantry and armor, not wings.

Thus were the warring powers equipped with seaplanes when the war began, France with its multiplicity of aging designs, Britain with less—but with the formidable Sunderland—and Germany with a handful, but with little interest in extensive overwater operations. Meanwhile, too, the United States tentatively on the sidelines had a number of flying boats and awaited the outcome of the fighting.

The single word that crews have applied to long stretches of patrolling over water is "monotony." Months of dreary operations were now and then livened by action— attacking a U-boat, an enemy ship, or an enemy plane. Or the weather could dispel all tedium for several hours, while the crew fought to save the plane and perhaps their lives. But the major enemy was boredom.

"With luck," a British pilot wrote during the war, "we arrive at our patrol area in six hours. On the other coast of England the bombers are arriving home. Our work is just beginning—the hunt for submarines. . . . Sometimes we imagine they are a myth. It is not easy to go on believing in something you have never seen. . . . We are forever searching for signs of the enemy. But nothing appears. Even the waves are formalized into the monotony: each one exactly like its predecessor. The wireless operator is receiving and sending, but his woodpecker taps are drowned by the engines. The navigator is bent over the chart table, plotting courses—sometimes going for'ard to check the aircraft's drift. One of the fitters is working on the clocks and gauges, noting down temperatures, pressures, and petrol consumption. The air gunners lead the most frustrated existence of

all. They sit and wait and watch and wait, hour after hour, day after day, month after month. They lean on their guns praying for a glimpse of the enemy." Still, the pilot did add, "We have helped twenty great ships today to bring armaments and food to England. That is our reward."

The strain of flying for hours on end over a trackless sea had its effect. "I have more than once," yet another pilot admitted, "found myself making a sudden, steep bank when five hundred miles out in the Atlantic under the impression that I was avoiding a mountain. One of my friends, shortly before he went on his rest, swore he saw a man riding a motor-bicycle 450 miles off the west coast of Ireland."

But the big flying boats helped to keep the Battle of the Atlantic under control, and the appearance of a Catalina or Sunderland over a convoy had its immediate and salutary effect. A merchantman paid a tribute to the men in the boats above from the men in the boats below when he wrote, "I know it must be very monotonous at times to the men of the Royal Air Force Coastal Command being on patrol duty, but I would like them to know what a thrill it is to us seamen—I know I speak for all— to see them around us and what confidence it gives us. I would also add that we enjoy their company after trudging along at slow speed for twenty days or more; it heartens us."

The two outstanding flying boats of the war were the Consolidated Catalina and the Short Sunderland, both of which went into action with the RAF early in the war; the Sunderland was ready at the very beginning and the Catalina, though ready, was not exported to Britain until early in 1941. Shortly after the first deliveries the Catalinas began making history when two of the aircraft, one from No. 240 Squadron and piloted by Pilot Officer D. A. Briggs, and another from No. 240 Squadron, piloted by an American lieutenant, Smith of

From monotony to tedium: members of a Sunderland aircrew on patrol over the Atlantic. (Imperial War Museum)

the U. S. Navy, who assisted in bringing about the destruction of the German battleship *Bismarck* in May of 1941. Smith had been sent by the U. S. Navy on detached service to check out British pilots on the new craft. He thus had stumbled inadvertently into the battle (and became known thereafter as "Bismarck" Smith).

Briggs told his story over the BBC: "We left our base at three-thirty in the morning, and we got to the area we had to search at nine forty-five. It was a hazy morning with poor visibility, and our job was to contact with the *Bismarck,* which had been lost since early Sunday morning. About an hour later we saw a dark shape ahead in the mist. We were flying low at the time. I and the second pilot were sitting side by side and we saw the ship at the same time. At first we could hardly believe our eyes. I believe we both shouted 'There she is,' or something of the sort.

"There was a forty-knot wind blowing and a heavy sea running, and she was digging her nose right in, throwing it white over her bows. At first, we weren't sure that it was an enemy battleship, we had to make certain. So we altered course, went up to about fifteen hundred feet into a cloud, and circled. We thought we were near the stern of her when the cloud ended, and there we were, right above her. The first we knew of it was a couple of puffs of smoke just outside the cockpit window, and a devil of a lot of noise. And then we were surrounded by dark brownish black smoke as she popped off at us with everything she'd got. She's only been supposed to have eight antiaircraft guns, but fire was coming from more than eight places—in fact, she looked just one big flash. The explosions threw the flying boat about, and we could hear bits of shrapnel hit the hull. Luckily only a few penetrated.

"My first thought was that they were going to get us before we'd sent the signal off, so I grabbed a bit of paper and wrote

A Catalina on patrol; hundreds were used by Coastal Command during the critical Battle of the Atlantic period of the war. (Smithsonian Institution, National Air and Space Museum)

out the message and gave it to the wireless operator. At the same time the second pilot took control and took avoiding action. I should say that as soon as the *Bismarck* saw us she'd taken avoiding action too, by turning at right angles, heeling over, and pitching in the heavy sea.

"When we'd got away a bit we cruised round while we inspected our damage. The rigger and I went over the aircraft, taking up floor boards and thoroughly inspecting the hull. There were about half a dozen holes, and the rigger stopped them up with rubber plugs. We also kept an eye on the petrol gauges, because if they were going down too fast, that meant the tanks were holed and we wouldn't stand much chance of getting home.. However, they were all right, and we went back to shadow *Bismarck.* Then we met another Catalina. She'd been searching an area north of us when she intercepted our signals and closed. On the way she'd seen a naval force, also coming towards us at full pelt through the heavy seas. They were part of our pursuing fleet.

"When we saw this Catalina we knew she was shadowing the ship from signals we'd intercepted and because she was going round in big circles. So I formated on him and came close alongside. I could see the pilot through the cockpit window and he pointed in the direction the *Bismarck* was going. He had come to relieve us: It was just as well, for we couldn't stay much longer, because the holes in our hull made it essential to land in the daylight. So we left the other Catalina to shadow *Bismarck*. You all know what happened after that.

"We landed just after half-past nine at night, flying for over eighteen hours. But one of our Catalinas during this operation set up a new record for Coastal Command of twenty-seven hours on continuous reconnaissance."

The plane in which Smith was flying had an almost similar experience—dodging anti-aircraft fire, getting the message off to the fleet in pursuit of the big battleship, being lightly struck by pellets from the *Bismarck*. "None of the crew was hit, though a piece of shell passed upwards through the floor between the two pilots as they were changing places. The only casualties occurred in the galley, where one of the crew, who was washing up the breakfast things, 'dropped two china RAF plates and broke them.' "

The shadowing was touch and go on that May 26, 1941, as the battleship and the Catalinas eluded each other in the tossing, misty elements. Then at about the time Briggs was approaching his base Swordfish torpedo-bombers from the carrier *Ark Royal* closed in on the elusive *Bismarck* to begin the final chapter of its story, and the end of its career as one of the most menacing of all of Germany's battleships then extant. It sank, a blazing wreck, on May 27 on what had been its first sortie.

American Catalinas served well with the RAF's Coastal Command—as did other American-made planes, such as the Lockheed Hudson and the Consolidated B-24

A Sunderland I of No. 210 Squadron, one of the first to fly the boat in action. (Imperial War Museum)

Liberator (both, of course, land-based craft capable of extended-range flights), but the backbone of Britain's flying boat fleet was the great Sunderland.

Three squadrons—Nos. 204, 210, and 228—were equipped with Sunderlands when the war began; by war's end there were nearly thirty. It was No. 210 Squadron's lot to score a number of "firsts" during the early confused days of the war. On September 3, 1939, one of its Sunderlands completed the first (uneventful) patrol of the war; the next day one of its boats suffered the doubtful distinction of being the first to come under attack from ground gunners, being in this case British antiaircraft gunners and, finally, on the eighth of September Flight Lieutenant E. L. Hyde, piloting a Sunderland, spotted and attacked the first German submarine in the watery approaches to England. The attack produced no results.

These were tentative, familiarizing, near-training missions as contenders measured each other and learned, under combat conditions, to use their equipment. But very quickly all elements—men and machines—united in achievements of outstanding accomplishment. One of the earliest occurred later that first September of the war—on the eighteenth—when two Sunderlands of No. 228 Squadron, piloted by Flight

Lieutenants Thurstan Smith and John Barrat, landed in troubled seas to rescue the crew of the tramp steamer *Kensington Court,* which had been torpedoed by a German U-boat in the Atlantic. Dividing the thirty-four survivors among them, Smith and Barrat took their overloaded Sunderlands off from a swelling sea and returned to their base at Mount Batten.

The German submarine was the Sunderland's prime objective, for the Atlantic wolfpacks threatened to strangle the British war effort as well as starve its population. The lifeline from the United States and Canada had to be kept intact, the convoys carrying supplies had to get through. The Sunderlands became the wide-ranging protectors of the ships and the scourge of the submarines in the Atlantic and the Mediterranean.

U-boats, in fact, were elusive objectives, and early operations were frustrating, partly because of inexperience and partly because there was much yet to be learned about arming the flying boats for antisubmarine work. Credit for the first near "kill" went to No. 228 Squadron when one of its Sunderlands came upon the submarine U-55 in distress after it had surfaced because of damages suffered in an attack by Navy depth charges. Rather than undergo further attack the German captain scuttled the submarine. The first actual destruction of a submarine occurred some months later, on July 17, 1940, when an Australian crew of a Sunderland of No. 10 (RAAF) Squadron sank a U-boat.

An unidentified Sunderland pilot described for the BBC audience a typical action in which a German submarine was sunk. Early in his talk he mentioned that "I have known of crews that have gone out for a year and not even seen a U-boat, so we've been rather lucky. . . ."

"The first U-boat that we knew for certain that we had sunk was in the Mediterranean when I was operating from Gibraltar. . . . We were out on patrol to cover an area where a U-boat had been attacked the previous day. There was a dead flat calm. We sighted a big Italian U-boat dead ahead cruising fast on the surface. I immediately dived at maximum speed. There was the mad moment of feverish activity that always follows my sounding the submarine attack alarm, which blares throughout the aircraft and startles everybody into action. Everyone jumps to their routine job at action stations.

"An extraordinary number of things get done in a surprisingly few seconds. We dived at maximum speed to get him before he crash-dived. When we were about half a mile away, he showed no signs of crash-diving, so we thought we'd taken him by surprise, coming dead astern. But suddenly there was a bright flash and a loud explosion as a big shell burst dead ahead of us. We got a terrific surprise and pulled away into a steep climbing turn, which shot us up about two thousand feet, with flak and machine-gun bullets bursting all round us and sometimes hitting us. My tail gunner was so furious that, unconsciously taking up his microphone, he reeled off a string of good Australian abuse in such a loud voice that I had to stop him because he was monopolizing the wire without realizing it.

"We circled the submarine and studied every detail of its construction, especially the placing of the guns, so as to plan an attack which would be safe as possible. We attacked him with bombs and machine-gunned him heavily, but he turned sharply to port and we missed him. We were under machine-gun fire throughout the attack. Our port bomb racks were not working, but during the action and while we were under fire, my armourer, L.A.C. Bob Scott, with the help of some of the crew, carried the bombs from the port racks to those on the starboard side, which were now empty, so that we could make another attack. He well deserved the D.F.M. that he got for

A Sunderland patrols over a convoy in the Atlantic. (Imperial War Museum)

this action. In fact, the whole crew were simply marvellous.

"We made a second attack, but the U-boat's fire forced us to turn aside before we could drop any bombs: however, my gunners poured a hail of accurate fire at point-blank range into the U-boat's conning tower, which was very crowded.

"Finally we attacked him with our remaining bombs, diving very low over him, in spite of his accurate fire. A stick of bombs fell diagonally across him and plumb centre. That stopped him all right, and he lay with no movement for some minutes while we machine-gunned him heavily. We had to return to base, but we know that the U-boat never got home. Our Sunderland was fairly badly shot up, but none of us had a scratch."

Not every, in fact only a few, sorties resulted in a victory; and aircraft were lost for reasons other than enemy action. A sudden change in weather, mechanical prob-lems—these too could prove lethal. One such incident involved a Sunderland that had set out from its base in Scotland at five in the evening in October 1940. Two hours out over the Atlantic the plane flew into a sudden, and unpredicted, electrical storm of unusual fury. Almost immediately the radio went haywire and the compass became all but useless. After five more hours of flying the crew was able to begin sending messages, informing their base that they were returning—but there was no reply from the base. Another five hours went by —they had been airborne for twelve hours—and the crew began sending distress signals and requests for bearings, which were picked up at the base; but the base could not communicate with the plane. It was morning of the next day; the Sunderland, without a compass and without complete radio communications, was lost over the gale-lashed Atlantic and practically out of fuel. The pilot then decided to bring

Sunderland over Gibraltar. (Charles E. Brown, FRPS)

the big boat down onto the ocean before they splashed into it.

An eighty-mile-an-hour gale was blowing near the surface, and one of the crew estimated that waves twenty feet high were running. To assist the landing three flame-floats were dropped into the seething waves, but they were immediately extinguished. A parachute flare managed to stay lighted long enough to give some indication of the wind direction. The pilot then brought the Sunderland down in a trough between two waves. The plane was lifted bodily up by one of the waves, air speed was immediately dissipated, and the big plane splashed back into the water without damage. Then began a nine-hour ordeal best told in the dispassionate language of the official version:

"The crew were at once prostrated by violent sea-sickness, and this endured for many hours. The wireless operator began to send out signals, not knowing if any would be received. One was, and they presently picked up a message telling them that a warship would arrive in eight hours.

"The Sunderland continued to drift in tumultuous seas at a speed of about eight miles an hour. How long she would endure the buffeting it was hard to say. The wireless set was dismantled, repaired, and reassembled. The signals subsequently made were picked up by the warship, faint at first, but strong after midday. At 2:20 P.M. the Sunderland signaled: 'Hurry, cracking up.' Fifteen minutes later she was sighted and the look-out on the bridge of the warship read the word 'hurry' flashed by a lamp. At that moment as the crew caught sight of the warship a wave larger than the rest struck the Sunderland head on.

She began to break up and the crew—there were thirteen of them—were flung into the water.

"The captain of the warship maneuvered her so as to approach the wreckage of the flying boat from the lee quarter. He took the way off his ship as the crew swept past abreast of, and almost as high as, his bridge. A naval commander and twelve ratings with lines secured to them went over the side and pulled on board nine of the crew, who had then been fifty minutes in the sea. The other four were lost. The Sunderland had remained afloat in a full gale for not quite nine hours. The name of the warship was H.M.A.S. *Australia.*" The official account, for reasons best known to the British in wartime, failed to name the men who had undergone the long adventure.

The Sunderland was a tough craft, as was proved in several such adventures, not all so fatally ended. When it was not fighting

On a takeoff run, a Sunderland leaves a foamy wake. (Imperial War Museum)

Off the step: a Sunderland heads out on patrol. (Imperial War Museum)

the weather or German submarines the Sunderland could be counted on to make a good showing in air battles as well. It literally bristled with guns from its several turrets in the bow, tail, upper fuselage, and sides and earned the nickname of *Stachelschwein* from the Luftwaffe, for it was indeed a flying "Porcupine." The one major vulnerable spot was the underside, so that it was necessary to keep that somehow protected from attack, often by hugging the water. Sunderlands frequently encountered German fighters and fighter-bombers, and particularly the U-boat's friend, the Focke-Wulf *Condor,* over the Atlantic and engaged in aerial combat with them, either driving the enemy off or into the sea.

Besides its assigned functions, the Sunderland, as did practically every flying boat, participated in rescue missions to ships in distress or airmen who had come down in the sea. They were also used in mining those ports that the Germans needed to supply themselves. The Sunderlands proved to be one of the most versatile and effective of any wartime flying boat.

As the Sunderland was the backbone of the British flying boat fleet, so was the Catalina the backbone of the U. S. Navy. It flew over all waters, ranging from the Arctic to the tropical Pacific. Catalinas were based at Pearl Harbor when the Japanese struck on December 7, 1941. Even before the attack came, Ensign William P. Tanner, on patrol in his PBY of Patrol Wing 1 (Patwing 1) assisted in sinking a submarine that had been found lurking in the waters around Pearl Harbor—this was, in fact, the opening action of the war in the Pacific, an hour and twenty-two minutes before the bombs began falling upon American installations in Hawaii. The submarine was Japanese and not, as young Tanner and his copilot, Ensign Clark Greevey, feared, one of their own, a victim of mistaken identity.

After administering the *coup de grâce*

War comes to the Pacific: Naval Air Station, Pearl Harbor, December 7, 1941. (Navy Department, National Archives)

with depth bombs, Tanner rather unhappily returned to his base at Kaneohe, about twenty miles east of Pearl Harbor. Incidentally, the commanding officer of Patwing 1 was Commander Knefler McGinnis, who had led the six-plane flights of the PY2-1s in the early thirties. He too had his doubts about the nationality of the submarine that his boys had sent to the bottom.

The main headquarters for the PBYs was on Ford Island, where Patwing 2 was based, and by 7:55 A.M., when the first Japanese dive bomber screeched down upon Ford, all doubts were canceled. So was most of the American air strength in the Pacific. Both PBY bases were struck, with Kaneohe suffering the worst; of the thirty-six Catalinas that had been stationed there, only three escaped damage—and these because they happened to be on patrol when

the attack came. Of the remaining thirty-three, twenty-seven were destroyed and six were damaged.

In the Philippines the fortunes of Patwing 10, commanded by Captain Boyd D. Wagner, were no better. Comprised of two squadrons of fourteen PBYs each, Patwing 10 was employed in wide-ranging reconnaissance before the outbreak of hostilities, later in frantic attempts at bombing missions, and finally—with its three surviving planes—in evacuating Navy and Army high-rankers out of the Philippines. But even before this could happen, one of the PBYs was damaged in a collision with a small boat and lost the left wingtip float. While it was under repair it and the two surviving PBYs, earmarked to fly out Admiral Thomas C. Hart and his staff, were strafed by Japanese planes. One burned and the other sank at its moorings. The single survivor, though shot full of holes and minus one engine, managed to fly to another, hopefully safer, port. When time came for Admiral Hart to leave, however, the plane was abandoned (and eventually destroyed to prevent its falling into Japanese hands), and the admiral left Manila Bay on the day after Christmas 1941, skulkingly, in the submarine *Shark*.

Those men of Patwing 10 who had to remain behind—now without aircraft—assembled at the Pan American base at Cavite, useless now to the *China Clipper*, to plan their resistance to the coming Japanese invasion. Most were fated to continue the war bitterly at Corregidor and Bataan. Those few PBYs that had gotten away during the last confused weeks of the hopeless fight in the Philippines continued to operate as Patwing 10 on small reconnaissance patrols out of the Celebes, Java, and, eventually, for the tattered survivors, Australia.

The PBY had proved to be a tough aircraft and its pilots indomitable, but neither were absolutely invincible. The battle appeared rather hopeless until American forces, reeling from one defeat after another, could strike back. This came at Midway, another action in which a Catalina, piloted by Ensign Jewell (Jack) Reid, played an important role. Reid was the first to spot elements of the Japanese fleet on the way to Midway, thus alerting all American forces for the battle that would end all hopes of a Japanese victory in the Pacific.

And so went the saga of the Catalina in the waters of the Pacific and the Atlantic as well. Though slow and vulnerable to the more nimble Japanese fighters, they proved to be exceptionally reliable, adaptable, and capable of operating under conditions that might have wrecked a less rugged aircraft.

Probably no worse theater of operations for aircraft could have been imagined than the foggy, gusty, freezing, and generally

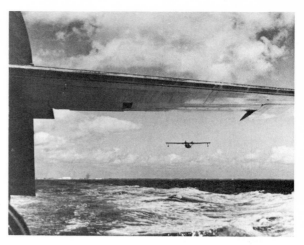

PBYs set out on patrol; the Catalina was operated in every theater of war within reach of water. (Smithsonian Institution, National Air and Space Museum)

The world's worst flying weather: in the Aleutians, where besides nearly eternal fog, pilots had to contend with the williwaw and ice. (Navy Department, National Archives)

miserable Aleutians, which the Japanese attempted to invade as a diversion for their major action at Midway. This was the province of Patwing 4, and whose province and its natural elements were Patwing 4's chief adversaries—the Japanese, at times, appeared to be little more than incidental. They, of course, suffered through their own nature-made problems.

Aircraft engines had to be heated (sometimes even by blowtorch) in order to get them to fly—and flying weather was invariably changeable and most often bad. This made it difficult to patrol and to strike at Japanese positions if they were found. High winds, called williwaws, reached a velocity capable of overturning an aircraft—and operating from ice-filled bays was its own hazard. Coming down at sea meant death from exposure unless rescue came immediately. Mist-covered mountains were a menace.

In the tropical Pacific, beginning with the assault on Guadalcanal in the summer of 1942, the Catalinas operated under conditions diametrically opposite to those in the Aleutians. Heat, dampness, a fine dust to grind away the engines, and glutinous mud provided the setting for the PBYs, as well as Marine, Navy, and Army airmen and craft in the Solomons. The PBYs were generally used for reconnaissance and bombing in the Pacific, but were even more frequently employed, as the war progressed, as rescue craft for pilots down at sea. By early 1943 a rejuvenated Patwing 10, based at Perth, Australia, and joined by Patwing 17 (Brisbane) began ranging the Pacific waters, not only dropping bombs on Japanese shipping, but also plucking airmen out of the sea—often under the very guns of the enemy.

It was around this period that the PBY became affectionately known as the "Dumbo," after the Walt Disney cartoon character, a flying elephant. The PBYs were also called P-boats and Cats by their crews.

A "Black Cat" sets out on a night-search mission from a base in the Pacific. Darkness came suddenly in this theater. (Smithsonian Institution, National Air and Space Museum)

A special variant was the darkly hued, radar-equipped PBY used first in the Solomons by Patrol Squadron 12, "The Black Cats," which did not take off until after dark and covered the infamous "Slot," a stretch of water between New Georgia and Santa Isabel Islands through which the Japanese ran their reinforcements and supplies into Guadalcanal. The Black Cats, later joined by another Squadron, VP-54, covered the "Slot" in search of shipping to bomb, or spotted enemy surface ship gunfire and radioed fire directions to American gunners.

The Atlantic PBYs were used primarily in antisubmarine patrols. The U-boat was a serious menace during 1942–43 particularly—and the area of search stretched from Iceland to South America. The South Atlantic was an especially dangerous section, which had been assigned to Patrol Squadrons 83, 94, and 74 (equipped with Martin Mariners). If submarine activity had picked up in the waters off Brazil, so did the willingness of submarine commanders to duel with their nemesis, the flying boat. One Patron 94 pilot, Lieutenant (j.g.) Frank F. Jare, was killed in such a duel although he was avenged by squadron mate Lieutenant (j.g.) S. E. Auslander, who sank the submarine, *U-590,* two hours later with bombs.

Attempts were made, with no great success, to stop the submarines in their own nests in the Bay of Biscay off western Europe. The Navy joined the U. S. Army Air Forces and the RAF in these assaults with its PBYs equipped with Magnetic Airborne Detectors (MAD), which invariably led to the nickname "Madcats" for Patrol Squadron 63. Operations were begun on July 31, 1943, without serious incident—or results, for that matter. But the Bay of Biscay area, particularly in the vicinity of sub pens, was ringed with antiaircraft guns and within easy reach of the Luftwaffe. On August 1 VP-63 returned to the bay and came under concentrated fighter attack. One PBY, named *Aunt Minnie,* became the target for at least eight Junkers-88s. The crew attempted to fight off the swarm of German planes, even succeeded in shooting one down, but the Ju-88s were faster, more heavily armed—and there were still a half dozen chipping away at *Aunt Minnie.*

The Catalina, trailing smoke, splashed into the Bay of Biscay. There were only three survivors (of a crew of seven) who were rescued; one of them was Lieutenant William P. Tanner, who as an ensign had contributed to the sinking of a submarine off Pearl Harbor.

The Catalina units were not the only ones, certainly, to fight the war; it is only that their ubiquitousness might make it appear so. There were squadrons of Martin Mariners—American as well as British—plying much of the same waters and whose crews experienced similar adventures and the boredom. Nor were the planes flown only by Navy and Army crews, particularly

A PBY-6A, last of the Catalina line; fuselage is two feet longer than in earlier models and vertical tail surface has been redesigned. This model was used by the U. S. Navy as well as the Army—and by the Russians, who received forty-eight and based their own GST flying boats on the Catalina. (General Dynamics, Convair Division)

A Mariner in the Pacific being serviced by its tender. (Martin Company)

Mariners in British colors; in 1943 twenty-six of these PBM-3Bs were delivered to No. 524 Squadron, RAF, but the disbanding of the squadron a few weeks later prevented the Mariner from being used operationally by the RAF. (Martin Company)

Three of the smaller amphibians: the Douglas Dolphin (wingspan: sixty feet), the Grumman Gray Goose (span: forty-nine feet), and the Grumman Widgeon, with a wingspan of forty feet. (Douglas Aircraft/Grumman Aircraft)

in the U.S. service. The Coast Guard operated off the coastal waters patrolling for submarines (especially in the infested Atlantic), dropping bombs when an objective was found, and just as often flying mercy missions to rescue pilots or ship crews that had gotten into trouble.

Generally the Coast Guard used smaller

aircraft, since their missions rarely carried them far out to sea—the long-range jobs were given to the bigger boats. Among the smaller craft were the venerable Douglas Dolphin (originally an eight-place commercial amphibian—the one, in fact, with which Pan American initiated its flying inside China in the early thirties). The Dolphin was also employed by the Army, the Marines, and the Royal Australian Air Force and, with the U. S. Coast Guard, served in a variety of roles: transport, trainer, and observation.

Another small amphibian was the Grumman G-21 Gray Goose, which had also begun its story as a commercial flying boat (in 1937) and then with few modifications was converted into a military aircraft—first for the U. S. Army (designated OA-9); the Navy attached the letters JRF to the Gray Goose and used it for, among other things, photography. The Coast Guard used them widely as air/sea rescue craft, and some models carried bombs for antisubmarine work. The RAF used the Goose as a trainer. A newer Grumman amphibian, the G-44 Widgeon, appeared in 1940 and was almost immediately taken over by the Coast Guard. In its conversion the G-44 could carry a single depth bomb under the starboard wing close to the fuselage. It was learned, however, that the Widgeon was limited in its ability to lift too great a load or to cover much distance should one of its engines go out. It suffered then from what pilots called "a negative rate of climb." The Widgeon was used more widely as a utility transport or trainer than as a subchaser. The Army designation was OA-14, the Navy's J4F-2, and the British dubbed it the Gosling.

A Boeing wartime contribution to the solution of the submarine menace was the XPBB-1 *Sea Ranger,* which flew for the first time in the summer of 1942. It was a unique aircraft, a very long-range two-engined flying boat. When originally con-

The Boeing Sea Ranger, *the flying boat sacrificed to the B-29 Superfortress. The land-plane had proved to be more efficient by the middle of 1942 when the* Sea Ranger *arrived. (Boeing Company)*

ceived the *Sea Ranger* was to have been built at Boeing's Renton plant, which was erected solely to produce the far-ranging plane. With a wingspan of 139 feet, eight inches, the plane was the largest twin-engined aircraft of its type anywhere. It bristled with guns (eight in various positions), carried a bombload of ten tons of bombs, and could remain airborne for no less than three days.

But by the time the plane had materialized the need for its type had lessened—and the emphasis had turned to the production of landplanes. Boeing's Renton plant, after having completed but one *Sea Ranger* (and which came to be called the *Lone Ranger*), was turned over to the production of B-29s.

The Lone Ranger *in flight over Seattle, Washington, summer of 1942. The wing of this flying boat and that of the B-29 were similar. (Boeing Company)*

Like their Axis partner, the Germans, the Japanese had not concentrated a good deal on flying boats. The emphasis was upon fighters, such as the outstanding Zero, and bombers. The Japanese, an island people, did not ignore the use of seaplanes, and several types of floatplanes were standard equipment in the Imperial Fleet. But when the war began the Japanese Navy could only count on one first-line long-range boat, the Kawanishi Type 97 (eventually code-named Mavis). It was big (131-foot span), slow (top speed: 239 mph; cruising speed: 161 mph), and like so many Japanese aircraft, lacked armament and protective armor for the crew. Nor was the Mavis furnished with self-sealing fuel tanks, which made it highly vulnerable to Allied fighters—and fire. Initially employed as a patrol bomber, as well as a transport, the flying boat's liabilities eventually led to its withdrawal from daylight operations by the middle of the Pacific war.

By this time its replacement, the Kawanishi Type 2 (Emily), one of the finest flying boats of the war, appeared. The Emily, the largest four-engined flying boat produced by the Japanese, was a vast improvement over the Mavis; its speed was a third more than that of the predecessor craft and it had a range increase of 50 percent. Its wing spanned nearly 125 feet, and it had a top speed of nearly three

Japan's only first-line flying boat at the time of the war's beginning, the Kawanishi H6K, code-named Mavis by Americans later in the war. First flown in 1936, the big plane was comparatively slow and was eventually withdrawn from daylight operations and used primarily as transports rather than as reconnaissance craft. (Smithsonian Institution, National Air and Space Museum)

A Kawanishi H8K Emily, one of the finest flying boats ever built by any nation, a tough contender and an excellent aircraft. (Smithsonian Institution, National Air and Space Museum)

hundred miles an hour (it was, in fact, the fastest flying boat of the war) and a range of well over four thousand miles, depending upon the payload. The Emily was heavily armed (no less than five .20-mm cannons and four 7.7 machine guns), armored, and fitted with protected fuel tanks. It was no mean adversary, although no match for the American fighters that fought in the Pacific in the latter months of the war: the Republic Thunderbolt and the

North American Mustang. But in its own category it was a superior conception.

The Emily suffered from early teething problems, a tendency to porpoise to the point of capsizing. Modifications corrected this defect: The depth of the hull was increased from fourteen feet, nine inches to sixteen feet, 4.75 inches; an inboard step was added to the planing bottom; and the vertical tail fin was enlarged. The first Emily was ready for testing at the end of 1940; the modified Emily went into production in 1941 and made its operational debut on March 1, 1942. This was to have been the first attack on Hawaii since Pearl Harbor, but thanks to poor weather conditions, it did not work out. The objective was Oahu Island (on which Pearl Harbor is situated), although no account of the attempt has specified the actual target. Some also say three Emilys participated, others two. However—and whatever the number—the Emilys never found Pearl Harbor (or whatever the target) because when they arrived over the island it was covered with thick clouds.

Following this abortive attack, the Emilys were used extensively in the Pacific as reconnaissance planes, as bombers, and as transports (of the total of 167 built, thirty-six were used as transports). All but one were eventually destroyed, either in operations, by strafing, or by occupation forces following the surrender of Japan. The surviving Emily was shipped to the United States in order to be studied for its superior hydrodynamic and flying characteristics.

But the heyday of the flying boat was over. Even during the war, many of the jobs that had once been assigned to the boats had been taken over by landplanes. With the proliferation of bases throughout the world, the need for water bases diminished—and the faster, more efficient landplanes were more economical to operate. They could lift heavier loads and they could carry them farther. The romantic but not always practical marriage between the ship and the aircraft was broken up by the Second World War. This was not obvious at the time, for there were still fleets of PBYs, Sunderlands and its several variants, there were Mariners and the Mars —there was even a single DC-3 mounted on floats, a hybrid that somehow symbolized the end of an era. The honored old "Gooney Bird" did not look comfortable on the water; it belonged on the ground on its own three wheels—or in its true element, the air. And the vast network of air bases that had mushroomed during the war placed airfields in practically every country on earth—beyond the wildest dreams of Juan Terry Trippe—the wide basis for a new birth in the postwar life of commercial aviation. But it also eliminated the need for the beautiful, but slow, flying boats that carried their own airports on their bottoms. They, like so much else of value, were casualties of war.

The "Gooney Bird" (military C-47, commercial DC-3) begins to encroach upon the province of the flying boat. This was the XC-47C mounted on Edo floats, of which only one example was built. By this time in the war there were plenty of landing strips in practically every spot on the globe. (Douglas Aircraft)

11: Swan Song,
Variations and a Coda

The coming of peace did not immediately halt the development and production of flying boats; there was an inevitable time lag before the significance of the great network of military airfields was noted. To have attempted such an undertaking in peacetime would have been economically ridiculous, but war and the important role played in it by aircraft—particularly bombers and fighters—had created a prodigious base upon which civil airports could be built.

The transition from war to peace had begun even as the war raged on: There were order cutbacks and as far as the production of flying boats was concerned, these were curtailed in favor of bomber and fighter production. Transition also from cargo planes, such as the C-54 (the Douglas DC-4, which evolved into the DC-6) into the airliners of the future actually began during the war. These planes, among them also the Lockheed Constellation and the Boeing 377 Stratocruiser, were to replace flying boats and would even be called "clippers" by Pan American.

The last of the large commercial flying boats was the Short S-45 Solent, a 1946 development of the Seaford, which in turn had evolved from the Sunderland. The military craft was converted into a civil airliner by a change of engines, crew accom-

The Short Solent, last of the large civil air transports of the flying boat type to see service in Britain. Its span was 112 feet, nine inches and fuselage length, eighty-seven feet, eight inches. A total of twenty-one were built. (BOAC Photo)

modations, and provision for as many as thirty passengers on its two decks. Like the old prewar Pan American clippers, the Solents were luxuriously appointed, complete down to a library and a cocktail bar on the upper deck. The Solents were used in the Southampton to Johannesburg run, the first of which was accomplished by a Mark 2 Solent *Southampton* on May 1, 1948.

Including night stops, the flight took four and a half days and was made three times a week. This was operated until 1950, when the route was taken over by landplanes and the Solents began shifting around to other quarters of the watery globe. Finally all British commercial flying boat use ceased in September 1958. As far as Britain was concerned the age of the large flying boat was ended.

But not quite. As late as 1966 Sunderlands were still operating in the waters around New Zealand. Although eventually replaced by more efficient land-based aircraft, the Sunderlands of the New Zealand Air Force were kept in service for emergency operations in the island communities around New Zealand.

Shortly after the Solent appeared, Saunders-Roe, in Britain, produced a revolutionary design—a small military fighter-boat, the SR-A/1. The design itself, the work of H. Knowler and Dr. D. M. Smith, was as sleek as a fighter, but the most revolutionary aspect was the use of turbojet

Saunders-Roe A/1, the unique fighter flying boat of 1947. Power was supplied by two Metropolitan-Vickers F2/4 Beryl axial flow turbojet engines. Despite remarkable high speed, this design was abandoned when the general trend toward landplane jet fighters decided against military watercraft. (U. S. Air Force)

engines for propulsion. Small—the wingspan was forty-six feet and fuselage length, fifty feet—the SR-A/1 was operated by a single pilot and was capable of speeds unheard of in water-based aircraft. The plane took off after a run of twelve seconds and, in early tests, reached a speed of four hundred miles an hour. Only three of the SR-A/1s were built, and only the first survived the general scrapping of flying boats in Britain.

The last word in flying boat giantism, meanwhile, had been under construction in the United States—for years, in fact. Aviation pioneer and mystery man Howard Hughes had joined forces with manufacturer Henry J. Kaiser to produce massive aircraft for use in wartime as transports. Hughes' conception was staggering: The span of the stabilizer alone was ten feet greater than that of the B-17 (113 feet, six inches), the wingspan stretched an unbelievable 320 feet, six inches, and the hull measured 218 feet, six inches—it dwarfed any aircraft built to that time and for years to come (the Boeing 747 approaches the Hughes flying boat—its span measures 195

feet; the fuselage is 231 feet long). Obviously, when it was conceived in 1942 the Hughes flying boat was ahead of its time by several decades.

And, of course, they said it couldn't fly.

It was germane to Hughes' concept that the big plane would not consume precious metals, so difficult to get in wartime, so that the chief materials in the boat's construction were wood. The skin was laminated plywood—and those who believed it was a "contraption that can't even fly" also called it the "Spruce Goose." Hughes encountered a number of obstacles, among them the problem of working on such a creation with a committee when he was by nature a loner; the other was the very important one that as work progressed on the big transport, so did the war. About three-quarters along, the need for the plane evaporated and, after an expenditure of some forty million tax dollars, appropriations for experimental aircraft were cut off, as was all official interest in flying boats.

While Hughes carried on with the work, using his own money, the heat began to rise in the halls of the Senate and Congress

The Hughes flying boat under construction near Long Beach, California, 1946. Some idea of its 320-foot span is suggested by this aerial view. (Navy Department, National Archives)

questioning the use of all that money; accusations rang forth and the cry of "boondoggling" was heard throughout the land. It was at this point that it was also suggested that the thing would never fly. What is of further interest is that the thing had not been intended to fly—it had been designed to study the conception itself as the first step in a series of such aircraft; the prototype was intended for taxi tests and careful evaluation of design.

However, the cries that Hughes heard made him unhappy. He was an airman of no mean ability and a designer who knew what he was doing. The accusations and lawsuits (in which the government attempted to retrieve its forty million dollars —to some extent on the grounds that the plane could not fly) goaded Hughes into action. About five years after work had begun the *Hercules,* as the behemoth was named, was run into the waters of Los Angeles Bay near Long Beach. The date was November 2, 1947.

The *Hercules* was gassed up, the eight engines started, and Hughes took his place in the pilot's seat. Before an interested audience that included government officials, aviation enthusiasts, and batteries of lawyers, Hughes began to taxi the plane across the bay. It exhibited excellent handling characteristics in the water; response to controls was exemplary. Suddenly Hughes gunned the engines and the plane skimmed across the bay, lifted onto the step, and rose into the air. Hughes kept the *Hercules* airborne for about a mile at an average height of twenty feet or so—at a speed of less than a hundred miles an hour! This in itself was remarkable considering the size and weight (though practically empty for the test) of the plane.

Hughes then set the plane gently in the water. He had made his point. The *Hercules* was then stored away at Long Beach, where it remains to this day, and never flew again.

About the same time that Howard Hughes formulated his plans to prove the *Hercules* could fly, Grumman, on the other coast, introduced one of the few successful new amphibians, the HU-16 Albatross. The company had already, the year before, produced its first postwar commercial amphibian, the G-73 Mallard. This craft could

The Hughes flying boat, with Hughes at the controls, makes its one and only flight, November 2, 1947. (U. S. Information Agency, National Archives)

*Transition from war to peace: the wartime **Grumman Gray Goose** (center) preceded by the Widgeon in civil colors and followed by the postwar Mallard. (Grumman Aircraft)*

carry ten passengers and was widely used after the war as executive craft and by small airlines. Although production of the Mallard ended in 1951, the plane enjoyed a long flying life.

The Albatross was developed initially for the U. S. Navy as a rescue craft and utility transport. In time, with modifications, the rugged little amphibian was serving in a number of roles other than that for which it had been originally designed. Among these were antisubmarine patrols, space vehicle recovery, training, and cargo transport. The Albatross was used by literally dozens of countries besides the United States. And in 1962–63, in a three-way venture, the U. S. Navy, Coast Guard, and Air Force set out to set new records for amphibious aircraft (six of which were then held by the Soviet Union). By the time the venture ended, on March 20, 1963, the United States held nine records for speed, altitude, load, and distance—breaking the six Soviet-held marks, one by Italy, and two that had never before been attempted. New life was given the Albatross in 1970 with a change-

over from the original piston engines (Wrights) to Rolls-Royce Dart turboprop engines.

While the lifespan of the Albatross might indicate that perhaps the swan song of the seaplane was prematurely sung, the fate of the British final fling into the big boat field could prove otherwise. But then, the advent

Grumman Hu-16 Albatross, a versatile, long-lived postwar flying boat. This particular aircraft, an Hu-16E, was one of a group of planes that broke numerous records in 1962–63. (Grumman Aircraft)

A Princess flying boat off Dover during a test flight in 1952. Aircraft pictured was the first of the three built by Saunders-Roe; none was ever used commercially. (U. S. Air Force)

of the Saunders-Roe S-45 Princess was in itself premature. Like the Hughes *Hercules,* the Princess was an ambitious idea, again that of H. Knowler, who had conceived the revolutionary SR-A/1. The design was begun during the war as a patrol craft, but by 1945 was switched to a possible contender for the Atlantic routes after the war was over. The original suggested name was an un-British Dollar Princess (for no doubt its function would be to acquire dollars for Britain), but characteristic British decorum prevailed and the plane was simply referred to as Princess.

The name was curiously diminutive for so grand a conception, for the Princess was another in the line of giant flying boats. The wing spanned 219 feet, six inches and the fuselage measured 148 feet from nose to tail. The plans called for the accommodation of more than a hundred passengers in two decks; two cargo holds had a capacity of eighteen thousand pounds.

Like the Hughes plane, the Princess project devoured money—the three built used up more than eight million pounds—although it did not generate the public outcry of the *Hercules.* The first Princess was ready for testing in August 1952. This was already nearly two years after British commercial aviation had abandoned the flying boat. Although the Princess proved to be a perfectly sound aircraft during the tests, it was also obvious that some mechanical problems were present and that it had evolved before the engines it needed had materialized. This last would necessitate expensive modifications; an order for four more Princesses was canceled, and two of the completed boats were cocooned and stored. Only the prototype continued to fly for a while, appearing at air shows until it too was beached. This really closed the chapter on Britain's large flying boat activity, for nothing has been done with the three big Princesses after they joined the Hughes *Hercules* in limbo.

Official recognition of the seaplane had not yet quite died in the United States, however. This was the result of the new look in hull design brought forth by Martin in their P5M Marlin. With a longer, more slender hull the Marlin could equal, and even surpass, the performance of land-planes. The old problem of bulk, of having to push air before it, thus limiting speed and endurance, was alleviated in the new concept, mainly the reduction of frontal area. At the same time the equally old advantage of being capable of operating from sea bases continued to be important in the event that the worldwide network of air terminals should be attacked. This was, of course, the era of the Cold War.

The first Marlin, the P5M-1, appeared in 1948—the wing obviously that of the wartime Mariner, but the long, narrow fuselage a new idea in flying boats. Equipped with the most modern electronic detection

A Martin Marlin—the P5M-2—comes in low to scrutinize a junk in the coastal waters of Vietnam. Powerful radar equipment was mounted in the nose and also in the tail. Navy pilots regarded the P5M a superb watercraft, possessing the best rough-water hull ever designed. (Martin Company)

gear, the Marlin was an effective antisub-marine craft; the first production models began flying by the end of 1951, in time for use in the war in Korea.

The P5M-2 appeared during the Korean War, its chief modification being in the change from a conventional fin-and-rudder to a T-tail, with the horizontal elevators mounted on top. These improved craft also saw service in Vietnam as elements of counterinfiltration patrols along the thousand-mile South Vietnamese coastline. Both steel-hulled ships and even junks come under the sharp-eyed scrutiny of Marlins in the campaign to prevent the delivery of war goods to the Viet Cong. With a range of well over two thousand miles the Marlin could traverse a good deal of water—and with the cooperation of a single seaplane tender and small support ships was capable of being water-based away from its home station for as long as two months at a time.

Shortly after the Marlin appeared, Convair (actually Consolidated-Vultee in 1950; it would become Convair in 1954) introduced their new concept in flying boats, the XP5Y-1. Powered by four Allison gas turbine engines (which turned six-bladed propellers), the new slender craft was designed as a Navy patrol seaplane. First flown in the spring of 1950, the plane revealed a number of "bugs," particularly in connection with the engines. Despite the fact that the prototype suffered an accident and was destroyed in 1953, the design was not immediately rejected and the plane, named Tradewind, was developed into a transport. These were given the Navy designation R3Y, of which eleven were built and used by the Navy. This design proved the practicability of a high-speed transport seaplane. The plane was also known as the "Flying LST," since in its transport version the bow of the craft could be opened for the loading of troops and equipment. The plane was also used as a flying tanker for refueling of jets in the air. Production of the

Consolidated-Vultee (later Convair) XP5Y-1 Tradewind, in its original form as a fast (388 mph) patrol boat, with radar scanner mounted in the nose. The fixed wingtip floats were the only anachronism. Span measured 146 feet, ten inches and length of fuselage was 127 feet, eleven inches. Most used of this design were the R3Ys—transport and tankers. (General Dynamics, Convair Division)

Tradewind did not continue beyond the original dozen, as funds for this type of aircraft were not forthcoming. In 1952 Consolidated-Vultee offered another design, a jet-propelled seaplane, but the competition was won by their traditional rival, Martin.

Success with the Marlin inspired what must be the most sophisticated seaplane ever built, the Martin P6M SeaMaster. Employing the hull concept introduced in the Marlin, the design was further refined by joining this idea to swept-back wings and jet engines: four Allison J-71 turbojets. These engines were mounted atop the wings, keeping them clear of the spray during take-off and landing. The wings, measuring a hundred feet from angled tip to tip, were mounted anhedrally, bringing them practically into the water. At each tip was a plastic float for balance while taxiing. Perhaps the most striking fact about the Sea-Master was its speed—which was in excess of six hundred miles an hour.

The first flight tests were carried out in the summer and winter of 1955, and by the following year announcements were made that the U. S. Navy would order thirty of

the P6Ms, but by June 1957 the first in a series of cutbacks was announced. A total of a dozen were built (including the initial two prototypes, which were destroyed during tests, and four modified P6M-2s) before the Navy terminated the entire project in the summer of 1959. Within eight years, on November 6, 1967, the Navy went out of the seaplane business altogether, marking the event with a last operational flight by a Marlin; this ended the brief renaissance of

The Martin P6M SeaMaster, last in Martin's seaplane line and one of the most advanced aircraft of its type ever built. Order cutbacks ended its life before it really began. (Navy Department, National Archives)

the flying boat, which had, in fact, begun with the Marlin in 1948.

But to suggest that the demise of the flying boat is at hand is to beg the issue. When the swan song appears to have reached its closing, another coda appears to prolong the life of the bird. As late as the spring of 1970 word arrived from Japan that the Shin Meiwa Industry Company was preparing its PS-1 amphibian for various roles. Its history actually went back to 1953, when restrictions were lifted by the Allies upon Japanese military aviation research and production. Shin Meiwa was the successor to Kawanishi Aircraft, which had produced the successful Emily. The new firm, in 1961, began working on a Short Take-Off and Landing flying boat based on the long-lived Grumman Albatross—although with ingenious variations—in the Shin Meiwa UF-XS. This led into the PS-1, the first prototype of which appeared in the autumn of 1967. Primarily designed and built for the Japanese Maritime Self-Defense Force as an antisubmarine warfare patrol plane, the PS-1 eventually evolved into several variants. One, the SS-2, is an air-sea rescue amphibian that could carry a crew of nine (four of them nurses) with places for thirty-six litters. Otherwise, in a transport version, the amphibian could carry as many as 115 passengers. Another version of the plane would be a landplane, also capable of carrying 115 passengers, and which could take off from relatively short runways; the commercial transport version of the seaplane would perform about the same, but from waterways.

The design of the PS-1 incorporates a number of innovations never before used as successfully and that make it possible for the aircraft to remain stable even in rough water, to take off and land in a short run (STOL) and that eliminate the possibility of water spray engulfing the engines during takeoffs and landings. These desirable conditions are achieved by a Shin

Shin Meiwa SS-2, amphibious configuration of the PS-1 flying boat, a major contribution to the resurgence of postwar flying boats and amphibians by the Japanese. The PS-1 was designed as a rescue craft, transport, and for antisubmarine operations. Power is supplied by four turbojet engines. Interestingly, the wingspan and fuselage length are the same: 110 feet. (Shin Meiwa Industry Company, Ltd.)

Meiwa-designed spray suppressor built into the hull of the plane that channels the water alongside the fuselage to a point behind the wing, where it cannot strike the engines or propellers. The other innovation is called Boundary Layer Control (BLC), and is used to deflect the slipstream from the propellers to assist in taking off, particularly in rough seas. Air is forced, by a General Electric three-stage axial flow compressor, across the control surfaces of wing and tail. This adds to the normal thrust of the propellers, practically triples the lift of the wing, and contributes also to the plane's stability, making it possible to take off, after a very short run, in seas with waves running as high as fourteen feet. The Shin Meiwa was designed for a number of uses: antisubmarine patrol, air/sea rescue, weather and oceanography research, and transport (in a projected landplane version). An aircraft of great versatility, the Shin Meiwa is innovational in the effectiveness of its modern technology—and may very well be the first in the renaissance of the military seaplane.

Contemporary devotion—in the noncommercial and nonmilitary sense—to flying off water is not dead either. A perhaps not very large but a dedicated number of pilots confess to a love for their "water birds." These are relatively tiny (with an average wingspan of barely forty feet) amphibians in the two- to four-place category, with low operating cost and that are reasonably inexpensive to acquire to begin with; some even are home-built.

Such a design is the Anderson Kingfisher, the work, fittingly enough, of a Pan American clipper pilot (Boeing 707), Earl W. Anderson. "Wilderness fishing, designing, and craftsmanship," Anderson has said, "have always been my principal off-the-job interests; the Kingfisher is a natural outgrowth of these inclinations." Beginning work on the design in the early sixties, Anderson completed the plane and flew it for the first time in April of 1969. "While my airplane isn't the last word in aerospace technology," Anderson admitted, "it is a nice flying example of what can be built by a homecraftsman." The Kingfisher, if not strikingly the "last word," is beautifully nostalgic in that its configuration conjures up the classic planes of the thirties.

A bit more sophisticated (and no subject

Thurston Teal prototype Model TSC-1A. Landing gear is manually retracted (saving on weight plus complexity of retracing mechanism). Wingspan is thirty-two feet; length of fuselage, twenty-three feet, seven inches. Cruising speed is 108 mph; range, 250 miles. (Thurston Aircraft Corporation)

for the homebuilder) is the Thurston Teal, the design of veteran David B. Thurston, once a Grumman project engineer, later the designer of the Colonial Skimmer and the Lake amphibian. The Teal (the amphibian; a T-Boat version is not equipped with wheels) carries two people and its single Lycoming engine and deep-step hull design make it possible for the craft to rise off the water in as little as fifteen seconds. This characteristic makes the craft especially excellent for short pond operations. A unique design feature is the "T" tail. The prototype of the Teal flew in August of 1968; manufacturing was begun in the spring of 1969 and steady production in 1970.

Perhaps "waterbug" rather than "bird" would be more appropriate to George Pereira's Osprey I, a tiny, homebuilt seaplane (wingspan: twenty-three feet). Pereira, a former Second World War B-17 pilot, has said, "Before testing the Osprey, I had absolutely no seaplane time; we sort of learned together." The main idea behind this one-man craft is mobility. For transportation Pereira also designed a special trailer that enables the pilot to haul the plane to "any convenient launching ramp, put the plane into the water unassisted, fly for as

Anderson Kingfisher, a homebuilt amphibian for the sportsman flier. Power is provided by a 100-hp Continental engine. The plane uses the standard wing of the Piper J-3, the span being thirty-six feet, one inch. Plane cruises at around eighty-five miles an hour and has a maximum range of 270 miles. The hull is of fiber glass-covered spruce and plywood. (E. W. Anderson)

Pereira Osprey I, homebuilt, one-man seaplane, one of the smallest of contemporary private seacraft. Brochure in which plane is described states "Once in the air, the climb angle can be quite startling," a point well made in this photograph. (G. Pereira)

The Spectra, in its two-place test vehicle form. The final production model will carry four passengers and will be amphibious. (Island Aircraft Corporation)

long as you like, then take it home for storage in a garage or carport." The wings are designed to fold for transport and storage. Pereira has summed up an emotion shared by many advocates of water birds when he said, "This aircraft has been a source of more personal enjoyment than anything I have ever flown. For some reason, flying from the water adds a whole new dimension to aviation."

Unusual configurations are not unique in the more recent designs. One such is the Spectra, the product of Island Aircraft Corporation of Florida. The most spectacular aspect of the design is the placement of the engine in the T-tail. With its drooping wings, the tiny craft (thirty-two feet, eight inches in span) resembles an offspring of the SeaMaster. The little plane is, interestingly, the brainchild of a group of engineer-pilots from Grumman, headed by Le-Roy Lopresti, and thus represents the fusion of the pilot's dream with the engineer's practicality. Testing of the craft was done with a one-sixth scale radio-controlled model, which, by early 1971, had made some forty successful flights and had completed its test program, including spin recovery.

The full-sized Spectra will be a four-place amphibian. One other interesting feature of its design is a retractable hull step. Controlled from the cockpit, the step may be lowered to the correct takeoff position, depending upon water conditions; in flight it then can be retracted to reduce drag. The top speed of the production Spectra is expected to be more than two hundred miles an hour, with a maximum range (with auxiliary tank) of twelve hundred miles. To a great extent the Spectra represents a distinct new look in seaplane design.

But, of course, to the romantic stickler these water birds are not the great, graceful clippers of old, the classic aircraft that created a legend. Most of them have gone —no Martin or Boeing clippers survived,

nor any Ugly Ducklings by Sikorsky—or S-42s; all have been devoured by time and the evolution of aviation history. Still one Sikorsky S-43 continues to exist in Houston, Texas, the property of Howard Hughes. He had used the plane to practice water landings and takeoffs just before he proved to his critics that his *Hercules* could fly. Like the *Hercules,* however, the S-43 is mothballed and inactive.

Some glimpse of the past may be experienced when in various parts of the world an old PBY is seen, especially in the remoter watery areas of the United States, Canada, or South America.

The last of the four-engined flying boats —which was still flying in the middle sixties —was the surviving (of three) Vought-Sikorsky VS-44s. The first of these planes flew in 1942 and, instead of being bought by Pan American (already having turned to the Boeing 314), all three planes were purchased by American Export Airlines. Later the planes went to American Overseas Airlines—two of the planes, meanwhile, being destroyed, one during a night landing in South America, the other during a takeoff at Botwood, Newfoundland.

The remaining VS-44, the second completed, was saved from a rusty end by

Last of the operational classic flying boats, the Vought-Sikorsky 44A of Avalon Air Transport (later Catalina Air Lines), which flew the plane between Long Beach and Catalina Island. The 44A was the last fixed-wing aircraft to bear the Sikorsky name. By 1967 this plane, after being damaged, was no longer flying. (Sikorsky Aircraft)

Wilton Probert, president of Avalon Air Transport (later Catalina Air Lines), who found the plane abandoned in Ankon Harbor, Peru. After a good deal of toil and money the plane was flown to California and modified to carry as many as fifty-three passengers (over the original forty) for hops from Long Beach to Catalina Island. Since the inception of this mere twelve-minute run thousands of passengers, including devotees of antique aircraft, have made the flight. Probert has given the boat the majestic name of *Excalibur*, evoking another, more enchanting period in time and redolent of the halcyon days of an aerial Camelot.

Acknowledgments

The idea for this book originated with my friend and editor Harold Kuebler, who then patiently waited until all the photographs were assembled and all the words (such as they are) were hammered out, one at a time, on paper. Work was done on *Seawings* over an extended period of time and not a little space, beginning in New York (where the bulk was done) and continuing in its pleasanter aspects (namely, research and culling picture files) in London, Baltimore, Seattle, Stratford, Connecticut, Washington, D.C., and Beaverton, Michigan.

Throughout, and from the beginning, I have had patient and understanding help from Harold Kuebler. Second only to him, and free and easy (plus accurate) with advice and aid to me, has been Pan American's Althea Lister, Curator of Clipper Hall, and veteran of some of the first flights mentioned in this book as well as a witness to several of the historic events. Miss Lister's memory, as well as her bulging files, were at instant and good-humored beck and call during much of the writing of this book. Miss Lister, I might add, is responsible only for the correct facts; the slips are mine, as are the views on Pan American's contribution to the early development of the flying boat and to the expansion of commercial aviation in the Caribbean, Latin America, the Pacific, and the Atlantic.

Certain individuals employed (at least when I came upon the scene) by several of the manufacturers of flying boats deserve more than passing mention because they rendered more aid than I had a right to ask for. These were Mark E. Nevils, formerly of the Boeing Company, now of Forest Hills, New York; Michael J. Marlow, the Martin Company; Robert R. Rodwell and James White of Short Brothers & Harland, and Frank A. McClung of Sikorsky Aircraft.

A special note of loving gratitude is owed to my wife, Edith, who, despite the fact that she has her own deadlines to meet, patiently stole time from her own work to make mine a bit more presentable. This was only one form of aid and comfort, among many, that she has always given during the long hauls of putting a book together. My son, David, always my research assistant, helped me on several details of fact and in the selection (and finding) of several pictures. My daughters, Carla, to whom this book is dedicated, and Emily, helped too by curbing some of their natural joyous exuberance (even on Saturdays and Sundays) to give me a reasonably serene atmosphere in which to work. Too much quiet wasn't good either (for it makes me restless), so they saw to it that there was not too much quiet.

My thanks to them all and also to:

Earl W. Anderson, Mahwah, New Jersey

Art Beltrone, Fairchild Hiller, Republic Aviation Division, Farmingdale, Long Island, New York

Fred Bettinger, General Dynamics, New York

Sigrid Bjornson, Boeing Company, Seattle, Washington

Larry Booth, Title Insurance and Trust Company, San Diego, California

M. Brennan, Imperial War Museum, London

Denise V. Broncato, British Overseas Airways Corporation, New York

Charles E. Brown, FRPS, Worcester Park, Surrey, England

Harold E. Carr, Boeing Company, Seattle, Washington

Vern L. Carstens, Chanute, Kansas

City News Bureau, St. Petersburg, Florida

Rachel Cunningham, British Overseas Airways Corporation, London

Miguel Deluccio, Aerolineas Argentinas, New York

Virginia Fincik, Det. 5, AAVS, Arlington, Virginia

E. J. Finley, Braniff International Airways, Dallas, Texas

F. R. Fowler, Deputy Chief and Historian, Norton Air Force Base, California

Gerald M. Holland, Lieutenant Colonel, USAF, Chief, Magazine and Book Branch, Department of the Air Force, Washington, D.C.

Gordon Jackson, San Diego, California

Roberts Jackson, Culver Pictures, Inc., New York

William Kavanagh, USM, Rockaway Park, New York

F. R. Kniffen, General Dynamics, New York

Karl H. Koepcke, Lufthansa German Airlines, New York

Lynn Lavner, J.H.S. 62, Brooklyn, New York

LeRoy P. Lopresti, Island Aircraft, Merritt Island, Florida

Ian Mackersy, British Overseas Airways Corporation, London

William D. Martin, Commander, U.S.N., U. S. Naval Air Station, Brooklyn, New York

Mary McCarthy, Pan American World Airways, New York

R. Mercier, Musée de l'Air, Paris

Elliot H. Miller, Martin Company, Baltimore, Maryland

Kurt H. Miska, Grumman Aerospace Corporation, Bethpage, Long Island, New York

G. A. Osbon, National Maritime Museum, Greenwich, London

George Pereira, Sacramento, California

W. R. "Dick" Probert, Catalina Seaplanes, Inc., San Pedro, California

Captain Basil L. Rowe, Coral Gables, Florida

Markoto Shimomura, Shin Meiwa Industry Company, Ltd., Tokyo, Japan

Wanda and Jerry Simpson, Saginaw, Michigan

James C. Sparks, Boeing Company, New York

David B. Thurston, Thurston Aircraft Company, Sanford, Maine

Arnold I. Turkheimer, British Overseas Airways Corporation, New York

Paul L. White, National Archives and Records Service, Washington, D.C.

C. M. Withington, Sikorsky Aircraft, Stratford, Connecticut

Robert B. Wood, National Air and Space Museum, Washington, D.C.

BIBLIOGRAPHY

Burden, William A., *The Struggle for Airways in Latin America,* Council on Foreign Relations, New York, 1943.

Davies, R. E. G., *A History of the World's Airlines,* Oxford University Press, London, 1964.

Delear, Frank J., *Igor Sikorsky—His Three Careers in Aviation,* Dodd, Mead & Co., New York, 1969.

Duval, G. R., *British Flying Boats and Amphibians, 1909–1952,* Putnam & Co., Ltd., London, 1966.

Gibbs-Smith, Charles H., *The Invention of the Aeroplane, 1799–1909,* Taplinger Publishing Co., New York, 1965.

Green, William, *War Planes of the Second World War,* Vol. 5—*Flying Boats,* Doubleday & Company, Garden City, New York, 1962.

Grooch, William Stephen, *Skyway to Asia,* Longmans, Green & Company, New York, 1936.

Josephson, Matthew, *Empire of the Air,* Harcourt, Brace & Company, New York, 1944.

Palmer, Henry R., Jr., *The Seaplanes,* Morgan Aviation Books, Dallas, 1965.

Roseberry, C. R., *The Challenging Skies,* Doubleday & Company, Garden City, New York, 1966.

Rowe, Basil L., *Under My Wings,* Bobbs-Merrill Company, Indianapolis, Indiana, 1956.

Sikorsky, Igor I., *The Story of the Winged-S,* Dodd, Mead & Company, New York, 1938.

Smith, Henry Ladd, *Airways Abroad,* University of Wisconsin Press, Madison, 1950.

Still, Henry, *To Ride the Wind, A Biography of Glenn L. Martin,* Julian Messner, New York, 1964.

The following articles published in the invaluable *Journal* of the American Aviation Historical Society were especially helpful:

Klaas, M. D., "Last of the Flying Clipper 'Ships'" (Boeing 314), Vol. 13, No. 2, Summer 1968.

Mayborn, Mitch, "The Ugly Duckling—Sikorsky's S-38," Vol. 4, No. 3. Fall 1959.

Scheppler, Robert H., and Anderson, Charles E., "The Martin Clippers," Vol. 10, No. 3, Fall 1965.

Index

'Untin' Bowler (S-38), 64
Uppercu, Inglis M., 25, 26, 41

Van Dusen, C. A., 114, 115
Van Dusen, W. I., 56, 57–58
Van Zandt, Parker, 129
Vanderbilt, William H., 18, 20
Vargas, Getulia, 94
Versailles Treaty, 17, 150
Viaçao Aérea Rio Grandense, 36
Vichy government, 211
Vickers, Mr., 161
Vidal, E. L., 91
Viet Cong, 240
Vietnam War, 240
Virginia Company, 24
Voisin, Charles, 2
Voisin, Gabriel, 2–3
Voisin-Archdeacon design of 1905, 2
Voss, Walter, 59
Vought 02U Corsair, 195, 196
Vought-Sikorsky VS-44, 245–46

W. R. Grace & Company, 33, 39, 40
Wagner, Captain Boyd D., 226
Walker, Mayor James, 154
Wallach, Mrs. Charles, 144
Wanamaker, Rodman, 9–10, 26
Warner, Edward P., 35
Watson, Captain, 76
Wedemeyer, General Albert S., 182
Weick, Frederick, 199
Wells, H. I., 20
Werber, Max, 120
West Indian Aerial Express, 22, 28
West Indian Air Express, 42
West Indies Airways, 26
Western Air Express, 64

Westervelt, Conrad, 172
Westfalen (ship), 149–50
Whitbeck, J. E., 23
White, Francis, 40
Whitney, Cornelius V., 18, 20, 21, 140–41
Whitney, Mrs. Cornelius V., 140–41
Williams, Red, 52
Wilcockson, Captain A. S., 167–68, 171
Wilkins, Sir Hubert, 202
Willgoos, Andrew, 90
Wong, T., 172
Wood, Robert, 64
World War I, 10, 12–13, 16, 81, 161, 172
World War II, 77, 78, 143, 154, 158, 166, 187, 209–33; Africa Korps, 216; in the Pacific, 225–29, 231–32; Sunderland patrols, 221–25, 233; U-boat warfare, 185, 192, 218, 222, 223, 225, 228
Wright (ship), 127
Wright, C. D., 124, 132
Wright, Orville, 3, 7, 11, 29
Wright, Victor, 124–29, 132; China Clipper flight, 119–37
Wright, Wilbur, 3, 7, 11, 29
Wright Company, 11
Wright Flyer, 11
Wright Model B, 11
Wright Model G Aeroboat, 11
Wright Twin Cyclone engines, 175–76, 178, 180, 206

Yale Flying Club, 18, 20
Yale University, 18
Yancey, Lewis, 202–4
Yankee Clipper, 180, 181, 182, 187–88

Zeppelins, 12–13, 149–50, 160, 182, 194